symbol, pattern
& symmetry

symbol, pattern & symmetry

the cultural significance of structure

Michael Hann

B L O O M S B U R Y
LONDON • NEW DELHI • NEW YORK • SYDNEY

Bloomsbury Academic

An imprint of Bloomsbury Publishing Plc

50 Bedford Square   1385 Broadway
London   New York
WC1B 3DP   NY 10018
UK   USA

www.bloomsbury.com

Bloomsbury is a registered trade mark of Bloomsbury Publishing Plc

First published 2013

British Library Cataloguing-in-Publication Data
A catalogue record for this book is available from the British Library.

ISBN: HB: 978-0-8578-5488-9
      PB: 978-1-4725-0312-1
      ePDF: 978-1-4725-3900-7
      epub: 978-0-8578-5490-2

Library of Congress Cataloging-in-Publication Data
A catalogue record for this book is available from the Library of Congress.

Typeset by Apex CoVantage, LLC
Printed and bound in India

To Nell and Peter Hann

contents

acknowledgements

The author is indebted to Ian Moxon for his constructive review, useful commentary and helpful advice; his instinct for identifying errors, simple or complex, subtle or blatant, was crucial to the development of the manuscript to this book. Thanks are due also to Chaoran Wang, Kevin Laycock, Jean Mitchell, Emelia Clay, Roy Daykin, Alice Humphrey, Kholoud Batarfi, Joseph Lyons, Josh Caudwell, Victoria Moore and Marjan Vazirian for their substantial efforts in assisting with the production of large quantities of illustrative material. Gratitude is extended also to David Holdcroft, Christopher Hammond, Jeremy Hackney, Hywel Coleman, Dirk Huylebrouck, Margaret Atack, Rory McTurk, Jill Winder, Briony Thomas, Ben Whitaker, Edward Spiers, Margaret Chalmers, David Geekie, X. (Roger) Lin, A. Nagori, Ian Murphy, Hong Zhong, Jae Ok Park, Young In Kim, Myung-Sook Han, Sookja Lim, Catherine Docherty, Cigdem Sini, Caroline Mason, Annmarie Sanderson, Nicola Kirby, Biranul Anas, Behnam Pourdeyhimi, Myung-Ja Park, Kyu-Hye Lee, Chil Soon Kim, Jin Goo Kim, Mary Brooks, Peter Speakman, Kenneth Jackson, Percy Grosberg, Gerald Leaf, Damian O'Neill, Gordon Thomson, Sangmoo Shin, Eun Hye Kim, Patricia Williams, Biranul Anas, Sandra Heffernan, Barbara Setsu Pickett, Kahfiati Kahdar, Eamonn Hann, Teresa Hann, Mairead O'Neill, Barney O'Neill, Jim Large, Moira Large, Kieran Hann, Roisin Mason, Tony Mason, Donald Crowe, Dorothy Washburn, Doris Schattschneider, Jay Kapraff, Michael Dobb, Keum Hee Lee, Haesook Kwon, Young In Kim, Sophie Nurse and Simon Longman, editorial and production staff at Berg, as well as gallery staff at the British Museum, the Victoria and Albert Museum, the Ulster Museum (Belfast), the National Museum of Korea (Seoul), Leeds Museum, Walters Art Museum (Baltimore), the Art Institute of Chicago, the Metropolitan Museum of Art, and the following student contributors: Ashley Warren, Alice France, Deasy Camiladini, Mohammad Rizki, Herry Putra, Septia Andini, Menur Ardanareswari, Desiree Btari Siregar, Mega Saffira, Olivia Listyani, Fadhila A. Arimurti, Menur Ardanareswari, Ni Putu Padmi, Sari Astiti, Hasri Haryani Direja, Anastasia Anette Djauhari and Andhieza Tsalashra.

The author accepts responsibility for all omissions, inaccuracies and incorrect statements. Last, and by no means least, gratitude and thanks are extended to Naeema, Ellen-Ayesha and Haleema-Clare Hann. Every effort has been made to extend acknowledgement where it is due and the author apologizes in advance should such acknowledgement be omitted. Unless otherwise specified, photographic images were produced by the author.

list of illustrations

Graphic and scanning work associated with geometric and other images is by Chaoran Wang (CW), Kevin Laycock (KL), Emmelia Clay (EC), Joseph Lyons (JL), Victoria Moore (VM), Alice Humphrey (AH) and Alice France (AF). Photographic contributions were made by Marjan Vazirian (MV), Josh Caudwell (JC), Hywel Coleman (HC), Ashley Warren (AW), Sophie Nurse (SN), Mairead O'Neill (MO'N) and Roy Daykin (RD). Unless stated otherwise, additional photographic material is by the author.

plates

figures

preface

This book explores and analyses the origins, development and diffusion of symbols, motifs and patterns in visual art forms across a selection of (predominantly non-European) cultures and historical periods. The focus is on explaining and illustrating the nature of various visual art forms and how they may be classified, analysed and compared, particularly with reference to their underlying structural characteristics, though, where appropriate, commentary relating to thematic content is also included. The universal importance of visual symbolism is recognized and the role played by geometric structure as a means of encoding meaning is discussed.

The book embraces a number of academic traditions, develops insights proposed by various eminent observers and suggests methodologies of value to modern scholars concerned with structural analysis in the visual arts. An emphasis is placed on showing how the visual arts are underpinned invariably by strict geometric structure and on explaining how reference to such structures can allow classification and comparison of data from different cultural or historical sources. The topics selected for the series of case studies reflect some of the research interests of the author and his research students over the past few decades. Research data and information from past reviews, student projects, conference presentations, exhibition booklets and catalogues have been developed, updated or supplemented and associated with new material. In a 2012 publication entitled *Structure and Form in Design*, the present author reviewed and discussed a range of geometric concepts and principles which are summarized also in this present publication. In the former case the focus was largely (though not entirely) on the needs of student design practitioners, and in this present case the focus is on analysis in the visual arts, with a coverage which deals with a wide range of cultural and historical material, including textiles, ceramics and other designed and crafted objects as well as notable buildings and monuments. The intention is to encourage student readers to create a connection between basic geometric structures (including symmetry arrangements) and the visual arts design and architecture. A series of 37 case studies (denoted by initials cs) is presented in chapters 3 to 14.

It should be noted that often in general texts concerned with developments in the visual arts and design the immense contributions made by Egyptians, Greeks and Romans are an early focus, and sometimes the starting point for discussion. This book steps outside this well-worn convention and focuses attention on developments to the east of the Mediterranean. The choice of subject matter has been influenced by a number of factors. Cultures and countries located along the trade routes from west to east, from the Mediterranean to China, Korea and Japan, offer ideal platforms from which to consider diffusion in the visual arts. Relevant objects are well represented in museums and galleries and are often well displayed on museum websites. The British Museum and the Victoria and Albert Museum (both in London) were inspirational jointly in the development of lecture material to service the lecture course from which this publication springs. It is hoped that students will be inspired to visit both of these great institutions, or provincial or other national museums which may be more accessible. Many of the geographical zones covered are of course accessible (in the physical sense) to modern-day students. Another factor in the selection of case-study material was the ready access to large quantities of unpublished material held at the University of Leeds International Textiles Archive (ULITA), a resource largely unknown to scholars worldwide. It is also worth remarking that the selection of topics covered has been very much geared to the preferences and interests expressed by students over the past decade.

It should be noted that assigning dates and giving precise geographical boundaries to events or developments in the ancient world is problematic and is a source of controversy among scholars. To ensure a degree of consistency (and, it is hoped, dependability), reference is made throughout to dates, periods and geographical boundaries as specified, at the time of writing, by the British Museum (scholarly and exhibition publications and website pages).

The organization of this book is as follows. Chapter 1 reviews the nature of stylistic adoption and diffusion, and Chapter 2 presents an appraisal of concepts relating to structure and form in the visual arts with a particular focus on the nature of geometric symmetry and the value of this and related concepts to the classification of visual art forms. Each subsequent chapter (Chapters 3 to 14 inclusive) consists of an introductory

section and this is followed by a series of case studies which relate to the theme of the chapter. Each of these case studies focuses on one particular object, a group of related objects or a monument of some kind. Each case study offers scope for development as a student dissertation (especially at undergraduate level). Where appropriate, key literature is listed and relevant objects and monuments are identified. A series of topics or questions, suited for discussion or as a basis to guide the development of student assignments, is included at the end of chapters. These can be adjusted, developed, edited, lengthened or shortened, depending on the requirements of a particular class.

Selections of well-known symbols are identified, their thematic or symbolic content explained and, where appropriate, underlying geometric structures recognized. Geometrical concepts and principles are illustrated by simple line drawings and by reference to various classes of designed object, comprising ceramics, textiles and carpets, metal and wood work, architectural motifs, symbols and other figures, patterns, tilings and other forms of regularly-repeating structures, as well as floor plans, sections and façades of a selection of notable buildings or building complexes. Consideration is given to symbols, motifs, patterns and signs from a range of cultures including Babylonian, Neo-Assyrian, Persian, Moorish, Turkish, Indian and Pakistani, Southeast Asian, Japanese, Korean and Chinese. Common characteristics are highlighted and accounted for, and the apparent relationship between geometry and culture is debated.

A particularly important characteristic of this book is the emphasis on geometric analysis. Consideration is given to forms of visual art, motifs, symbols and patterns, and their apparent diffusion from one cultural context or historical period to another. The book demonstrates how the consideration of underlying structure, particularly geometric symmetry, can be used to analyse, classify and compare data from different historical and cultural contexts. A small contribution is made also to the debate on how geometric structure has been used to encode meaning in various cultural settings.

The objectives are, first, to explain and illustrate how simple and complex motifs, surface designs, regular patterns, product and architectural forms, cross-sections and other constructions are underpinned by a strict geometric structure and, second, to show that identification of this underlying geometric structure can act as a basis for classification, analysis and comparison. The aim of the book is to introduce a simple and readily usable means of classification, appropriate to structural analysis in the visual arts and design, and to show how such a system of classification subject to the availability of suitable and representative data can be used to develop unique methodological perspectives allowing (for example) intercultural comparisons, identification of origins, or the pinpointing of periods of cultural adherence, continuity and change. Classification in the visual arts, based on consideration of symmetry characteristics, using categories formulated by mathematicians, is well established. However, despite the efforts of scholars from a range of disciplines, this means of classification has not been readily picked up by the wider population of art and design analysts and historians, anthropologists and archaeologists. The means of classification presented in this book does indeed rely on symmetry identification, and is based on a simple square template which can be used as an aid to detect the presence of reflection symmetry in nonrepeating compositions. Formal mathematical content is thus kept to an absolute minimum and appropriate literature is identified throughout.

It should be noted also at this stage that the term *decorative art* is avoided in this book; rather the term *visual art* is used instead. This is due to the fact that in the popular mind motifs, symbols, patterns and visual compositions of one kind or another, all lumped under the title *decorative arts*, are deemed purely decorative or ornamental in function and somehow not worthy of serious scholarly attention. Washburn (2004: 49) observed that the titles of the renowned works by Owen Jones (*The Grammar of Ornament*, 1987[1856]) and Flinders Petrie (*Decorative Patterns of the Ancient World*, 1974 [1930]) implied that surface patterns served the purpose of embellishment and decoration rather than communication. Further to this she commented that 'non-representational patterns not only decorate, but also act as visual voices that, in conjunction with verbalized speech and song, communicate important cultural information' (Washburn 2004: 49). This perspective that underlying structure encodes information is a theme which occurs several times in the present book. Each case study (cs) gives an introduction to the subject, and is designed to act as a starting point for students interested in developing expertise in the relevant area.

MAH, Leeds, 2013

stylistic diffusion, adoption and adaptation

The image presented in Figure 1.1 was taken in 2009 in Seoul, Korea, a city located at the far east of Asia, and the photograph shown in Figure 1.2 was taken in 2007 in Cordoba (Spain), a city located in the south-west of continental Europe. Figure 1.1 depicts modern ornamental brickwork which reproduces a key pattern (also known as a fret pattern), considered by Koreans to be traditional to Korea. Meanwhile, Figure 1.2 portrays Arab-influenced brickwork showing a number of key patterns (located in the arches shown in the image), regarded by Western architectural historians as characteristic of southern Spain. Clear similarities are evident in the two images. It is the contention here that some form of diffusion of ideas, maybe operating in a time frame extending over several centuries and also involving several intermediary locations, ensured the similarities of the designs.

Similar designs depicted in different contexts and created at different times may result from one of two causes and, on occasion, from a combination

Figure 1.1 Detail of traditional brickwork, entrance to National Museum, Seoul

Figure 1.2 Detail of an exterior portal of the Great Mosque of Cordoba, Spain

of the two: (1) a process of diffusion which may be followed by a degree of independent development or (2) processes of independent discovery, construction, evolution and development. The author's position is that a vast range of designs resulted at least in part from a process of cultural diffusion, though, at the same time, in many instances something local and familiar also was imposed to allow the new to sit comfortably with the old. *Cultural diffusion* is the process by which cultural traits, material objects, ideas, artistic styles, inventions, innovations or patterns of behaviour are spread from one social or geographical context to another. Such a process is a key aspect of *globalization*, a term coined in modern times to refer to the increased interconnectivity between countries, generally expressed through trade and facilitated through developments in technology and communication. Many examples of visual art forms from different cultural or historical domains exhibit similarities in terms of structure, form and thematic content, and are attributable to a common identifiable source. A process of diffusion seems clearly at work in such instances. However, it may well be the case that key-type motifs and patterns such as those illustrated are examples from a class of designs developed largely on an independent basis across many cultures, time zones and geographical locations.

In cases where it is clear that diffusion has occurred and that motifs, symbols, designs, patterns or visual compositions of one kind or another have been transmitted from one culture to others, the great challenge for the analyst is to identify the road of transmission; this, when considering historical material, is exceedingly difficult. Wittkower, in his renowned work *Allegory and the Migration of Symbols*, recognized the challenge: 'In considering the transplantation of forms, designs and styles, we are faced with a triple challenge, from the simplest cases—the trading of objects and the migration of artisans—to the assimilation and adaptation of imported material, and then to its complete transformation' (1977: 14).[1]

Wittkower observed that there was a substantial quantity of symbols and motifs, from many time periods and produced across a wide geographical area, which had origins 'lost in the early dawn of history' (1977: 14). Examples of such symbols include: key-type motifs, the tree of life, eagles or other birds of prey, mythical heroes taming or hunting wild beasts, circular devices seemingly associated with the sun, various dragon motifs and a wide range of mythical beasts often created from a mixture of physical attributes of various animals. Of particular note are certain basic geometric figures: the circle, the square, various types of triangle and rectangle, the hexagon and the pentagon. Selections of symbols are identified in various parts of this book and, where possible, an account of their significance is given. Such commentary relies largely on examining the thematic content of relevant symbols and making comparisons between different geographical zones. Also of importance in this book are the identification and explanation of various underlying structures which can be associated with forms of visual art; these structures and their classification are explained in Chapter 2.

The objectives of this chapter are to review aspects of diffusion and adoption in the visual arts by identifying the main literature and by proposing a framework which will assist in the classification of the illustrative material and case studies that follow.

the process of diffusion

Prior to discussing the process of diffusion, it is worth remarking that there is a substantial quantity of literature which focuses on the nature of independent discovery, invention and innovation. These important issues, and their associated concepts and explanations, may be of some use when considering changes in the visual arts; relevant literature and perspectives were considered previously by the author in the context of technological change (Hann 1982: 3–8). The consideration of the processes by which a particular idea or physical object can transfer from individuals, groups, production units or centres of power of one type or another (physically located in place A or culture A) and be introduced, accepted, adopted, adapted, applied or used by other individuals or groups (located in place B or culture B) has intrigued scholars from various disciplines since the nineteenth century.

Anthropologists were early participants in the diffusion debate, and several of the relevant theoretical perspectives are associated with eminent scholars from this academic discipline. The word *diffusion* has been used to refer to the spread of ideas or innovations of various kinds, and has become associated with a school of anthropology which (in its early years) proposed that civilization spread from one culture to others and that human beings largely lacked the inventiveness to stimulate independent development. At the extreme end of this perspective were those scholars who considered Egypt the source for all other ancient civilizations. This type of diffusion, which focussed on one source only, became known as *heliocentric diffusionism*. Wider-ranging diffusion perspectives were forthcoming, and these included cultural circles or cultural areas.

Cultural diffusion is best considered as the process by which cultural traits, material objects, artistic ideas, techniques, styles, motifs and symbols are spread between individuals or groups of individuals within a single culture (intracultural diffusion) or from one culture to another (intercultural diffusion). It is widely accepted that cultural change manifests itself through changes in the visual arts. As a result the visual arts are regarded as an ideal source from which to generate data to determine various aspects of adoption and cultural change.

Generally cultural traits originate in a particular area and, from there, spread outward. After diffusion and adoption, the trait will invariably not appear identical in its new location; rather, it will be adapted to the new circumstances. Historically, migrating populations have often brought with them new ideas and innovations. Transcultural diffusion agents may include traders, adventurers, explorers, slaves, diplomats, soldiers and hired artisans, craftspeople and labourers. In literate societies, letters and books can communicate innovations and ideas, and thus encourage diffusion. In the modern era, various forms of mass media have fulfilled the same function. The best example of worldwide diffusion in the early twenty-first century is fast food and other forms of mass catering (e.g. McDonald's, Kentucky Fried Chicken and various coffee chains such as Starbucks and Costa) with many companies becoming geographically widespread in a few decades.

The study of cultural diffusion thus concerns the spread of culture and the factors that account for that spread, including migration, communications, trade and commerce. As mentioned previously, cultural traits originate in a particular area and, from there, diffuse outward. A cultural trait will not keep spreading. Rather it will encounter barriers which limit the spread. Barrier effects may be physical or social. Physical barriers include the natural environment (seas, mountains, deserts, forests and extremes of climate). Social barriers are those characteristics that differentiate groups and potentially limit interaction, including language, religion and ethnicity. In recent years, barrier effects have been overwhelmed by modern means of communication. Adoption of the new is often accompanied by disuse of the old; hence the apparent decline of cultural diversity.

Among the leading theoretical contributors to the development of diffusion theory and its associated concepts and perspectives are Franz Boas (1858–1942), a pioneering anthropological field worker; Leo Frobenius (1873–1938), the originator of the concept of cultural circles; Fitz Graebner (1877–1934), a leading diffusion theorist; A.C. Haddon (1855–1940), a Cambridge zoologist and anthropologist who produced an important book entitled *A Short History of Anthropology*; Thor Heyerdahl (1914–2002), a twentieth-century Norwegian adventurer; A.L. Kroeber (1876–1960), a student of Boas; Freidrich Ratzel (1844–1904), who contributed significantly to nineteenth-century theories of migration and diffusion; and W.H.R. Rivers (1864–1922), a strong supporter of diffusion perspectives who spoke strongly against evolutionist explanations. Diffusion theory therefore had its origins in the discipline of anthropology. In more recent times diffusion concepts have been used in the areas of archaeology, cultural geography, business studies and marketing. The work of Rogers and Shoemaker (1971) is of particular importance in introducing diffusion concepts to researchers from a wide range of disciplines.

The initial use and development of concepts seems to have focussed simply on understanding how societies change because of the spread of culture traits, innovations or inventions. On considering the links between the arts of Europe and of non-European civilizations, Wittkower

(1977: 10) observed that there were two antagonistic theories (both identified briefly in the introduction to this chapter) which dominated the thinking of ethnologists and anthropologists over the course of the twentieth century: diffusion of technology and associated techniques, ideas, concepts and art forms, versus independent and spontaneous invention in different parts of the world, possibly thousands of miles apart. This latter outlook was embraced by a competing school of anthropology, which became known as the evolutionist school, a theoretical outlook which became associated with various ethnocentric ideas and, in particular, focussed to a large degree on how human societies progressed from primitive social positions. So from one dogmatic corner (the diffusionist extreme) anthropologists believed that all human civilization was from one source. From the other corner (the evolutionist extreme) they maintained that all human beings shared psychological traits which permitted equal inventiveness, and that inventions had arisen independently in different geographical locations; hence diffusion had little or no effect on human development. A good critique of the evolution–diffusion debate in the context of the visual arts can be found in Munro's *Evolution in the Arts* (1963).

Zeitlin (1994), in his study of ceramic styles and appropriate analytical procedures of value in accounting for diffusion between neighbouring societies in pre-Columbian America, highlighted the importance of distinguishing between the diffusion of style and the diffusion of associated technology: 'In the latter case, technological concepts may be adopted across social or political boundaries, even by unfriendly neighbours who perceive some advantages in their use. The same would be less likely when it comes to the spread of stylistic concepts.' It may indeed have been

the case that certain techniques of manufacture, such as bronze casting, ceramic manufacture or weaving, all associated with the visual arts, may have been adopted in some circumstances where motifs, symbols, patterns or other components of visual composition were rejected and indigenous forms were used instead, but applied or created using the adopted technique of manufacture.

So it seems to be the case that technological ideas or materials for making useful objects (particularly weapons or tools) would be readily adopted by societies that became aware of them, whereas motifs, patterns, signs, symbols or other forms of visual statement, particularly when used for personal adornment, would be less likely to be adopted speedily by cultures which might not wish to be associated with the initiating culture. On the other hand, where one culture might wish to imitate another, then adoption of forms of visual art associated with the initiating culture might well be speedy.

Friedrich (1970) noted the tendency of archaeologists (e.g. Deetz 1965; Hill 1966; Longacre 1968; Whallon 1968) to deduce the extent of social relations between neighbouring societies by making reference to stylistic variation in material objects associated with those societies. Focussing on a relatively modern context (late twentieth-century San José, a Tarascan-speaking village in the state of Michoacán in Mexico), Friedrich considered how variation in painted decoration on pottery might serve as an indicator of intensity of social contact between pottery painters. Sackett (1977) reviewed the usage of the term *style* and developed a model of style applicable especially to archaeological contexts. Watson observed that the study of pottery had been at the centre of archaeological research for more than a century, and presented a survey of a selection of publications concerned with the analysis of pottery from the Near East and the south-western United States, noting that past studies seemed concerned largely with chronological placement as well as stages of technological awareness and aesthetic achievement rather than possible avenues of diffusion (1977). Eminent anthropologist Franz Boas (1924) presented a concise and well-argued case for the role played by diffusion in cultural change and development. In an impressive article published in 1940, Kroeber distinguished between various types of diffusion process and focussed particular attention on what he called 'idea diffusion' or 'stimulus diffusion', a process which he claimed would normally leave a minimum of historical evidence. He commented that, 'in a great many cases in history . . . evidence as to the process of diffusion is much more scant than its effects' (Kroeber 1940: 19). He gave several examples, including the 'invention' of porcelain in Europe after a few hundred years of using imported porcelain from China. He observed that the problem was to find the necessary materials at home and to develop the required technical skills. Ultimately in the early eighteenth century (initially in Germany) deposits of the necessary kaolin were found and techniques of manufacture developed. So the innovation, in this case, was original from a European viewpoint but not totally independent. Kroeber commented further: 'If it were not for the pre-existence of Chinese porcelain and the fact of its having reached Europe, there is no reason to believe that Europeans would have invented porcelain in the eighteenth century, and perhaps not until much later, if at all' (1940: 19).

Rands and Riley (1958) reopened the debate on diffusion and independent invention. D'Azevedo (1958) debated the nature of art as perceived by anthropology scholars and noted the difficulty in arriving at an all-encompassing definition. Fischer (1961) questioned the widely held belief among anthropologists that there are connections between art forms and sociocultural conditions. He examined the relationship between social stratification in societies and variations in art style and, on examining the distribution of design elements in works of art, proposed positive associations: between visual repetition, empty space, and symmetry in design and egalitarian societies, and between enclosed figures and hierarchical society. Kirk (1975) considered long-term cultural diffusion in the context of the Indian subcontinent.

Silver observed that several important schools of anthropology 'were rooted in a basically diffusionist philosophy and . . . diffusionist schools were basically incompatible with most evolutionary theory' (1979: 267). He maintained that Boas's contribution to the study of art styles should be considered against this background, and that 'Boas was instrumental in dispelling many evolutionist dogmas' (Silver 1979: 267).

In the 1979 article 'Ethnoart', Silver observed that the literature concerned with the anthropology of art revealed a substantial variation in terms used to describe the actual subject under investigation. Where reference was made to non-European art from the second millennium CE, terms such as *primitive*, *tribal*, *non-Western* and *traditional* were employed often and invariably without definition. Further terminology used to refer to the same material included *preliterate*, *folk*, *native* and *ethnic*. By way of alternative, Silver suggested the use of the term *ethnoart* (felt by this author to be just as unsatisfactory) to describe the visual art from all continents other than Europe. The term *visual art* is employed in this book to refer to the historical, traditional or modern output of all cultures and societies whether European or not.

Silver (1979) noted that many of the pioneers of anthropology considered the visual arts of non-European cultures in their quest to develop or support preferred theoretical perspectives. Studies concerned with the development and distribution of artistic styles or traits were used as platforms for debate between the evolutionist and diffusionist schools (Silver, 1979). In the context of the term *style*, Silver (1979) observed the necessity for social scientists to define adequately what is meant by it, and also the necessity to determine the exact relationship that art styles bear to the civilizations which produced them. Silver proposed what he referred to as a 'common-sense' definition of style: that 'which attends to formal features characterizing individual works of art' (1979: 267).

Kroeber, a student of Boas, argued that 'historic styles' went through a series of stages of growth and decline. Styles were thus considered by Kroeber as inherently dynamic, going from inception through stages of growth and then deterioration, and he claimed that a stylistic revolution occurred when influential individuals sensed that an existing style had exhausted its potential and needed to be replaced (1948: 126).

Silver (1979), on reviewing the work of eminent anthropologist Lévi-Strauss (1962; 1967) and his contribution to the development of structuralism, confirmed the substantial influence of Lévi-Strauss on studies which drew relationships between structural characteristics of artwork and structural aspects of societies.

Structuralism is one possible approach to the study of symbols. Another is through psychological and psychoanalytical interpretation (Silver 1979). An important contribution to the study of style was made also by Arnheim (cited by Silver 1979: 285), who urged that research should consider the formal aesthetic elements of symmetry, line and balance. Silver added that 'each culture recognises canons in these areas' (1979: 290).

Mundkur (1978) presented an impressive review and discussion of evidence suggesting Hindu influences from India, around the middle of the first millennium CE and later, on cultures existing in pre-Columbian Mesoamerica., He dealt particularly with lunar hieroglyphs of the Maya and certain groups of deities of the Aztecs and the Zapotecs, drawing parallels with various symbols and deities of Hindu origin.

Haselberger, though critical of the use of terms such as *primitive*, *tribal*, *traditional*, *native*, *indigenous*, *folk* or *popular*, offered yet another term, *ethnographic art*, to denote 'the tribal and tourist art of those peoples in Africa, America, Asia, Australia and Oceania who were the objects of ethnological (or as it is called in the Anglo-American tradition), anthropological study' (1957: 342). A comprehensive review of diffusionism was given by Blaut (1987), and Hegmon presented a well-focussed review of 'the analytical process that links material culture variation, style and human activity' (1992: 517). From the discipline of design history, the book by Adamson, Riello and Teasley (2011) was particularly notable. Their work provided a fascinating and well-focussed assessment, discussion and appraisal of the cultural interactions which have influenced developments in design from the early-modern era.

components of diffusion, adoption and adaptation

A substantial review article by Davis (1983) still stands as an informative and well-balanced survey of the subject area. He noted that while diffusion theory had reached a position of impasse in the field of anthropology by the middle of the twentieth century, other disciplines such as economic geography, industrial economics, sociology and marketing had made great strides in considering various kinds of diffusion and, in particular, those factors which enhance rates and levels of adoption among recipients (or adopters). Various general frameworks, developed to assist in the study of the diffusion of innovations, can be identified.

To assess the extent to which diffusion theory may be useful in characterizing adoptive behaviour relating to visual art types, it is of value to consider further the use of relevant terms and their definitions. Even a superficial survey of literature relating to visual art styles will indicate that the terminology relating to concepts of style, decoration, innovation and diffusion has often been used in ambiguous ways, and more precise definitions are required.

A *style* is the sum total of aesthetic attributes which place an object within a particular range of types. Probably the most important aesthetic attributes are the shape and form of the object itself and its surface patterning, texture and colouration. Underlying structure or composition is also important. Artefacts of the same style share aesthetic attributes. In the context of this book, the term *style* does not account for raw material type, technology, techniques or means of production except where these may impart a characteristic aesthetic feature such as that achieved through the use of an ikat or a batik technique: a feathered visual effect on the surface of the woven textile in the case of ikat, and a cracked, hairline-like appearance occurring occasionally on the surface of a batik textile where dyestuff has penetrated through a broken or cracked resist (generally

wax). Style may thus include constituent motifs, symbols, pattern types, textures, colour palettes and, in particular, compositional arrangements such as proportion and degree of symmetry or asymmetry. This book (as was Davis's review) is largely concerned with the adjectival use of the term *style* in phrases such as stylistic attribute, stylistic variation and stylistic change.

Diffusion theory presents a systematic description of the process of adoption over time of a new idea or innovation by individuals, groups or other adopting units (Hann 1987: 19). Rogers and Shoemaker observed that the crucial elements were '(1) the innovation which was (2) communicated through certain channels and (3) adopted over time by (4) individual members of a social system' (1971: 18).

It seems most sensible to consider the first stage of adoption (and diffusion) to occur when the adopter obtains the object (or drawing) and a further stage when the adopter replicates the object including its stylistic features, or alternatively commissions an outside craftsperson to create the relevant architectural or product style. It seems best to refer to this latter stage as *full diffusion*. Buying or trading the object and placing it within a display cabinet or cupboard does not constitute stylistic diffusion in this full sense, but rather suggests that the object has simply been acquired as a curio of one type or another, probably through trade, exchange, gift, purchase or theft. Such an acquisition does indicate a broadening appreciation of the style, but not full stylistic diffusion of the type that is the principal focus of this book. So a process of imitative manufacture by the adopter is necessary to confirm that adoption and diffusion have actually taken place.

Perspectives from various disciplines can shed light on identifying the determinants of stylistic diffusion, adoption and change. The monumental work produced by Rogers and Shoemaker (1971) still stands as the most important treatise in the subject area. They synthesized several hundred studies of diffusion and presented a comprehensive model based on this synthesis; this served as a platform for numerous subsequent diffusion studies in many social-science areas.

An important concern in many diffusion studies is the identification of factors involved in the acceptance of an innovation—though this is not the principal concern here. Rather it is to identify subject themes, motifs, symbols and, where appropriate, their underlying structures and evidence for their spread from one setting to another. On considering the relevant literature, Davis noted that 'the success with which a cultural trait diffused was highly context-dependent and that such intangibles as symbolic value or prestige associations were important factors in determining acceptance or rejection of outside traits' (1983: 58).

Hann (1982) considered the diffusion of technical innovations in the context of twentieth-century textile manufacture, and focussed in particular on identifying and reviewing factors which determined the rates and levels of diffusion of different types of process innovation. Although the concepts and principles were largely specific to technological change brought about by adoption in the context of relatively modern factory production, the terminology used and theoretical perspectives employed may be of some value in developing a model or framework to consider forms of stylistic change and adoption. Likewise, consideration of late twentieth-century marketing studies concerned with product innovations, especially modern-day fashions and their marketing and diffusion (Hann 1987), may be of some value.

Sproles, on reviewing the nature of modern clothing and its adoption, considered a design to be a unique combination of characteristics which, within a given class of product, distinguishes one item from another. Carpets, carved-ivory containers, cast-bronze mirrors, painted mandalas and block-printed cottons can each be considered an individual class of products with a vast number of design possibilities achievable within each class. In most cases, this large number of possibilities or designs within each class are achievable through the use of unique combinations of visual elements (including motifs, symbols, colours and textures) and compositional arrangement. As observed by Sproles, 'each separate design exists as a highly individualistic creation' (1979: 13).

Assembling data from a wide variety of scholarly disciplines, Rogers and Shoemaker (1971) identified certain characteristics that seemed to be associated with widespread diffusion. These characteristics, which they believed determined to varying degrees the rate and extent of adoption within a population of potential adopters, included relative advantage, compatibility, complexity, divisibility, communicability (or observability) and availability (1971: 18–19). Hann explained and discussed each of these further (1987: 20). In the context of the present book, when the spread of art styles, motifs, symbols, patterns and compositional arrangements is considered, the extent to which these characteristics were of greater or lesser importance to adoption is at best open to conjecture. Nevertheless it seems appropriate to develop a list of factors which may have influenced adoption; these are derived from Rogers and Shoemaker's list of characteristics which, although not fully satisfactory in terms of their scholarly rigour and their appropriateness to the visual arts, may act as a basis for further development and consideration.

Relative advantage

This is the extent to which an innovation of some kind is perceived as more satisfactory than the object, techniques or visual forms that it may replace. Rogers and Shoemaker observed that the degree of relative advantage 'may be measured in economic terms, but often social prestige factors, convenience, and satisfaction are also important components' (1971: 22). It does indeed seem to be the case, in the context of the visual arts, that social and economic factors play an important role. The acquisition of luxury goods, such as multicoloured porcelains, highly coloured cotton textiles or exquisitely embroidered silks, can be seen to have substantial social prestige value. Further to this, the economic value of an acquired object may relate to its practicality and utility, and this may be influenced by its constituent raw materials. For example, in certain climates, wool may be more appropriate than linen and vice versa; an iron blade may be more useful than one of stone; a building of stone will have more permanency than one of mud and wattle, but if supplies of stone are not readily at hand then adoption may not make sense. Acquiring the object is one level of diffusion, but the deeper level of adopting the processing or production procedures, obtaining the necessary raw materials and actually producing the object and applying the relevant stylistic features to it arguably constitutes full diffusion (of the idea as well as the object) within the society or culture as a whole.

Compatibility and degree of fit with accepted norms and values

This is the extent to which an object or form of visual art is perceived as consistent with the existing beliefs of potential adopters. In circumstances where an innovation in the visual arts demands great changes in existing behaviour and attitudes, then the necessity for these changes acts as a force against speedy adoption.

Adaptability

This is the extent to which an innovation can be used readily and integrated into a society. Often, various symbols, in the process of adoption, may undergo a transformation in meaning but are thus readily adapted to existing norms and value systems. Religious iconography is an important example. It was certainly the case that Buddhism, a few centuries after its introduction, adopted (and then adapted) certain emblems, symbols and perspectives from Hinduism. This calls to mind the view of Boas (1924): 'The introduction of new ideas must by no means be considered as resulting purely mechanically in addition to the cultural pattern, but also as an important stimulus to new inner developments.' Adaptability may relate also to underlying technology; examples may include techniques for forging or working metals, application of ceramic glazes or use of various fibre dyes, all of which may fit alongside existing techniques (though gradually displace them). This possibility relates to the next factor of technological appropriateness.

Technological appropriateness

This refers to the physical nature of the product itself and, after it has been adopted or accepted, the extent to which its ultimate production can be carried forward using existing skills, technological and production knowledge, as well as familiar processing techniques. Knowledge relating to ceramic firing and glazes, fibre types, metals, armaments production and architectural-engineering principles are important examples. In cases where pre-existing technological knowledge is adequate to produce a given innovation, adoption can be facilitated more readily. In cases where further technological knowledge needs to be acquired, full diffusion can be delayed. Such knowledge would seemingly come most appropriately from attracting individuals or groups with the relevant skills and know-how, rather than simply adopting an object produced using some unfamiliar processing technique or raw material.

Complexity and ease of imitation

Complexity refers to the degree to which a potential adopter has difficulty in comprehending the innovation and learning to use it. Rogers and Shoemaker (1971: 22) observed that, where certain innovations were readily understood by members of a social system, then a rapid rate of adoption prevailed. For full diffusion and actual production of the innovation (in addition to acquiring it and using it), the complexity of production arrangements is an important factor which influences the rate of full adoption. In cases where detailed explanations and instructions need to be comprehended before using a product, initial diffusion can be seen to be held back. As recognized by Sproles, the adoption of an innovation involves a learning process and, if this learning process is quick and easy, the innovation has a greater chance of speedy adoption, whereas if the learning process is too complex then this acts as a force against adoption (1979: 102). Ease of imitation relates partly to technological appropriateness (listed earlier). Assuming that an innovation of some kind is readily acceptable and the desire

for adoption exists, then adoption proceeds more readily in circumstances where production is most easily carried out using existing technological knowledge. So if it is a matter of adopting the use of a particular symbol, pattern or composition which can be achieved using current technological know-how, then the barriers against adoption are fewer and full diffusion can follow.

Perception of benefits (compared to what is available)

Where an innovation is perceived as more beneficial in some way to the object, belief, symbol, motif, sign, pattern, visual composition or building type which it may replace (or may be used alongside), then this acts as a force favouring adoption, use and ultimate production with full diffusion.

Communicability, trialability and availability

The essence of adoption and ultimate diffusion is communication, not only between outsiders (who may introduce the innovation) and members of the target culture or social group (who may adopt it), but also among those from within the target group itself. Where innovations are visible objects, these have a greater chance of undergoing early adoption than when the innovation is not readily communicated visually. *Trialability* is the extent to which a society may experiment with an innovation on a limited scale. As recognized by Rogers and Shoemaker (1971: 23), those new ideas which can be tried on an instalment basis are adopted more readily than innovations that are not divisible. Finally, on the assumption that potential adopters have judged all of these factors positively, the availability of an innovation must then be adequate to meet demand. This may involve items made available through trade or, at a more advanced stage of diffusion, may be through home production addressing home needs. During the latter half of the twentieth century, the bulk of diffusion research focussed on the nature of the adoption process and the characteristics of the adopting population. Often based within the conceptual framework proposed by Rogers and Shoemaker, much empirical work focussed on identifying the characteristics of adopters, particularly early adopters who exhibited innovativeness or leadership and who, as a consequence, were in a position to make the innovation more visible and thus influence the subsequent desire to adopt. In the context of the present book, where the focus in the main is on adoption and change which occurred over a remote past time frame, there is little value in pursuing a detailed discussion of further aspects of adoption. The author previously provided a review of some of the important literature (1982: 10–15, 1987: 19–23).

To characterize a process of adoption, change and adaptation, and to assess the effects of this process, it is essential to identify precisely what has been changed and how it has been changed. The author believes certain underlying structural characteristics are unique to, and underpin, all societies and that the visual arts of the given culture encapsulate and express these characteristics with great subtlety. Underlying structures thus retain information relating to the culture that holds them. These underlying structures change in response to wider cultural changes (such as the widespread adoption of a new religion). To explore this outlook (or hypothesis) further, Chapter 2 presents an identification and explanation of the various geometrical measures, concepts and principles which are of value in identifying these underlying structural features; note that the author previously explained many of these

geometrical features in some detail (Hann 2012). Also of importance in considering the process of change in the visual arts is the adoption, adaptation and use of certain symbols, signs and motifs. The identification of these is more immediate and obvious than the assessment of underlying structure, and the following section includes further explanation.

motifs, symbols and symbolism

Motifs are considered generally to be visual building blocks, often found in regularly repeating compositions. As will be seen in Chapter 2, motifs can be classified by reference to their symmetry or underlying structural characteristics. They may be free-standing, may form a repeating unit in a regular pattern or may form a component of a larger nonrepeating composition. Motifs, whether obviously representational (e.g. a rose) or abstract and non-representational (e.g. a circle drawn around a pentagon), may possess an inherent symbolism, though in the popular imagination they may often be deemed to fulfil a purely decorative or ornamental function.

Visual symbols are important features of all cultures at all times. The pioneering perspectives of Carl Gustav Jung (1875–1961) did much to shape late twentieth-century and early twenty-first-century thinking on the subject of symbols and symbolism. The Jungian insights were inspired largely by research concerned with dreams and the analysis of their content. An important observation was the recurrence of various symbolic images. Jung observed a surprising similarity between dream-based symbols and the symbols associated with the major world religions, myths and legends. From this, Jung concluded that certain symbols retained a universal significance (Fontana 1993: 13). Jungian perspectives consider the human psyche to be built of conscious and unconscious elements as well as a deeper collective unconscious shared by all humans across space and time. The collective unconscious, Jung believed, was the source of various symbols or 'archetypes', and these were expressed in some dreams (Fontana 1993: 14). Much of the present book concerns symbols rather than signs, though there seems to be a common tendency to confuse the two. They are indeed different, as recognized by Jung, who made the informative and well-observed differentiation: 'The sign is always less than the concept it represents, while a symbol always stands for something more than its obvious and immediate meaning' (1968: 41). Several useful compendia of symbols present alphabetical lists with explanations of use, possible origins and significance for different cultures. The work by Cooper (1978, reprinted in 1998) is of particular value in this regard. It is worth noting that similar symbols can have substantially different meaning in different cultures, and also within a given culture a symbol may be prone to more than one meaning depending on how or where it is used. This calls to mind Silver's observation, when considering symbolism in the visual arts, that 'context often clarifies a symbol's significance where several meanings are possible' (1979).

a nine-point framework

The intention in this book is to identify the characteristics of the visual arts and architecture across a selection of cultural and historical contexts.

Relevant symbols, motifs, patterns and compositions and, where appropriate, their thematic or symbolic content, as well as their underlying structural characteristics, are noted. Some of this is possible within cataloguing frameworks used in museums.

The headings which form the components of the framework presented in this section have been developed from those used typically in a twenty-first-century museum environment (although substantial cross-referencing with other objects, relevant projects, literary references and identification of relevant historical markers or points of concern to the production source of the object are invariably also included, particularly in large national museum environments). This nine-point framework draws on ideas Munro (1970) expressed several decades ago, though greater overall simplicity is the aim here. This present book stresses the shape of objects and the structural analysis of their underlying forms. Attention also focuses on thematic content and apparent symbolism. The framework provides scope to classify these and related features.

1. Title and nature of object or collection.
2. Provenance (geographical and historical source and subsequent history) and current location.
3. Period or date.
4. Specific location of production.
5. Physical measurements (dimensions and weight).
6. Visual features or subject matter (narrative aspects, symbols, motifs, signs, patterns and other obvious compositional characteristics).
7. Raw materials, technology, technique, colours and textures.

8. Associated ideas, beliefs and attitudes, as well as mythical or mystical aspects, thematic content and apparent symbolism (may have some overlap with the sixth point above).

9. Structural and visual analysis (proportions, symmetry and other underlying geometric features, as well as line, form and graphic elements).

This is an outline to aid the classification of a variety of objects. The important addition to standard classification frameworks is point 9, identification of the structural features of the object. It is believed here that cross-referencing (with other objects) of this particular feature may help to identify paths of diffusion, in that different cultural settings may express similar geometric selections. It should be stressed that flexibility is the intention, that with some objects not all headings are appropriate, and that in some cases the relevant information may simply not be available. The order of headings can be adjusted and further headings added. In fact the reader is encouraged to develop the system further by adding subheadings where felt appropriate to the project at hand.

summary

Cultural diffusion is the process by which cultural traits, material objects, ideas, inventions, innovations or patterns of behaviour are spread from one social or geographical context to another. A substantial body of literature has been created over the course of the twentieth century, initiated largely by anthropologists such as Boas (1924) and Kroeber (1940, 1948). This chapter has highlighted the principal components of diffusion theory and adoption. Researchers have suggested that often an innovation, after adoption, will undergo adaptation so that adopters can conform to prevailing norms and values. Cultural changes in a society are expressed in subtle ways through changes in the structural characteristics of the visual arts. Structural analysis therefore offers the potential to identify changes in culture which may have occurred through diffusion.

DISCUSSION TOPIC

Making reference to the more important theoretical literature, explain and discuss the nature of cultural change and diffusion. Give examples from the visual arts and other forms of artistic expression, during one or more historical (or modern) periods or cultural contexts of your choice. Organize your response into numbered and headed sections. State your precise intentions in an introduction. Define the terms *cultural change* and *diffusion* and identify and briefly review relevant literature. It is of importance that you identify relevant nineteenth- and twentieth-century diffusion theorists and their contribution to the development of diffusion theory and its associated concepts and perspectives. Give a range of examples; these may be from ancient, historical or modern times. Provide a summary of the main points.

further reading

Adamson, G., Riello, G. and Teasley, S. (2011). *Global Design History*, London: Routledge.

Boas, F. (1924). 'Evolution or Diffusion', *American Anthropologist*, 26 (3): 340–4.

Davis, D. D. (1983). 'Investigating the Diffusion of Stylistic Innovations', *Advances in Archaeological Method and Theory*, 6: 53–89.

Fischer, J. L. (1961). 'Art Styles as Cultural Cognitive Maps', *American Anthropologist* (New Series), 63 (1): 79–93.

Friedrich, M. H. (1970). 'Design Structure and Social Interaction: Archaeological Implications of an Ethnographic Analysis', *American Antiquity*, 35 (3): 332–43.

Jung, C. G. (ed.) (1968). *Man and His Symbols*, New York: Dell.

Kroeber, A. L. (1940). 'Stimulus Diffusion', *American Anthropologist*, 42 (1): 1–20.

Kroeber, A. L. ([1948] 1963). *Anthropology: Culture Patterns and Processes*, New York: Harcourt, Brace and World.

Lévi-Strauss, C. (1962). *The Savage Mind*, Chicago: University of Chicago Press.

Lévi-Strauss, C. (1967). *Structural Anthropology*, Garden City, NJ: Doubleday/Anchor.

Liungman, C. G. (1991). *Dictionary of Symbols*, New York and London: Norton.

Munro, T. (1963). *Evolution in the Arts*, Cleveland, OH: Cleveland Museum.

Munro, T. (1970). *Form and Style in the Arts: An Introduction to Aesthetic Morphology*, Cleveland, OH and London: Case Western Reserve University Press with Cleveland Museum.

Wittkower, R. (1977). *Allegory and the Migration of Symbols*, London: Thames and Hudson.

Zeitlin, R. (1994). 'Accounting for the Prehistoric Long-Distance Movement of Goods with a Measure of Style', *World Archaeology*, 26 (2): 208–34.

note

1. The word *migrate* is used occasionally rather than the word *transfer*, though this hardly seems appropriate in all cases as migration indicates leaving (or removing from or re-locating). In this book *migration* will be avoided where possible and *diffusion* will be used instead, because it is recognized that migration has had a chequered history among anthropologists.

2

geometric patterns of culture

This chapter concerns the geometric aspects of structure in the visual arts and design (including architecture). It focuses first on explaining and illustrating a range of geometrical structures which underpin surface images, designs, regularly repeating patterns, product and architectural forms, floor plans, façades and cross-sections, and, second, on explaining how the identification of these underpinning structures can act as a basis for classification, analysis and comparison. Various geometric characteristics, constructions, comparative measures and ratios are of particular importance to visual artists, architects and designers. Since the mid-twentieth century, scholars have generated a range of theoretical literature aimed at identifying the use of these constructions, in both historical and modern times, in the visual arts, including design and architecture. This chapter identifies the relevant structures and explains possible means of classification. This chapter also reviews a range of relevant literature but makes minimal reference to mathematical terminology and symbol. Subsequent chapters introduce a selection of the measures identified here in the analysis of a wide range of objects and constructions, drawn from architectural details, tiles, domestic and religious artefacts, sculpture, ceramics, inscriptions, metalwork, carpets and other textiles.

principles, concepts and constructions

A substantial body of literature examines the geometrical aspects of art and design, though much of this is not readily accessible to an audience of visual art and design students who, on the whole, are less mathematically inclined than their engineering or scientific peers. Accessible sources dealing with analysis (as opposed to explaining principles and concepts) are found mainly in the scholarly literature of anthropology and archaeology. It seems to be the case that considerations of the type dealt with in this book are deeply unfashionable in the early twenty-first century among the majority of professional art-and-design analysts and historians, at least within the United Kingdom.

The present examination of the literature dealing with the structural aspects of the visual arts, design and architecture places stress on various geometric principles, concepts, constructions, comparative measures, ratios and proportions. These include the following: the circle; the square; various triangles (equilateral, isosceles, right-angled, scalene); various rectangles (based on certain length and width proportions); regular polygons (particularly pentagons and hexagons); various grid structures; a range of ratios and proportions; geometric symmetry. Reynolds (2001) listed many of these in

'The Geometer's Angle. An Introduction to the Art and Science of Geometric Analysis'; reference to this and other articles by Reynolds (2000, 2002, 2003) may prove of value to students wishing to pursue projects aimed at structural analyses in the visual arts. Readers may also wish to refer to Hann (2012), who identified and explained the full range of relevant underlying structures. For the convenience of the reader, this chapter illustrates and explains briefly the more important figures, measures, concepts and principles.

A circle is the easiest geometrical figure to draw with a high degree of accuracy, and in many cases it acts as an aid in the construction of various other geometrical figures. Historically, it has had many uses in the visual arts and has clear associations with, for example, rose windows in cathedrals, halos of saints and deities, marriage rings and bangles, ancient stone circles and Buddhist mandalas, prayer wheels and stupas. Circular-type designs, often referred to as *rosettes*, have been in use since ancient times, and their use can be detected worldwide. Various related constructions are also of importance. One of these is the *vesica piscis* (or fish bladder), a construction consisting of two circles of the same radius, overlapping in such a way that the centre of each lies on the circumference of the other. Figure 2.1 provides an example. The area of overlap (enclosed within the emboldened arcs in the illustration) is the *vesica piscis*, a construction of ancient origin found, for example, in early depictions of Christ (Calter 2000), as well as in many non-Christian Asian contexts. Lawlor discusses briefly the mysticism of the figure in his text *Sacred Geometry* (1982: 31–4).

The *vesica piscis* can initiate other constructions such as an equilateral triangle or a regular hexagon (Figure 2.2). Further (equal) circles added can yield an alternative means of constructing a regular hexagon (suggested in Figure 2.3). Four circles overlapping with a central circle can create a four-petal motif (Figure 2.4). Hann previously explored these and related constructions (2012: 34–5).

Wittkower observed that 'the equilateral triangle, the right-angled isosceles triangle, the square and the pentagon and derivative figures like the octagon and decagon formed the basis of medieval aesthetics [although his focus was primarily on various European contexts]. Most medieval churches were built *ad quadratum* or *ad triangulum*' (1977: 112). A triangle is a polygon with three sides and three interior angles. In the context of

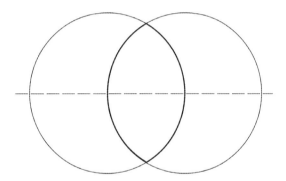

Figure 2.1 *Vesica pisci*s (CW)

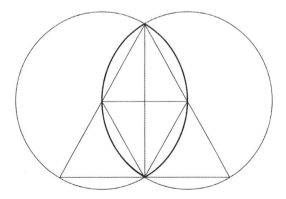

Figure 2.2 Equilateral triangle construction (CW)

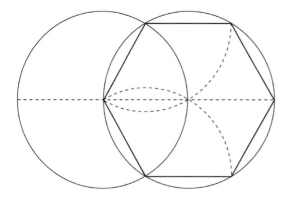

Figure 2.3 Hexagon construction (CW)

polygon (with equal sides and equal angles). A regular pentagon has five equal-length sides and angles (Figure 2.8), and a regular hexagon has six equal-length sides and angles (Figure 2.9).

From the viewpoint of the visual arts, the most important non-equilateral triangle is the right-angled triangle with sides of three, four and five units (Figure 2.10). Also known as the Egyptian triangle, the 3–4–5 triangle was used in the construction of various Egyptian pyramids (Kapraff 2002: 181). Scholars believe ancient Egyptian

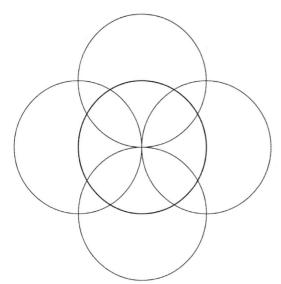

Figure 2.4 Four circles over one (CW)

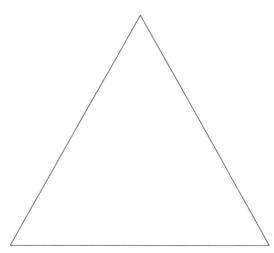

Figure 2.5 Equilateral triangle (CW)

the visual arts, whether European or Asian, the most commonly used types of triangle are the equilateral triangle, with three sides and three angles equal (Figure 2.5); the isosceles triangle, with two equal sides and two angles equal (Figure 2.6); the right-angled triangle, with one angle equal to 90 degrees (Figure 2.7). A regular polygon has equal-length sides and equal angles (Hann 2012: 15–17). A square is thus a four-sided regular

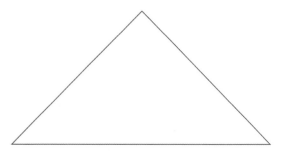

Figure 2.6 Isosceles triangle (CW)

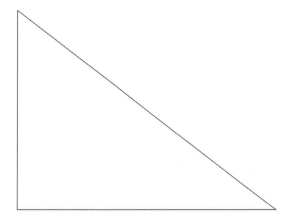

Figure 2.7 Right-angled triangle (CW)

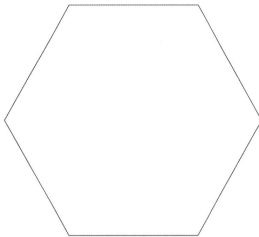

Figure 2.9 Regular hexagon (CW)

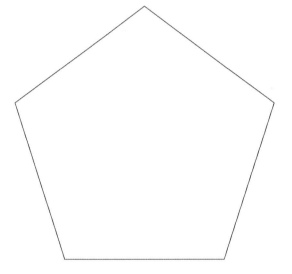

Figure 2.8 Regular pentagon (CW)

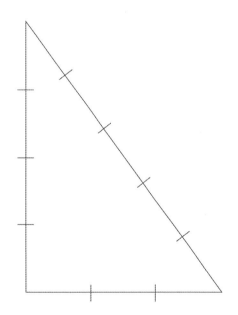

Figure 2.10 5–4–3 triangle (CW)

engineers used a measuring stick of some kind plus a rope with twelve equal divisions (suited to create a right-angled triangle of sides 3, 4, and 5). Subsequently, the ancient Greeks and Persians used the 3–4–5 triangle (Ghyka 1977: 22).

A further important triangle from the viewpoint of the visual arts is the isosceles triangle with 36 degrees at its smallest angle (Figure 2.11). Ten of these triangles can fit exactly together to create a regular ten-sided figure or decagon (Figure 2.12), achievable since ten of the small angles, each of 36 degrees, fit exactly into 360 degrees.

Certain regular polygons, when combined, produce various tiling designs. In the context of this book, a *tiling* is an assembly of polygonal shapes which cover the plane without overlap or gap. Hann previously gave detailed explanations of tiling types (2012: 49–69). Each of the basic tiling types is comprised of component units of three distinct regular polygons: the equilateral triangle (Figure 2.13), the hexagon (Figure 2.14) and, most commonly, the square (Figure 2.15).

A further category of geometrical phenomena includes grids, which relate closely to tilings. Both have assemblies of polygons covering the plane without overlap or gap. Often a tiling is a final, finished statement, whereas engineers or artists often use a grid as a guideline for a composition or construction of one kind or another. A grid can thus be described as an assembly of lines, probably evenly spaced and with half running vertically and at right angles to the other half which

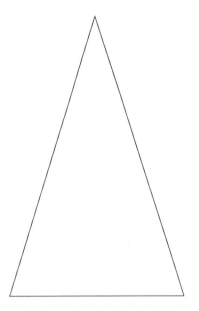

Figure 2.11 36-degree isosceles triangle (CW)

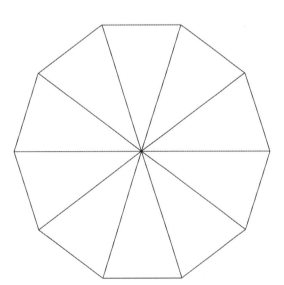

Figure 2.12 Ten 36-degree isosceles triangles (CW)

Figure 2.13 Equilateral triangle grid (CW)

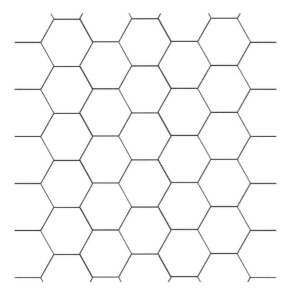

Figure 2.14 Regular hexagon grid (CW)

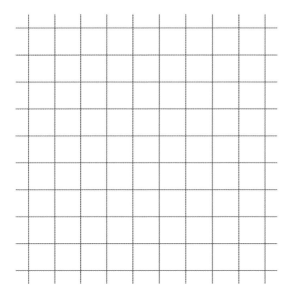

Figure 2.15 Square grid (CW)

runs horizontally across the plane. Grids provide structural frameworks to guide the development of visual compositions and the placement of component parts. Artists and engineers can employ them as organizational tools in, for example, the drawing of floor plans and building façades. Various grids are of value in organizing repeat units in patterns and tiling designs. Most common are grids with unit cells composed of equilateral triangles or squares or regular hexagons.

The square and its diagonal are the basis for generating a series of rectangles known as 'root rectangles'. According to Hambidge, various ancient civilizations used these in the design of monuments and sculptures ([1926] 1967: 19). A series of root rectangles is shown in Figure 2.16. Hann previously explained the construction of these and related figures in some detail (2012: 38–42). For further explanation, the reader should also refer to Hambidge's treatise *The Elements of Dynamic Symmetry* (1967: 84–98). Hambidge introduced a particular rectangle derived from a construction initiated by drawing a diagonal to a square's half, as shown in Figure 2.17. He referred to the figure as the *rectangle of the whirling squares* because of the series of successive squares that can be constructed within the figure itself (Figure 2.18). This rectangle is known commonly as a *golden-section rectangle*.

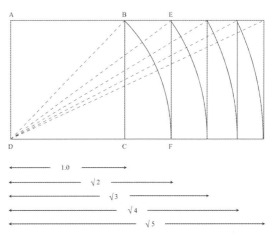

Figure 2.16 Square and root rectangles (CW)

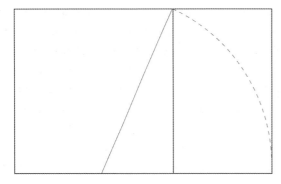

Figure 2.17 Diagonal to the half and construction of the golden-section rectangle (CW)

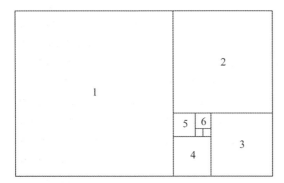

Figure 2.18 Whirling squares rectangle (CW)

While Hambidge (1926) focussed on the use of various rectangles (which he referred to as *dynamic rectangles*), other researchers argued the value to the art-and-design analyst of certain other geometric constructions. A construction known as the *Brunes Star* is an important example. Named after a Danish engineer, Tons Brunes (1967), the construction is an eight-pointed star, which engineers have commonly used as an underlying structural device. The construction is created through the addition of diagonals to the square, the subdivision into four equal component squares and the addition of various further diagonals (Figure 2.19).

When lines are drawn through intersection points (Figure 2.20), various equal segments result (e.g. on either side of the centre lines connecting opposite sides). The author believes this construction is of great potential value to the art-and-design analyst. Amazingly, when the Brunes Star is placed over a wide range of square-based visual compositions, key aesthetic points (a term introduced by Hann 2012: 157–9) of these compositions coincide with the intersections of the star diagram. Hann previously provided fuller explanation (2012: 42–4 and 157–9). Stewart, who referred to the construction as the 'starcut diagram', presented an extensive review of its use in ancient and relatively modern times (2009).

Great strides have been possible in visual analysis through reference to symmetry and by examining the symmetry characteristics of relevant objects. The term *symmetry* implies balance of physical form, and, in everyday usage, can be applied to an image, figure or object with

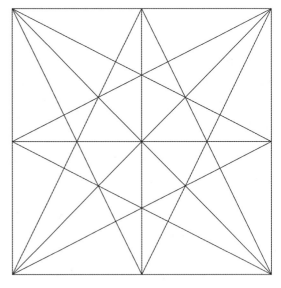

Figure 2.19 Square with Brunes Star–type divisions (CW)

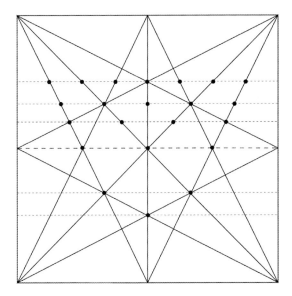

Figure 2.20 Brunes Star with intersection points (CW)

two equal parts, each of the same size, shape and content, one a reflection (as if in a mirror) of the other. Beyond this everyday usage, the concept of symmetry can be extended to include figures or objects consisting of more than two parts of the same size, shape and content. Also, various further geometrical actions, in addition to a perceived single reflection in a mirror, can be considered. Symmetry can be detected throughout much of the natural and created worlds. Over the years, researchers have published a wide range of scholarly literature focussed on the universality of the phenomenon. Washburn and Crowe provided an extensive bibliography (2004). The wideranging nature of symmetry and its applicability across academic disciplines are highlighted by the two-volume compendium, edited by Hargittai (1986, 1989), which consists of more than 100 papers from the arts, humanities and sciences, each paper focussed on one particular aspect of

the subject. Arnheim reviewed the two-volume work: 'As one reads what so many minds have thought and found out about the organisation of form, one is led to conclude that the inexhaustible complexity of inorganic and of organic shapes surrounding us derives ultimately from a few simple elements, so that, in principle, our vision is still akin to that of Plato, who derived air, earth, fire, water and the universe from the five symmetrical geometric solids' (1988).

Although symmetries can be recognized in many domains, it is, however, in the sphere of regular-pattern classification and analysis that interest in the concept among social anthropologists and archaeologists began to pick up momentum during the last few decades of the twentieth century. The increased interest in symmetry and its use in design analysis can be attributed firmly to the endeavours of Washburn and Crowe (1988) and their impressive treatise dealing with the theory and practice of pattern analysis. In particular, they brought about awareness among scholars of how academics and other researchers can use symmetry concepts in the analysis of designs from different cultural settings and historical periods. By the early twenty-first century, this work continued to be an important reference for anthropologists, archaeologists and art historians. A later publication, edited by the same authors, explored how cultures used pattern symmetry to encode meaning (Washburn and Crowe 2004). A further groundbreaking treatise, which Washburn (2004) also edited, again dealt with a range of symmetry attributes including how symmetry can encode meaning and how, when presented in various product forms, it can communicate messages relating to the societal structure of the culture that created the object. Developing this view, this chapter suggests that not only is symmetry capable of encoding meaning, but that other geometrical features (such as root rectangles), which may not be classified readily under standard symmetry headings, may also act as encoders of meaning and, like symmetry characteristics, may act as evidence of diffusion of ideas from one source to another, across cultures and their history. As noted previously, the author maintains that the geometric construction known as the Brunes Star (a highly symmetrical figure) can be found across numerous cultures and time periods; it too may prove of value to diffusion research.

Hann previously recognized that 'symmetry can be considered to have internal structural meaning and significance on the one hand as well as external function and application on the other'(2012: 73). For analysts to access this internal meaning it is of benefit to understand the external arrangement of component parts. In the visual arts, symmetry is an organizing principle which imposes constraints on physical construction.

Although of applicability to three-dimensional objects (such as buildings), symmetry concepts are most readily understood in the context of two-dimensional designs; the identification of

symmetry properties has proved of particular value in characterizing two-dimensional figures, motifs and regular repeating designs. Hann previously explained the technicalities of symmetry (1992, 2012), and these appear in summarized form below.

The identification of up to four geometric actions known as *symmetry operations* offers a means of classifying designs in two dimensions. These symmetry operations, known as *rotation*, *reflection*, *translation* and *glide reflection*, appear schematically with the relevant explanatory key shown in Figure 2.21. When considering the context of two-dimensional repeating designs, it is convenient to make reference to three distinct design types: motifs, which are either free-standing designs or the recurrent components or building blocks of regular repeating designs; frieze patterns (also known as border or strip patterns), which show regular repetition of a motif or motifs in one direction across the plane; all-over patterns (also known as plane or wallpaper patterns), which show repetition of a motif or motifs in two directions across the plane. We can classify all three design types in terms of their constituent symmetry characteristics. An

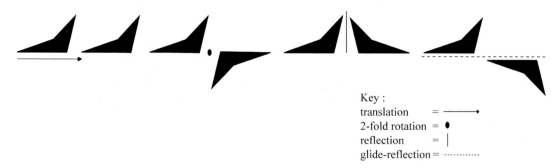

Key :
translation   = ———→
2-fold rotation = •
reflection   = |
glide-reflection = ············

Figure 2.21 Schematic representations of symmetry operations (CW)

explanation is presented below of the role played by symmetry in each of the three design types.

Motifs may be either asymmetrical or symmetrical. An asymmetrical motif consists of one part only, and thus is not deemed to have symmetry characteristics. Certain motifs exhibit either reflection symmetry or rotational symmetry. In the former category the motif consists of two or more component parts of the same size, shape and content, and each of these component parts is a reflection of an adjacent part. Best imagined inscribed within a circle, the classification of motifs with reflection symmetry relies on simply counting the number of imaginary reflection axes which pass through the centre of the imaginary circle surrounding the motif. Using the prefix letter d (for dihedral), motifs with reflection symmetry can be classified as d1, d2, d3, d4, d5, d6 and so forth, depending on the number of reflection axes which pass through the motif's centre (Figure 2.22). For example, class d2 motifs have bilateral symmetry around both their horizontal and their vertical axes, so they consist of four component parts (or fundamental units). Each d2 motif has two reflection axes, intersecting at 90 degrees; we can refer to this as *two-direction reflection symmetry*.

Where a motif exhibits rotational symmetry, two or more identical component parts can be identified also, but in this case each component part can be considered to be reproduced through rotation (rather than reflection) of its neighbours. Using the prefix letter c (for cyclic), motifs with rotational symmetry can be classified as c2, c3, c4, c5, c6 and so forth (Figure 2.23). Note that a motif in class c1 is an asymmetrical motif and needs to rotate through an imaginary 360 degrees before coinciding with a copy of itself. By

Figure 2.22 Schematic illustration of dx motifs (CW)

Figure 2.23 Schematic illustration of cx motifs (CW)

way of example, class c2 motifs possess twofold rotational symmetry and consist of two fundamental parts or units. Through a rotation of 180 degrees, each fundamental unit comes into coincidence with its neighbour. With a further 180 degree rotation, each unit is placed in exactly its original position.

When the four symmetry operations of rotation, reflection, translation and glide reflection are combined in designs which repeat (or translate) in one direction (i.e. between two parallel lines) a total of seven (and only seven) distinct frieze pattern classes can be produced (shown schematically in Figure 2.24). On combining the four symmetry operations in two distinct directions across the plane, a total of seventeen (and only seventeen) distinct all-over patterns can be produced (shown schematically in Figure 2.25). In terms of symmetry, we see seven types of frieze patterns and seventeen types of all-over patterns. The seven frieze-design classes are as follows: p111, p1a1, pm11, p1m1, p112, pma2 and pmm2. The letter and number components of the notation denote the presence or absence of the four symmetry operations. Hann previously gave an explanation of the notation and a fuller description of each class (2012: 83).

As noted earlier, combinations of the four symmetry operations yield a total of seventeen all-over pattern classes. In describing these, it is best to group them by making reference to the absence or presence of rotational symmetry (and, if present, the highest order of rotational symmetry): pattern classes p111 (or p1), p1g1, p1m1 and c1m1, which do not include rotation of any kind among their constituent symmetries; pattern classes p211 (or p2), p2gg, p2mg, p2mm and c2mm, which exhibit twofold rotation; classes p311 (or p3), p3m1 and p31m, which exhibit threefold rotational symmetry;

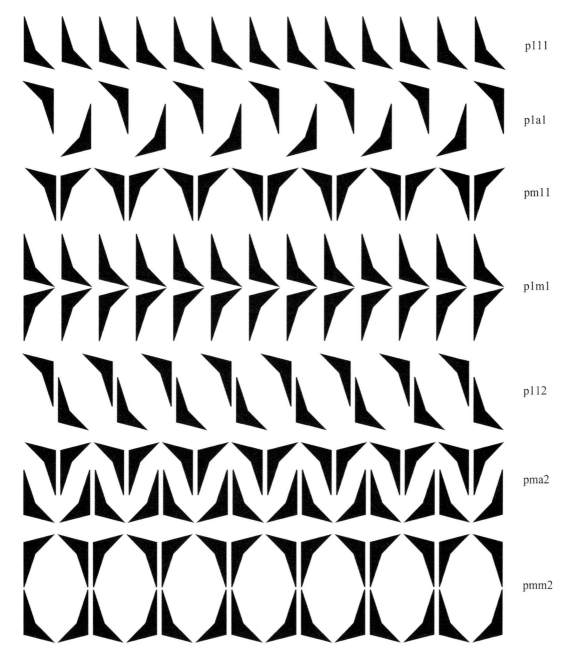

Figure 2.24 Schematic illustration of the seven frieze patterns (CW)

classes p411 (or p4), p4gm and p4mm, which exhibit four-fold rotation; classes p611 (or p6) and p6mm, which have a highest order of rotation of six. Although complicated, the notation used for each of the seventeen classes of all-over patterns simply indicates the relevant combination of symmetry operation from the seventeen possibilities. Hann previously gave fuller explanations of each

Figure 2.25 Schematic illustration of the seventeen classes of all-over pattern (CW)

class and the relevant notation (2012: 88–94 and 169–70). A good introduction to the subject is that by Padwick and Walker (1977), and Stevens (1981) also provided an accessible account.

Washburn and Crowe's 1988 work presents what is still the most accessible account for researchers wishing to develop a working knowledge to aid analysis.

geometric analysis in the visual arts

The earliest attempts to analyse structure and form in the visual arts seem to date to the era of the Italian Renaissance. In most cases, analyses focussed on understanding the inherent features of Greco-Roman orders of architecture and related forms of creative endeavour. The stimulus was the belief that such sources encapsulated in some unknown way the secrets of ancient Greek geometers and that success (in architectural design) was assured should such secrets be discovered and made the creative focus of fifteenth-century Italian practitioners (Chitham 2005). The present author is not aware that studies similar to those cited by Chitham have been conducted on non-European material. The perspectives taken in the analysis of European material may, however, be of some value in developing approaches for the analysis of visual arts from other areas.

In more recent times, Owen Jones's *The Grammar of Ornament* (1856) stands as the great nineteenth-century treatise dealing with artistic endeavours from a wide range of historical periods and cultural contexts. The focus of Jones's work and of a range of similar treatises published in the late nineteenth and early twentieth centuries (e.g. Racinet 1873; Speltz 1915) was the identification of the typical stylistic characteristics of visual art and design from various sources, cultures and periods, largely unfamiliar to the general public of the day. These treatises served as inspirational sources to designers. It is worth noting that newly established nineteenth-century museums—where newly accessioned designed objects of one kind or another were examined and analysed visually—also played an important role and ultimately acted as inspirational sources for newly created designs. For example, some of the work of William Morris and Lewis Foreman Day appears inspired by visits to the South Kensington Museum (i.e. the Victoria and Albert Museum, London). It is important to note that the visual analysis conducted by such individuals was not aimed primarily at understanding the relevant cultural or historical sources of selected objects, but rather at working out their underlying structure in order to apply this to newly created designs produced using Victorian processing techniques (as well as pre–Industrial Revolution hand techniques). Day and Morris were neither archaeologists nor anthropologists; they were designers with a keen awareness for innovative design.

Notable twentieth-century contributors to the development of methodologies of value to the analysis of the visual arts include Hambidge (1967 Dover ed.), whose examination of Greek art led to his proposal that all harmonious design exhibited what he termed 'dynamic symmetry' with proportions provided by various rectangles. Ghyka (1946) acknowledged the usefulness of Hambidge's perspectives, examined the relationships between geometry, nature and the human body and, making reference to Greek and Gothic art, proposed a theory of proportion which he believed would be of value to art and design practitioners. It seems that the most important published contributions to the increased understanding of structure and form in art and design during the twentieth century came from scholars concerned primarily with the geometric aspects of structures from the natural world. The works of Theodore Cook (1914) and D'Arcy Thompson (1917) are of particular note, and the bulk of publications concerned with structure in visual arts cite them frequently.

By the early twenty-first century, many mathematicians had taken a keen interest in the geometrical analysis of designed objects and constructions, including paintings, sculpture and architecture. A wide range of relevant literature resulted, but again the bulk was not readily accessible to typical art and design student audiences. There were, however, a few exceptions, including Melchizedek (2000), who examined cultural and historical aspects of what was referred to as 'the flower of life' motif (consisting of overlapping circles in hexagonal order); Ascher (2000), who considered the challenge of including 'ethnomathematics' (defined as the study of 'the mathematical ideas of traditional peoples') in high school geometry curricula; Elam (2001), who reviewed the use of geometry in art and design from ancient times and analysed a selection of twentieth-century product designs and posters; Kapraff (2002), who in his treatise *Beyond Measure* examined various geometric phenomena in cultural contexts, including the Brunes Star and how it may have been employed as a measure in ancient times; Fletcher (2004, 2005, 2006), who presented a series of studies which included consideration of the *vesica piscis*, assemblies involving six circles around one and the presence of golden-section measures in the regular pentagon and other figures; Marshall (2006), who considered the use of the square and related constructions in ancient Roman architecture; Stewart (2009), who (as mentioned previously) considered the use of the Brunes Star. Although a consistent, fully formed, replicable methodology for examining structural aspects of the visual arts has not emerged, some steps forward have been made by Reynolds (2000, 2001, 2002, 2003), who presented a range of useful articles dealing largely with the geometric analysis of designs. It is worthwhile consulting his 2001 article,

which outlined a series of procedures to assist geometric analysis in the visual arts.

Wittkower observed: 'Publications on proportion in the arts, searching, speculative, prophetic, assertive, and dogmatic, appear in a steady stream and in ever growing numbers', and noted further that a 1958 bibliography containing 900 articles was 'far from complete'(1962: 3). Scholars have published a vast number of attempts to identify how artisans and builders may have used geometry and knowledge of geometrical construction to provide some form of canon or structural guideline. For example, several important articles have focussed on explaining how ancient Egyptian and Near Eastern sculptors created renderings of humans (and human-like figures) by reference to a well-established system of proportion (Iversen 1960, 1968, 1976; Lorenzen 1977, 1980; Robins 1985, 1991, 1994; Hollenback 2005). A key piece of evidence, which most of these authors cite, is a rectangular wooden board held in the British Museum. It is believed that this object, which measures around 34 centimetres by around 54 centimetres, is a drawing board used by artisans in ancient times in Egypt. The front of the board depicts a seated human figure, in black ink, inscribed within a square grid. The board holds a few further drawings, including a representation of human arms, a small bird and a circular object. This drawing board suggests that ancient Egyptian craftspeople ensured that all human representations, in particular the location in drawings of particular parts of the human anatomy, conformed to this numbered grid system. Referring to the seated figure on the drawing board, Iversen (1960) commented: 'It is clear that the full theoretical height of the seated figure can be arrived at by counting the squares from the line at the feet up to the hair line (which was the upper measuring point in the . . . canon), following the line of the body around the bend of the knee.' Iversen continued: 'From the base-line to knee is 6 squares; along the thigh to the axis-line is 4 squares; from the level of the knee upward along the axis to the hair-line is 8 squares, the total being 18 squares, which exactly equals the number of squares in height required for the standing figure of a man' (1960). Note that there appears to be some confusion among scholars on whether the canon of proportion, at the time of the drawing board's use, was based on eighteen squares for an upstanding human male figure (as Iversen argued) or a canon of nineteen squares (as Lorenzen 1980 claimed). Although there appears to be some contradiction among authors (on the precise number of regular squares which should equate to the upright size of a sculpted male figure), the important issue is that they agreed that rules of proportion (referred to as a *canon of proportion*) were adhered to in ancient Egyptian times. It seems also to be the case that certain rules of proportion were used elsewhere, outside Egypt, in ancient times.

In the European context, Erickson reviewed the use of proportioning devices in pictorial composition and observed that systems of proportion were probably used first in ancient architectural planning, involving 'master diagrams and formulae evolved, largely in secrecy through generations of . . . planners and builders in the ancient civilizations of Egypt and Greece. After the Roman architect Vitruvius Pollio refined Plato's cosmological concepts of symmetry and proportion . . . and applied them specifically to architectural planning in the ten books of Architecture,

methods of proportioning and regulating design spread throughout Europe and diversified in the craft workshops of medieval master builders and masons' (1986).

When considering the available evidence relating to knowledge of proportions and geometry among visual artists, we should make reference to the *Medieval Sketchbook of Villard de Honnecourt*, a thirteenth-century sketchbook depicting a diverse range of material, including religious figures, birds, animals and insects, and architectural details, mainly from cathedrals at Chartres and Rheims, as well as mechanical devices of various kinds and church furnishings. The original sketchbook may well have been used as a source of reference by sculptors and artisans involved in wood carving and masonry and other crafts associated with Gothic cathedrals of the thirteenth century, although the precise role played by the sketchbook and the reasons for its production are unknown. Various forms of the publication appeared prior to a readily accessible and readable edition published by Dover, with an introduction and captions by Bowie (2006). Bucher, in his consideration of Gothic architecture and its design, examined a range of medieval plans and drawings, as well as various theoretical treatises and designs. Making reference to cathedrals in Austria, France and Germany, he concluded that it was likely that 'extensive, careful and detailed planning accompanied the erection of large structures at least from the beginning of the thirteenth century onward . . . In addition to the square and the two basic triangles [probably equilateral and isosceles], rotating polygons and circles inscribed in squares were used. The standard rectangle [probably a root-2 rectangle, where the longer side is equal to the diagonal of an initiating square] as well as the golden section were geometrically constructed at least from the twelfth century onwards' (1968). Padovan (1999) provided a comprehensive and highly enlightening review of the use of proportion in architecture. This is probably the best starting point for students intending to begin a research project concerned with proportion in the visual arts. Dudley produced an appraisal of the use of geometry in cathedral design, with specific reference to Canterbury Cathedral. His selected bibliography is ideally suited as a well-focussed starting point for all scholars involved in projects concerned with medieval architectural design, particularly the use of what Dudley referred to as 'sacramental geometry', that form of geometry used in religious buildings in medieval England (2010). It is stressed that, although these studies focus on a European context, the methods used and the perspectives taken may also be of value when considering material from a different geographical zone.

In *Embedded Symmetries, Natural and Cultural*, Washburn observed that, 'whereas the mathematics of symmetry has been understood for many years and psychological studies of the perception of symmetry have been conducted for some decades now, the acknowledgement by anthropologists that cultures actually recognise, use and prefer certain kinds of symmetrical order has not had widespread currency in cultural studies' (2004: 5). Since then, there appears to be some evidence (though only anecdotal) that the important breakthrough Washburn and Crow (1988, 2004) announced and expressed further, with support from various renowned authors, in

Embedded Symmetries, Natural and Cultural, had (by 2012) gained some currency of belief among cultural researchers. The fundamental issue is that 'patterns communicate many kinds of culturally important information' (Washburn 2004: 47), and also that 'in areas of the world where imagery rather than the written word remains as one of the primary means of communication, a proliferation of different forms and formats of imagery, both representational and non-representational, has arisen that visually projects ideas fundamental to the core concepts of those cultures' (Washburn and Crowe 2004: x). A further point to stress is that non-representational images have the capability of encoding 'important cultural principles and beliefs' (Washburn and Crowe 2004: x–xi). Attention is turned below to the symmetry of a well-known historical object.

Known as 'Queen of the Night' (a British Museum caption), this relief of a female figure dates to the early centuries of the second millennium BCE and is from Mesopotamia (Figure 2.26). The figure wears a horned headdress, typical of Mesopotamian deities. She holds a rod and a ring, together symbolizing her power to administer justice. The figure stands with talons as feet on two lions and her wings point downward, suggesting a connection with the underworld. A forward-facing owl is positioned beside each lion, at either side of the figure. The most remarkable aspect of this object, produced nearly four millennia ago, is that it expresses impressive bilateral reflection symmetry (two owls, two lions and two wings, in each case positioned at the same distance in relation to its partner from an imaginary mid-way vertical axis). This age-old geometric feature, reflection symmetry, is one of the principal concerns of this present book.

Figure 2.26 Queen of the night, plaque of baked clay, from early second millennium BCE, Mesopotamia (British Museum)

a small addition to a systematic analytical framework

As indicated previously, a highly productive avenue of design analysis and classification has been based on consideration of the underlying symmetry characteristics of designs. Important contributions were made by Washburn and Crowe (1988, 2004), Washburn (1983, 2004), Hargittai (1986, 1989) and Hann (1992, 2003c). Hann and Thomson (1992) previously provided a review of relevant literature, and Washburn and Crowe (2004: ix–xxx) provided an extensive (and very useful) bibliography. A key finding from the numerous research contributions

was that, when a representative sample of repeating designs from a given cultural setting (or historical period) is analysed with respect to its underlying symmetry properties and classified by reference to the various symmetry classes (seven frieze pattern classes and seventeen all-over pattern classes), we can see that different cultures (and historical periods) express different symmetry preferences. An important implication when considering the distribution of symmetry classes in any representative series of data is that symmetry classification is a culturally sensitive tool and can be used to detect continuity and change over time (subject to the availability of suitable data). The important point to stress, from the viewpoint of hypothesis testing and theoretical development, is that symmetry analysis and classification allow for replication of results from one researcher to another (Washburn and Crowe 1988). The intention here is to suggest a minor addition to standard symmetry classification by providing a means by which certain types of symmetry can be identified and recorded from consideration of nonrepeating designs, particularly those contained within a square frame.

Structural analysis in visual arts can proceed in numerous ways. Symmetry classification forms the basis of a substantial analytical framework which, in the longer term, may contribute to the further understanding of how geometry in general has been used in the visual arts historically and culturally and, in particular, how underlying geometry can encode meaning. Such understanding, in turn, may contribute to further knowledge of the diffusion process and to identifying possible time frames, places and avenues of diffusion.

In the visual arts, a large proportion of compositions are composed within a square framework. Further to this it is evident that a large proportion of these compositions exhibit reflection symmetry. Occasionally this reflection is in one direction only (simple bilateral reflection symmetry). It seems that there are many other occasions when reflection symmetry in a square relies on two or even four reflection axes. It seems, therefore, that square compositions may exhibit one of three orders of reflection symmetry: one-direction reflection symmetry; two-direction reflection symmetry; four-direction reflection symmetry. A square with four axes is presented in Figure 2.27. It is proposed that this simple figure be used as a template to assess the presence of reflection symmetry in square compositions.

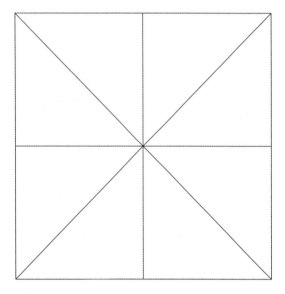

Figure 2.27 Square template with four-direction reflection axes (CW)

summary

Visual compositions are created and developed by reference to structural rules and, subsequently, they may be analysed with respect to their underlying structural features. This chapter introduced various geometrical constructions, including geometric symmetry, and presented a review of literature concerned with geometric analysis in the visual arts. Attention was focussed briefly on canons of proportion used by the ancient Egyptians and others later in history. This chapter pursued a short discussion of the nature of symmetry and on how associated concepts have been used to describe and classify designs, particularly regularly repeating designs, typically characterized by the systematic (or regular) repetition of a tile, motif or figure along a band (known as a frieze pattern) or across the plane (known as an all-over pattern). This chapter highlighted the value of symmetry classification as an analytical tool, and its potential to uncover a wide range of social, psychological, philosophical and cultural properties. This chapter also acknowledged the pioneering work of scholars such as Washburn and Crowe (1988, 2004) and Washburn (1983, 2004), and proposed a further addition to the analytical framework, based on square constructions. Where appropriate, subsequent chapters make reference to this and other symmetry measures in the case studies which follow.

Figure 2.28 The role of symbolism. All images by Joseph Lyons

Figure 2.29 Symmetry identification. Images by the following student contributors: Joseph Lyons, Alice France, Victoria Moore, Deasy Camiladini, Mohammad Rizki, Herry Putra, Septia Andini, Menur Ardanareswari, Desiree Btari Siregar, Mega Saffira, Olivia Listyani, Fadhila A. Arimurti, Ni Putu Padmi, Sari Astiti, and Hasri Haryani Direja

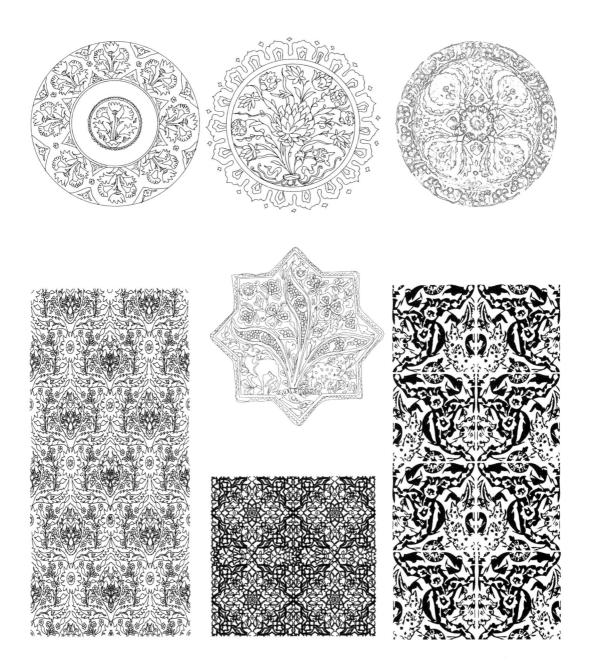

Figure 2.29 *(Continued)*

DISCUSSION OR ASSIGNMENT TOPICS

Symmetry of Motifs

Photograph or draw twenty motifs from your everyday environment. Consider the symmetry characteristics of each. Making reference to the notation of the form dx, or cx (where d denotes the presence of reflection, c the presence of rotation and x is a whole number), classify each of your twenty selected motifs.

Symmetry in Frieze Patterns

Photograph or draw twenty frieze patterns from your everyday environment. List and describe the symmetry characteristics of each.

Symmetry in All-over Patterns

Photograph ten all-over patterns from your everyday environment. List, describe and briefly compare the symmetry characteristics of each.

Detection of Reflection Symmetry

Photograph ten objects or buildings from your everyday environment which you believe exhibit reflection symmetry to varying degrees. Classify your images with respect to the order of reflection symmetry shown: one line of reflection; two lines of reflection (each in a different direction); three lines of reflection (each in a different direction); four or more lines of reflection (each in a different direction). Discuss your results.

Symbolism

Making reference to the examples provided in Figure 2.28, discuss the role of symbolism in the visual arts.

Symmetry Identification

Identify and list for each the symmetry characteristics of the motifs and patterns presented in Figure 2.29.

further reading

Arnheim, R. (1988). 'Symmetry and the Organisation of Form: A Review Article', *Leonardo*, 21 (3): 173–276.

Elam, K. (2001). *Geometry of Design: Studies in Proportion and Composition*, New York: Princeton Architectural Press.

Hambidge, J. (1967). *The Elements of Dynamic Symmetry*, New York: Dover.

Hann, M. A. (2012). *Structure and Form in Design: Critical Ideas for Creative Practice,* London and New York: Berg.

Hann, M. A. and Thomson, G. M. (1992). *The Geometry of Regular Repeating Patterns,* Textile Progress Series, 22 (1), Manchester: The Textile Institute.

Jones, O. ([1856] 1986). *The Grammar of Ornament,* London: Day and Son. Reprint, London: Omega.

Kappraff, J. (1991). *Connections: The Geometric Bridge between Art and Science,* New York: McGraw-Hill.

Washburn, D. (ed.) (1983). *Structure and Cognition in Art,* Cambridge: Cambridge University Press.

Washburn, D. (ed.) (2004). *Embedded Symmetries, Natural and Cultural,* Albuquerque: University of New Mexico Press.

Washburn, D.K. and Crowe, D.W. (1988). *Symmetries of Culture: Theory and Practice of Plane Pattern Analysis,* Seattle and London: University of Washington Press.

Washburn, D.K. and Crowe, D.W. (eds.) (2004). *Symmetry Comes of Age: The Role of Pattern in Culture,* Seattle and London: University of Washington Press.

3

cradles of civilization and initiators of trade

The established archaeological record of the region known as Mesopotamia extends several millennia BCE from the Bronze Age cultures of the Sumerian, Akkadian, Babylonian and Assyrian empires, superseded in the Iron Age by Neo-Assyrian and Neo-Babylonian empires. The Persian Achaemenid empire controlled the region from the sixth century to the fourth century BCE. Fertile land provided substantial agricultural surpluses which, when traded, allowed for importing metals, timber and precious stones to the area. Trade networks developed at least from the fourth millennium BCE onwards, connecting south Mesopotamia to the eastern part of the Mediterranean and with modern-day Turkey, Egypt, Iran, the Indus Valley (Pakistan) and Central Asia (Benzel, Graff, Rakic and Watts 2010: 17). Various durable art forms, especially in stone and clay, have survived and, in the early twenty-first century, are held in museums worldwide.

the development of international trade

When considering the visual arts of ancient Mesopotamia, scholars can observe certain consistencies and continuities. The motivation associated with the production of visual artwork appears consistent over many centuries, and was focussed largely on communicating religious or political messages. From the third millennium BCE until the outset of the Common Era, regional control waxed and waned among rival military powers, but trade with lands far and near developed steadily. International relationships were forged through the exchange of precious raw materials and luxury goods of various kinds, as well as diplomatic gifts, including horses and other animals. Trade facilitated the transfer of raw materials and the diffusion of associated technological knowledge of how to process or work these new raw materials, as well as the introduction of new forms of objects including armaments, household and palace furniture, mirrors, foodstuffs, styles of buildings, clothing, carpets and other textiles, and stylistic elements, motifs, symbols and patterns. By the late first millennium BCE, extensive trade networks had developed by both land and sea, linking Han China with Parthian Persia and the cities of the Near East and the Mediterranean region. Luxury goods such as Roman glass, Chinese silk, Indian dyed and printed cottons and Southeast Asian pepper were traded, and artistic traditions and religious beliefs were exchanged (Aruz and Wallenfels 2003; Bataille 2005; Benzel et al. 2010).

Mesopotamian visual arts, by the first millennium BCE, took many forms in various materials; predominant were relief sculpture, in the form of architectural and commemorative plaques, and other monuments, as well as furniture panels and stamp and cylinder seals. In the second half of the first millennium CE, a common visual language appears to have been shared across Mesopotamia and much of the Mediterranean coastal areas, probably due largely to the conquest of the Near East by Alexander of Macedon and the later Roman influence which continued for several centuries subsequent to the outset of the Common Era. Also, due largely to trade, substantial diffusion and adoption of motifs, symbols and compositional arrangements occurred, originating predominantly in the Near East, Egypt and Greece.

The contribution made to the visual arts by unsettled populations should also be acknowledged. Nomadic and semi-nomadic peoples in Central Asia created metal objects often used to adorn their horses (Aruz, Farkas, Alekseev and Korolkova 2001). Note that although it is often assumed that such metal objects fulfilled a purely decorative function (particularly in all other contexts where populations were largely without a writing system), this chapter suggests that these metal objects had an additional function as talismans, probably associated in some way with a tribal or other deity, believed to enhance performance and ensure success in battle. This book argues that many forms of visual art encapsulated cultural messages of some kind and had communication functions beyond the purely decorative. As noted previously, it is for this reason that the term *visual art* is employed here rather than the highly restrictive term *decorative art*.

motifs and compositions

In the visual arts of the Near East, for millennia up to the outset of the Common Era and for several centuries later, images of rulers (the majority male) conveyed one of two attributes: piety (as servant of the relevant deity) or might (as protector and ruler of the royal realm). Benzel and colleagues observed that the former types of representation, with the ruler depicted in a modest pose with hands clasped and head slightly bowed, were generally sculpted and presented in three dimensions (known as 'in the round') and the latter, of the mighty ruler, were often executed in relief, with various narratives unfolding across the surface of the object (Benzel et al. 2010: 34). Headdresses were an important attribute in the ancient Near East. According to Benzel and colleagues, 'the brimmed cap is the most widespread head attire during the later-third and early-second millennium BC[E], while later rulers depicted themselves wearing a fez-like cap' (2010: 34–5). Status was also communicated visually through the inclusion of various symbols, including rod and ring motifs (which indicated the power to make a judgement and to dispense justice) and weapons such as bows, arrows, swords and spears. Depictions indicating involvement in military campaigns, lion hunts and the performance of various rituals were also important. Representations of Neo-Assyrian rulers, for example, did not show real-life attributes, but rather qualities such as wisdom (associated with individuals who were 'wide eared' and became so through careful listening) and strength (indicated by bulging muscles).

In Near Eastern visual arts, motifs of animals, real or imagined, played a major role in the first millennium BCE and subsequently. Benzel and colleagues commented:

> [T]he art of the ancient Near East includes some of the most vivid images of animals to be found anywhere, appearing in forms ranging from painted pottery and clay sculptures to carved stone and sculpture in precious metals. Concepts of divinity, kingship, and the fertility of the natural world were frequently expressed through compositions depicting animals that decorated temple equipment, ritual and ceremonial objects. (2010: 30)

Portrayal of animals played a major role in royal hunt scenes, which depicted the ruler mounted on horseback or in a horse-drawn chariot, using bow and arrows, spears or swords aimed at running animals. For millennia, in the ancient Near East and subsequently elsewhere, royalty associated itself with lions. The motif of the royal hunt is of ancient origin. An illustration of a relief carving, excavated from Uruk and dated to around 3000 BCE, was included in Benzel and colleagues' work (2010) and is believed to be the oldest known representation of royal associations with the lion. Two components of the carving are: a 'priest king' with bow and arrow aimed at a lion-like animal and a figure which appears to be spearing an animal (which again seems to be a representation of a lion) (Benzel et al. 2010: 32). Benzel and colleagues observed that relevant cuneiform texts refer to the establishment by royalty of zoo-like parks that held various rare and exotic animals, including lions (Benzel et al. 2010: 33). In the visual arts, imaginary creatures were often composite in nature. Even the addition of a pair of wings to a lion brought it to the realm of the fantastic. Human-headed lions and bulls (that guarded

Assyrian palaces) wore horned headdresses. The sphinx migrated to Mesopotamia from Egypt, and the griffin, found initially in the Near East, travelled to Greece, Rome and much of Europe.

The visual arts also depicted various deities. Accumulated written records indicate a pantheon of deities extending to around three thousand names (Benzel et al. 2010: 39). Most deities were perceived in human form, could be either male or female and, like humans, required food, drink and shelter. Certain deities were associated with the sun, stars, moon, rivers, oceans or winds. Many were linked to certain animals. Benzel and colleagues listed the following as distinguishing attributes in the representation of deities: horned headdress, flounced robes, representation of a temple façade and associated animal or cosmic attributes (2010: 40). Artists often depicted gods or goddesses as of greater size when placed beside humans in the same composition.

the royal standard of Ur and other treasures (cs 1)

The Royal Standard of Ur (also known as the Standard of Ur or Battle Standard of Ur and held in the British Museum) was excavated from a tomb in the royal cemetery in the Sumerian city of Ur, one of the earliest Mesopotamian cities established in the fertile plains between the Tigris and Euphrates rivers. Figures 3.1–3.12 present relevant illustrations. The original wood that held the object together when found had rotted away. Reconstruction from the remaining materials (shell, red limestone and lapis lazuli) was a best-guess attempt at how the object may have been constructed originally. The intended function of the original object is not known, but Charles Leonard Woolley, who led the relevant archaeological dig, imagined it as a military or royal standard of some kind, possibly carried into battle at the end of a long raised pole. The object dates to the middle of the third millennium BCE. In its reconstructed condition, the box-like, wedge-shaped object, with truncated triangular sides and with a larger base than top, measures 21.59 centimetres by 49.53 centimetres. Various scenes, in mosaic form, created by assembling the excavated materials, appear on the four side panels. The two larger side panels, referred to as the war and peace panels, depict various scenes in frieze-type format, with each panel holding three parallel friezes, referred to as the top, middle and lower register. Peltenburg offered a good brief explanation (1995: 60–1), and MacGregor gave a discussion of the object (2012: 61–5).

Figure 3.1 Royal Standard of Ur detail (British Museum)

Figure 3.2 Royal Standard of Ur detail (British Museum)

Figure 3.3 Royal Standard of Ur detail (British Museum)

Figure 3.4 Royal Standard of Ur detail (British Museum)

Figure 3.5 Royal Standard of Ur detail (British Museum)

Figure 3.6 Royal Standard of Ur detail (British Museum)

Figure 3.7 Royal Standard of Ur detail (British Museum)

Figure 3.8 Royal Standard of Ur detail (British Museum)

symbol, pattern and symmetry

Figure 3.9 Royal Standard of Ur detail (British Museum)

Figure 3.10 Royal Standard of Ur detail (British Museum)

Figure 3.11 Royal Standard of Ur detail (British Museum)

Figure 3.12 Royal Standard of Ur detail (British Museum)

The war panel shows a representation of an army, with four high-fronted, four-wheeled vehicles pulled by what appear to be donkeys. Each vehicle has a driver and, standing behind him on a projecting platform, a person carrying a spear or axe. These are depictions of early forms of wheeled transport, with fixed-wheel axles; these vehicles were not easily manoeuvred. Also depicted are: enemies killed with axes or run over by the vehicles; infantry with cloaks carrying spears; captured enemy paraded naked and presented to some dignitary (a larger figure holding a spear).

The peace panel shows animals, fish and other goods carried in procession, seemingly to a banquet. Seated figures wear fringed skirts, drink and listen to music. A musician plays a lyre. Banquet scenes such as this can be found also on contemporary cylinder seals (such as that of Queen Pu-abi, also displayed in the British Museum). Woolley discovered further notable objects, three of which the following sections describe briefly.

Ram in the Thicket

The first of these objects is known as 'the Ram in the Thicket'. Woolley discovered this object, buried in one of the graves in the royal cemetery at Ur. The inspiration for this name was the biblical story of a goat caught in a thicket. The animal is depicted reaching up, possibly to access the tastiest fruits or leaves, a pose common among goats and sheep in modern times. The animal's head and legs are covered with gold leaf and its ears are made of copper. Lapis lazuli, shell and gold are used elsewhere on the figure, and the thicket or tree itself consists of gold leaf (Figures 3.13 and 3.14).

Figure 3.14 Ram in the Thicket (British Museum)

Queen's lyre

Woolley also discovered several lyres in the royal cemetery. The one found in the grave of Queen Pu-abi is probably the most famous. When found, the wooden parts of the instrument had decayed. Certain components of lapis lazuli, shell and red limestone, as well as a gold mask of a bull (positioned at the front of the instrument's sound box) have survived (Figure 3.15). The Royal Standard of Ur depicts a bull lyre of similar construction.

Figure 3.13 Ram in the Thicket (British Museum)

Figure 3.15 Queen's Lyre (British Museum)

The royal game of Ur

This is another Woolley find from the royal cemetery at Ur, in southern Iraq. The board game is one of several with a similar layout. Although the wood which formed the base had decayed, the inlaid materials (shell, limestone and lapis lazuli) had survived in position, thus allowing the original format to be restored. The board has twenty squares (Figure 3.16 shows a detail). References to ancient documents indicate that two players competed to move their pieces from one side of the board to the opposite side, and that each piece came into play only when a particular value of dice was thrown by the player. The gaming pieces do not survive (maybe they too were made from wood or from other perishable materials), but excavators have found examples of games using twenty squares dating from the third millennium BCE up to the end of the first millennium CE at various sites east of the Mediterranean, as far as India.

Neo-Assyrian sculptures (cs 2)

Neo-Assyrian palaces, such as those at Nimrud and Nineveh, became renowned in modern times because of their pictorial narrative reliefs depicting royal affairs, hunting and warfare and its aftermath. Massive stone sculptures of protective mythological figures flanked gateways and important entrances. The architectural configuration of buildings was around large and small courtyards.

Nimrud, located on the banks of the Tigris river, was made the Neo-Assyrian capital in the early ninth century by Ashurnasirpal II, who built a substantial palace and temples on the site of the ruined city of Kalhu. Colossal sculptures of mythological beasts with human heads guarded the entrances. Sculpted wall reliefs lined many of the palace's interior walls; these illustrated the ruler's victory in battle, his participation in various court matters and his hunting exploits. Figures 3.17–3.24 show examples of Nimrud sculpture and relief panels.

Figure 3.16 The Royal Game of Ur (detail)

Figure 3.17 Winged bull and lion with human heads, from Nimrud (British Museum)

Figure 3.18 Neo-Assyrian relief detail, Nimrud, 865–860 BCE (British Museum)

Figure 3.19 Neo-Assyrian relief detail, Nimrud, 865–860 BCE (British Museum)

Figure 3.20 Neo-Assyrian relief detail, Nimrud, 865–860 BCE (British Museum)

Figure 3.21 Neo-Assyrian relief detail, Nimrud, 865–860 BCE (British Museum)

Figure 3.22 Neo-Assyrian relief detail, Nimrud, 865–860 BCE (British Museum)

Figure 3.23 Neo-Assyrian relief detail, Nimrud, 865–860 BCE (British Museum)

Figure 3.24 Neo-Assyrian relief detail, Nimrud, 865–860 BCE (British Museum)

Nineveh was an ancient city on the eastern bank of the Tigris river. It was for a period the capital of the Neo-Assyrian empire. Its location, within a landmass between the Mediterranean Sea and the Persian Gulf, made it ideally situated to benefit from trade passing from one region to the other. Although the city was of more ancient origin, significant expansion and development took place particularly during the ninth century BCE with the start of large-scale architectural projects, leading ultimately, by the eighth century BCE, to the laying out of streets, squares, palaces and temples (Figures 3.25–3.40). Following civil wars and attacks from outside the empire, the city was sacked in the early seventh century BCE.

Figure 3.25 Neo-Assyrian relief detail, Nineveh, 645–635 BCE (British Museum)

Figure 3.26 Neo-Assyrian relief detail, Nineveh, 645–635 BCE (British Museum)

Figure 3.27 Neo-Assyrian relief detail, Nineveh, 645–635 BCE (British Museum)

Figure 3.28 Neo-Assyrian relief detail, Nineveh, 645–635 BCE (British Museum)

Figure 3.29 Neo-Assyrian relief detail, Nineveh, 645–635 BCE (British Museum)

Figure 3.30 Neo-Assyrian relief detail, Nineveh, 645–635 BCE (British Museum)

Figure 3.31 Neo-Assyrian relief detail, Nineveh, 645–635 BCE (British Museum)

Figure 3.32 Neo-Assyrian relief detail, Nineveh, 645–635 BCE (British Museum)

Figure 3.33 Neo-Assyrian relief detail, Nineveh, 645–635 BCE (British Museum)

Figure 3.34 Neo-Assyrian relief detail, Nineveh, 645–635 BCE (British Museum)

Figure 3.35 Neo-Assyrian relief detail, Nineveh, 645–635 BCE (British Museum)

Figure 3.36 Neo-Assyrian relief detail, Nineveh, 645–635 BCE (British Museum)

Figure 3.37 Neo-Assyrian relief detail, Nineveh, 645–635 BCE (British Museum)

Figure 3.38 Neo-Assyrian relief detail, Nineveh, 645–635 BCE (British Museum)

Figure 3.39 Neo-Assyrian relief detail, Nineveh, 645–635 BCE (British Museum)

Figure 3.40 Neo-Assyrian relief detail, Nineveh, 645–635 BCE (British Museum)

the Ishtar Gate (cs 3)

The Ishtar Gate was one of the entrances to the inner city of Babylon. Constructed to the north side of the city in 575 BCE by order of King Nebuchadnezzar II, the glazed brick edifice was dedicated to the goddess Ishtar and decorated with dragon- and bull-like motifs. Through this gate lay the Processional Way, also in glazed bricks and decorated with striding lion motifs. Parts of the Ishtar Gate and Processional Way were reconstructed from material excavated in the 1930s and, in the early twenty-first century, were on permanent display at the Pergamon Museum in Berlin (Figures 3.41–3.49).

Figure 3.41 Detail of Ishtar Gate, 575 BCE (Staatliche Museen zu Berlin)

Figure 3.42 Detail of Ishtar Gate, 575 BCE (Staatliche Museen zu Berlin)

Figure 3.43 Detail of Ishtar Gate, 575 BCE (Staatliche Museen zu Berlin)

Figure 3.44 Detail of Ishtar Gate, 575 BCE (Staatliche Museen zu Berlin)

Figure 3.45 Detail of Ishtar Gate, 575 BCE (Staatliche Museen zu Berlin)

Figure 3.46 Detail of Ishtar Gate, 575 BCE (Staatliche Museen zu Berlin)

Figure 3.47 Detail of Ishtar Gate, 575 BCE (Staatliche Museen zu Berlin)

Figure 3.48 Detail of Ishtar Gate, 575 BCE (Staatliche Museen zu Berlin)

Figure 3.49 Detail of Ishtar Gate, 575 BCE (Staatliche Museen zu Berlin)

the Cyrus Cylinder (cs 4)

This is an ancient clay cylinder which holds a declaration in Akkadian cuneiform script, prepared on the instructions of the Achaemenid ruler Cyrus the Great (Figures 3.50–3.51). The object dates from the sixth century BCE and was discovered in the ruins of Babylon in 1879. In the early twenty-first century, it was on display at the British Museum, the institution which sponsored the expedition associated with its discovery. The object is a barrel-shaped cylinder of baked clay, 22.5 centimetres by 10 centimetres (maximum diameter). Excavated in several fragments, the two main pieces were reunited and the object restored in the early 1970s.

Figure 3.50 Cyrus Cylinder, sixth century BCE, Babylon (British Museum)

Figure 3.51 Cyrus Cylinder, sixth century BCE, Babylon (British Museum)

The text of the cylinder refers to the victorious Cyrus as a great leader who came to the aid of the Babylonians, repatriated various displaced peoples and restored temples and sanctuaries. Scholars and others have disputed the exact interpretation of the cylinder's text. Focussing on the declared peaceful rule expressed within the text, some modern-day observers have referred to the cylinder as an early human-rights charter. Others have insisted that the concept of human rights, as understood in the latter half of the twentieth century and the early decades of the twenty-first century, is far removed from perceptions of the role of the individual in society during the sixth century BCE.

the Babylonian map of the world (cs 5)

This is a clay tablet, with cuneiform text and a schematic drawing, believed to be the first map of the world (Brotton 2012). This object, from Sippar in southern Iraq, dates to around the middle of the first millennium BCE, and measures just over 12 centimetres by just over 8 centimetres (Figure 3.52). The British Museum acquired the tablet in 1882. Brotton underlined the importance of the object when he observed that it presented 'an

abstraction of terrestrial reality' and it allowed the earth to be comprehended by 'categorising it in circles, triangles, oblongs and dots, unifying writing and image in a world picture at the centre of which lies Babylon' (2012: 2–3).

Figure 3.52 The Babylonian map of the world, middle of the first millennium BCE (British Museum)

Brotton (2012) outlines the context of the object's discovery in the late nineteenth century among tens of thousands of excavated pieces. An Iraqi-born archaeologist, Hormuzd Rassam, discovered the piece when on an expedition sponsored by the British Museum and aimed at gathering cuneiform tablets which excavators and scholars hoped would provide an account of the biblical flood (Reade 1986). The object was overlooked until the script was translated towards the end of the nineteenth century. The British Museum placed the object on display in the first quarter of the twenty-first century.

The front of the tablet shows the world, as known to Babylonians at that time, in plan, bird's-eye view. The object has an area of cuneiform script and beneath this appear two concentric circles, within which are shown a series of small circles, arcs and oblong shapes. A hole sits at the centre of the object's face, maybe created by an early pair of compasses. A few triangles (labelled *nagû* or *region*) are distributed around the circumference of the outer circle. Further legends note distances ('six leagues between where the sun is not seen') and regions where exotic animals such as chameleons, ibexes, monkeys, ostriches, lions and wolves live (Brotton 2012: 2). Schematic drawings of the object invariably fill in the parts believed to be missing, so generally these depict eight triangles drawn equidistantly round the outer circle (e.g. Finkel and Seymour 2008: 17). Though Brotton maintained that five triangles 'remain legible' (2012: 1),

observations made by the present author in 2012 identified two clear triangles (one a right-angled and the other isosceles) and a third incomplete figure, possibly originally a triangle prior to damage. Artisans may have engraved further triangles on the object during its manufacture, but this is by no means certain when considering the drawn image as it appears on the clay tablet. However note that the cuneiform text on the object is associated closely with the figure. In particular, text on the reverse mentions eight *nagû*, so the assumption that there were at some point eight triangular shapes, positioned equidistantly around the circumference of the outer circle, is understandable.

The outer circle is labelled *marratu* or *salt sea*, suggesting an ocean encircling the world represented within the concentric circles. The most prominent curved oblong running through the central hole on the object represents the Euphrates river, with origins in an arc shape labelled *mountains* and ending in a horizontally oriented rectangle, labelled *channel and swamp* (Brotton 2012: 2). A small rectangle, positioned just above the central hole, is drawn across the Euphrates and labelled *Babylon*. Horowitz (1988) presented a comprehensive transcription, and Finkel and Seymour (2008: 17) provided an interesting commentary. Commenting on the historical significance, Brotton observed: 'this is more than just a map of the earth's surface: it is a comprehensive diagram of Babylonian cosmology, with the inhabited world as its manifestation' (2012: 2).

DISCUSSION OR ASSIGNMENT TOPICS

Royal Standard of Ur

Making reference to the illustrative material presented in this chapter, discuss the imagery associated with the Royal Standard of Ur.

Neo-Assyrian Reliefs

Making reference to illustrative material of your choice, discuss the pictorial content of the narrative reliefs found at Nimrud and Nineveh.

Ishtar Gate

What is the Ishtar Gate? Where was it constructed first, and where is it located currently in reconstructed form?

Cuneiform Objects

Describe and discuss the significance of the following objects: the Cyrus Cylinder and the Babylonian map of the world.

---

further reading

Aruz, J. with Wallenfels, R. (eds.) (2003). *Art of the First Cities: The Third Millennium* B.C. *from the Mediterranean to the Indus,* New Haven, CT: Yale University Press.

Benzel, K., Graff, S.B., Rakic, Y. and Watts, E.W. (2010). *Art of the Ancient Near East: A Resource for Educators,* New York: The Metropolitan Museum of Art.

Curtis, J. (2000). *Ancient Persia,* London: British Museum Press.

Curtis, J. and Tallis, N. (2005). *Forgotten Empire: The World of Ancient Persia,* London: British Museum Press.

Finkel, I.L. and Seymour, M.J. (eds.) (2008). *Babylon: Myth and Reality,* London: British Museum Press.

Finkel, I.L. and Seymour, M.J. (2009). *Babylon: City of Wonders,* London: British Museum Press.

MacGregor, N. (2012). *A History of the World in 100 Objects,* London: Penguin and the British Museum.

4

---

facilitators and intermediaries in lands to the east

As the previous chapter highlighted, various Near Eastern civilizations participated in trade, principally with lands to the east, during the last few millennia BCE and subsequently. To state the obvious, trade is not possible without at least two willing participants, and each participant should have something to offer that the other participant wants to obtain. Certain ancient civilizations arose in other parts of the world (outside the Near East, Greece and Egypt), and these civilizations participated in the development and maintenance of various international trading networks. The example of particular relevance in the context of this book is the civilization that developed in the Yellow River Valley in China (around 2000 BCE). From the viewpoint of civilizations in the Near East and Mediterranean regions, during the second and first millennia BCE, China was an important, though distantly located, trading source. When referring to international trade in ancient times, the use of the word *network* is important as it was probably the case that traded goods changed hands at various stages. Some participants, because of their commanding geographical location, acted as go-betweens or as the bridge connecting trading partners located at geographical extremes (of say, east and west). Examples of important intermediaries between the trading Chinese and the Near Easterners in ancient times include, at different

time periods, the Parthians, the Sasanians and the Kushans. Various nomadic tribal groups such as the Scythians (known also as the Scytho-Siberians), who roamed the steppe lands of Asia, were also important. They facilitated trade over several thousand miles, across a northern expanse, before the establishment of a network which became known in later years as the Silk Route (discussed briefly in Chapter 5).

ancient trade networks (BCE)

Scholars have identified in the literature several routes by which individuals or groups engaged in trade, exchange, travel, conquest or the development of diplomatic relationships or communications. By the first millennium BCE, complex, interconnected networks of trade had developed. The Amber Road allowed the transport of amber from the coast of the Baltic Sea to Italy, Greece, the Black Sea area and Egypt. The Incense Route enabled the exchange of frankincense, myrrh, Indian spices, precious stones, pearls, ivory, ebony, silk, gold and rare feathers, and linked by land and by sea the shores of the northern Mediterranean region with eastern and southern sources or destinations across the Levant and Egypt, Arabia, North Africa and India. The Persian Royal Road linked key locations during the times of the Achaemenid Empire: the Ancient Tea Route, a network of mule caravan trails, connected Yunnan Province in southwest China with Burma (Myanmar), India and Tibet, and allowed trade in tea, salt and Tibetan ponies; the King's Highway, from Egypt to the Sinai Peninsula, Jordan, Damascus and the banks of the Euphrates River, functioned during the latter half of the second millennium BCE; several trans-Saharan caravan routes were the ways by which scholars estimate that several million slaves were forcibly marched northwards in ancient times (Fage 2001: 256); the Grand Trunk Road, in operation as early as the latter half of the first millennium BCE, stretched around fifteen hundred miles and linked present-day Chittagong (Bangladesh) in the east with Kabul (Afghanistan) in the west.

When the nature of each of these routes or roads is reviewed, much contradiction is evident from the literature, and some readers tend to assume that each trade path operated independently, within stated geographical boundaries and without interconnections with other regions or types of commerce or exchange. Rather than assuming clearly separated entities, each involved in its own world of commerce and trade within tightly specified geographical and time boundaries (probably in response to modern scholarship's tendency to feel more comfortable when historical events, facts, figures and concepts are placed in neat boxes of time and space), it seems best to consider a complex network, overlapping in not only time and space, but also in the types of goods traded.

Ample evidence exists for both intra-continental and intercontinental trade before the commonly accepted Year One of the Common Era. Well-developed trade networks linked Europe, from the shores of the Mediterranean to the Baltic Sea, with lands to the east and south, including North and Central Africa, Egypt, Arabia, India, Southeast Asia and the Indonesian archipelago, China, Korea and Japan, and numerous lands in between. So it is evident that a great trading network, with probable origins in the second or third millennium BCE, provided a platform for long-distance communication, trade and exchange, and linked lands to the east with lands to the west and vice versa, across the landmass often referred to as Eurasia, with numerous tributaries south and north, by land and sea. Scholars have found much evidence for substantial and well-developed international trade between east and west across this great trading network by the end of the first century BCE, involving that part of the Roman Empire east of the Mediterranean, the Parthian Empire (Iranian Plateau), the Kushan Empire (present-day Pakistan, north India and part of Afghanistan), a confederation of Central Asian nomads and the Han Empire (China).

examples of intermediaries

In the first millennium BCE, various nomadic peoples from the southern steppes, with common customs, formed a loose association. Their geographical scope of influence extended from the Black Sea to Central Asia and Mongolia, a three-thousand-mile-long corridor of pasture land necessary to meet the grazing requirements of large numbers of horses, cattle, goats and sheep. These people valued horses highly and traded them with the ancient Chinese and others. During the twentieth century, archaeologists discovered many Bronze Age burial mounds (or *kurgans*), and these yielded much evidence to suggest that the steppe nomadic groups, referred to here as *Scytho-Siberians*, engaged in trade (or gift exchange) with their neighbours, probably across a network of routes extending from the border of present-day China in the north-east to northern Turkey in the west, probably also a few centuries before the establishment of trade activity along the trade routes to the south; these latter routes were later known collectively as the Silk Road or Silk Route.

By the time of his death in 323 BCE, Alexander of Macedon had built an empire extending from the Mediterranean in the west to the banks of the river Indus in the east. Hellenistic visual arts and architecture permeated much of the Near Eastern world, and the Parthians rose to power in this climate (247 BCE–224 CE). Establishing a headquarters at Ctesiphon, on the banks of the river Tigris in southern Mesopotamia, the Parthians ruled for more than four centuries, influencing events across much of the Near East. Because of the shortage of written evidence, scant knowledge survives of the Parthians' society and culture, though it is evident that they controlled a commanding geographic position on the Iranian Plateau, at intersections of important trade routes between Rome in the west and Han China in the east.

Subsequently to the Parthians, the next important Persian-dominated power (from 225 CE) was that of the Sasanians (also spelled Sassanians). The Sasanian area of control waxed and waned over the course of around four centuries, and at its peak included present-day Iran, Afghanistan, Iraq, Syria, the Caucasus (Armenia, Georgia and Azerbaijan), parts of Central Asia, southwest Pakistan and parts of Turkey. Sasanian cultural influence, especially in the visual arts, extended to all of these regions and beyond. As was the case with their Parthian predecessors, the Sasanians were keen to maintain and develop diplomatic and trade relationships with China. Land and sea trade were important to each. Both shared a common

interest to protect and preserve trade along the routes connecting China to the Mediterranean, to the extent that they both built outposts in remote border areas to ensure the safety of trade caravans from various nomadic bandits. Arab forces defeated Sasanian armies in 642 CE.

The Kushans (c. second century BCE to the third century CE) controlled an empire known traditionally as Gandhara, which, at its peak, covered territory that included much of present-day Pakistan and parts of north India (as far as Benares in the east and Sanchi in the south), Afghanistan and Uzbekistan. Regarded as home to a multi-ethnic society tolerant of religious differences, the Gandhara region was much sought after because of its strategic location, which provided access to both overland and sea trade routes. An eclectic mixture is evident in Kushan visual arts, with the expression of Buddhist themes as well as adaptations from Greek and Roman mythology. Peshawar and Taxila, both in present-day Pakistan, were important capitals. The Kushans did much to facilitate trade using land and sea routes where appropriate.

Chinese dragon motifs (cs 6)

Probably the most potent symbol historically, in China as well as across much of Asia, is the dragon, a motif used commonly in the visual arts for over two millennia. Although associated popularly with China, the motif also appears to varying degrees in Korea, Japan, parts of Southeast Asia, and parts of central Asia, Mongolia and Tibet.

The dragon (or *long*) appears to be China's oldest mythological creature and was featured commonly on ancient bronzes long before the invention of writing (Walters 1995: 44). The creature is depicted in several guises and is considered an amalgam of various animals, real or imaginary: the head of a camel and the horns of a stag, the neck of a snake, the eyes of a demon, the ears of a cow, the claws of an eagle, the soles of a tiger, 117 scales from a carp, and either winged or wingless (Allane 1993: 107). According to Allane, there are male and female varieties; the male is deemed to have whiskers and a stubbier nose and is usually portrayed in association with a luminous pearl motif (1993: 107). The creature was deemed to be charged with yang, the positive force in the cosmos, and successive emperors commonly selected it as their symbol. When used in costume, depending on the rank of the wearer, dragon motifs had five, four or three bird-like claws. Historically, five-clawed dragon motifs were reserved for use, particularly in garment form, by the emperor and high-ranking officials (Hann 2004: 34). However, as J. K. Wilson observed, on the basis of the substantial numbers of garments available from the eighteenth and nineteenth centuries (late Qing dynasty) depicting dragons with five claws, much wider availability is suggested; so the exclusivity rule appears to have been relaxed in later times (1990: 18). Figures 4.1–4.25 present examples.

Figure 4.2 Dragon (JL)

Figure 4.1 Dragon with phoenix (JL)

Figure 4.3 Dragon (JL)

Figure 4.5 A dragon as an architectural feature, Shanghai

Figure 4.4 Dragon (JL)

Figure 4.6 Dragon, detail from nineteenth-century textile (Qing dynasty collection, University of Leeds International Textiles Archive)

Figure 4.7 Dragon, detail from nineteenth-century textile (Qing dynasty collection, University of Leeds International Textiles Archive)

Figure 4.8 Dragon, detail from nineteenth-century textile (Qing dynasty collection, University of Leeds International Textiles Archive)

Figure 4.9 Dragon, detail from nineteenth-century textile (Qing dynasty collection, University of Leeds International Textiles Archive)

Figure 4.10 Dragon, detail from nineteenth-century textile (Qing dynasty collection, University of Leeds International Textiles Archive)

Figure 4.11 Dragon, detail from nineteenth-century textile (Qing dynasty collection, University of Leeds International Textiles Archive)

Figure 4.12 Dragon, detail from nineteenth-century textile (Qing dynasty collection, University of Leeds International Textiles Archive)

Figure 4.13 Dragon, detail from nineteenth-century textile (Qing dynasty collection, University of Leeds International Textiles Archive)

Figure 4.14 Dragon, detail from nineteenth-century textile (Qing dynasty collection, University of Leeds International Textiles Archive)

Figure 4.15 Dragon, detail from nineteenth-century textile (Qing dynasty collection, University of Leeds International Textiles Archive)

Figure 4.16 Dragon, detail from nineteenth-century textile (Qing dynasty collection, University of Leeds International Textiles Archive)

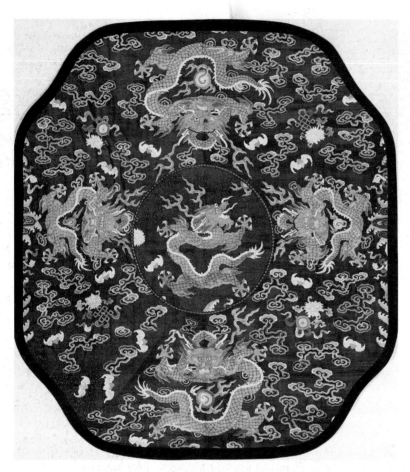

Figure 4.17 Dragon, detail from nineteenth-century textile (Qing dynasty collection, University of Leeds International Textiles Archive)

Figure 4.18 Dragon, detail from nineteenth-century textile (Qing dynasty collection, University of Leeds International Textiles Archive)

Popularly, Chinese dragons are associated with water, waterfalls, rivers and seas. Numerous types can be identified, most commonly horned dragons, winged dragons, celestial dragons, spiritual dragons, dragons associated with hidden treasures, coiling dragons, yellow dragons and the dragon king (which consisted of four separate dragons, each a ruler of a sea, to the north, south, east and west).

Carr (1990) identified over one hundred ancient Chinese names for dragons of various kinds, and rationalized these into seven categories: rain dragons, flying dragons, snake dragons, wug dragons (the term *wug* apparently referred to small reptiles, insects and worms), crocodile dragons, hill dragons and 'miscellaneous dragons'.

Figure 4.19 Dragon, detail from nineteenth-century textile (Qing dynasty collection, University of Leeds International Textiles Archive)

Figure 4.20 Dragon, detail from nineteenth-century textile (Qing dynasty collection, University of Leeds International Textiles Archive)

Figure 4.21 Dragon, detail
from nineteenth-century textile
(Qing dynasty collection,
University of Leeds International
Textiles Archive)

Figure 4.22 Dragon, detail from nineteenth-century
textile (Qing dynasty collection, University of Leeds
International Textiles Archive)

Figure 4.23 Dragon, detail from nineteenth-century textile (Qing dynasty collection, University of Leeds International Textiles Archive)

Figure 4.24 Dragon, detail from nineteenth-century textile (Qing dynasty collection, University of Leeds International Textiles Archive)

Figure 4.25 Dragon, detail from nineteenth-century textile (Qing dynasty collection, University of Leeds International Textiles Archive)

Historically, Chinese dragons were regarded as divine mythical creatures that brought prosperity, abundance and luck. When Buddhism spread to China, the symbolism associated with the dragon motif was absorbed into the mythology integral to the new religion (Walters 1995: 45).

Dragon motifs appear in the full range of Chinese visual arts, in painting, sculpture and in objects of bronze, lacquer, jade, ceramics and textiles). During the Qing dynasty, the motif was in prevalent use in traditional court and other formal garments. A particular class of Chinese garment became known among English-speaking museum curators and collectors in the late twentieth and early twenty-first centuries as *mandarin robes* or *dragon robes* (V. Wilson 1986: 12). The term scholars employ most commonly in the literature is *long pao*. *Long pao* were worn predominantly (though not exclusively) by men, and their use was associated with a range of accessories (J. K. Wilson 1990: 24–9). The use of several dragon motifs is the dominant surface-design feature of the cloth used in construction of these garments. Although intended as fabric for use in garment form, on many occasions the decorated cloth itself was sewn into rectangular panels and sold to Western buyers. As a result, many museums today include in their collections quantities of rectangular fabric panels.

Dragon motifs are associated with certain compositional arrangements, when considered in either sewn-up garment or rectangular panel form. Often, the lower part of the composition includes a substantial section of stripes, representing the earth. Stylized waves appear above these stripes, representing the seas and waters of the earth and, centrally within these, is positioned a stylized mountain motif. Above these decorative layers are depicted cloud-filled skies, with one or more pairs of dragons facing each other (in bilateral-symmetry format), with a flaming pearl positioned between each pair. Sprinkled throughout this upper layer are various good luck and longevity symbols, especially bats, but often also symbols associated with Buddhism, Taoism and Confucianism.

the Oxus Treasure (cs 7)

The Oxus Treasure is a collection of 170 gold and silver objects from the Achaemenid period. Scholars believe the discovery of the collection occurred close to the Oxus river. The British Museum and the Victoria and Albert Museum (both in London) hold pieces from the hoard. This case study makes reference to the following items from the collection: the Oxus chariot model and a pair of griffin-headed bracelets.

The Oxus chariot model

This item measures around 10 centimetres in length and is made from gold (Figure 4.26). Two figures are contained on the chariot's platform, one a driver and the other probably a regional political dignitary or governor whose task it was to enforce laws and to collect taxes. A notable feature is the symbol displayed on the front of the chariot: that of Bes the Egyptian dwarf-god, a popular protective deity. The display of a motif foreign to the Persian rulers is not unusual, for Cyrus and his successors apparently showed great religious and cultural tolerance. Provided conquered populations submitted to Persian rule, they were allowed to speak their own languages and to practise their own religions. Four horses or ponies pull the model chariot. The two figures wear Median-style dress. The Medes were from the north of the central part of the Achaemenid Empire.

Griffin-headed bracelets

This pair of griffin-headed bracelets is similar in form to some depicted on relief sculptures in the ruins of Persepolis. Semi-precious stone or coloured-glass inlays which probably filled the hollow spaces in the bracelet are now lost (Figure 4.27).

Figure 4.26 Gold model chariot, fifth to fourth century BCE, Oxus Treasure (British Museum)

Figure 4.27 Detail of gold armlet (one of a pair), fifth to fourth century BCE, Oxus Treasure (British Museum)

steppe art (cs 8)

To the west of the Central Asian steppes lived the Scythians (800–100 BCE), a semi-nomadic group that turned eventually to agriculture. Various small groups, including the Sarmatians (600 BCE–450 CE), inhabited the mid plains. In the east, located around the Altai Mountains, were the so-called Pazyryk people, named by Rudenko (1953 and 1970) from the local word for *mound*. Note that scholars continue to debate the degree of association among the various groups, the period of dominance of each, their significance historically and the extent of their geographical influence. The collective term *Scytho-Siberian* is probably the

most appropriate when referring to all of these groups. They appear largely to have adhered to common forms of decoration, dominated by the use of animal motifs, which were stylistically different from Chinese or Persian forms of the time. They were, however, familiar with both Persian and Chinese art styles. They valued horses highly as a source of transport as well as a source of food. The Scytho-Siberians were unrivalled as archers, skilled at using the powerful composite bow from horseback. To the west of their sphere of influence, they challenged the great invading army of Darius the Persian. Although each tribe within the larger Scytho-Siberian group probably roamed distances of several hundred miles, the tribes to the far east probably never came into direct contact with those to the far west. It seems likely, however, that the various groups formed a loose trading federation with influence extending from the perimeter of the Great Wall in the east to the shores of the Black Sea in the west. It seems that this network of nomadic pastoralists may have acted as crucial intermediaries between the settled and established (agrarian) civilizations to the east and west. Relatively recent publications edited by Aruz and colleagues (2001) and Davis-Kimball and colleagues (2000) provide comprehensive historical coverage.

The term *steppe art* covers a group of interrelated styles associated with objects found during the excavation of burial mounds (*kurgans*) on the Eurasian steppe from the shores of the Black Sea in the west to the north-western border of present-day China. The objects are portable, mainly of metal, bone or wood, and depict various animals and birds, some creatures probably familiar at the time of production

Figure 4.28 Bronze object depicting confronting animals, third to first century BCE, steppe art, Ordos area, Mongolia (British Museum)

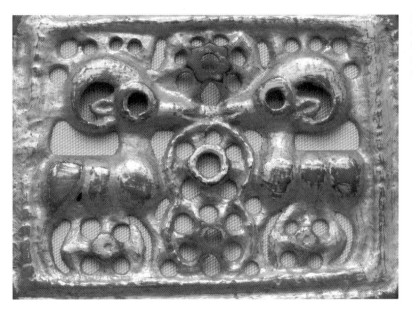

Figure 4.29 Bronze object depicting confronting animals, third to first century BCE, nomadic or steppe art, Ordos area, Mongolia (British Museum)

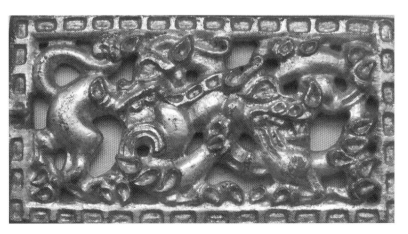

Figure 4.30 Bronze object depicting fighting animals, third to first century BCE, nomadic or steppe art, Ordos area, Mongolia (British Museum)

Figure 4.31 Bronze object depicting fighting animals, third to first century BCE, nomadic or steppe art, Ordos area, Mongolia (British Museum)

Figure 4.32 Bronze object depicting fighting animals, third to first century BCE, nomadic or steppe art, Ordos area, Mongolia (British Museum)

and others, such as griffins, taken from some mythological source. Animals unknown to the steppes, such as lions, appeared frequently. With only a few exceptions, preference was given to the representation of wild animals rather than domesticated animals (Figures 4.28–4.32). A characteristic steppe style appears to have prevailed around 700 BCE and survived into the early centuries of the Common Era. Although steppe art is regarded largely as isolated stylistically, there is evidence of both Greek and Persian influence in the art of the steppe in the later centuries of its production.

Gandhara sculptures (cs 9)

The name Gandhara is given to the ancient state located in parts of present-day eastern Afghanistan and northern Pakistan, though boundaries varied throughout its history. Peshawar Valley and the city of Peshawar, as well as Taxila and the Swat Valley, seem to have been important constituents of the state for the bulk of its history. Gandhara was an influential power for much of the first millennium BCE to around the middle of the first millennium CE. Its peak of significance came during the first few centuries of the Common Era, when it was under the influence of the Buddhist Kushan Empire. Gandhara was strategically located to benefit from international trade and acted as an important channel for commercial, cultural and religious communications between Central Asia, India and Iran. By the second century CE, Taxila had become an important centre for Mahayanan Buddhist scholarship and learning. Many stupas and other Buddhist monuments and statuary were created. It seems that it was in this region that the Buddha was first represented in human form (Figures 4.33–4.51).

Around the middle of first millennium BCE, the region came under the influence of the Persian Achaemenid Empire (especially during the reigns of Cyrus the Great and Darius I). This Persian influence remained in place until the expeditions of Alexander of Macedon in the fourth century BCE. The beginnings of what is recognizable as Gandhara-Greco-Buddhist art date largely from the late first to the fourth centuries CE. Note that Persian, Indian and various indigenous influences are also apparent. The Kushans (then known as the Yuezhi to the Chinese) migrated from Central Asia to the Gandhara region in the late first century CE, and the Kushan period, which extended to around 150 years, saw Buddhist scholarship and culture flourish in the region, and numerous monasteries were established and stupas built. From Gandhara, the Buddhist religion spread to

Figure 4.33 Buddhist sculpture, first to fourth century CE, Gandhara region (National Museum, Korea)

Figure 4.34 Buddhist sculpture, first to fourth century CE, Gandhara region (National Museum, Korea)

Figure 4.35 Buddhist sculpture, first to fourth century CE, Gandhara region (National Museum, Korea)

Figure 4.36 Buddhist sculpture, first to fourth century CE, Gandhara region (National Museum, Korea)

Figure 4.37 Buddhist sculpture, first to fourth century CE, Gandhara region (National Museum, Korea)

Figure 4.38 Buddhist sculpture, first to fourth century CE, Gandhara region (British Museum)

Figure 4.39 Buddhist sculpture, first to fourth century CE, Gandhara region (British Museum)

Figure 4.40 Buddhist sculpture, first to fourth century CE, Gandhara region (Victoria and Albert Museum)

Figure 4.41 Buddhist sculpture, first to fourth century CE, Gandhara region (Victoria and Albert Museum)

Figure 4.43 Buddhist sculpture, first to fourth century CE, Gandhara region (Victoria and Albert Museum)

Figure 4.42 Buddhist sculpture, first to fourth century CE, Gandhara region (Victoria and Albert Museum)

Figure 4.44 Buddhist sculpture, first to fourth century CE, Gandhara region (Victoria and Albert Museum)

Figure 4.45 Buddhist sculpture, first to fourth century CE, Gandhara region (Victoria and Albert Museum)

Figure 4.46 Buddhist sculpture, first to fourth century CE, Gandhara region (Victoria and Albert Museum)

Figure 4.47 Buddhist sculpture, first to fourth century CE, Gandhara region (Victoria and Albert Museum)

Figure 4.48 Buddhist sculpture, first to fourth century CE, Gandhara region (Victoria and Albert Museum)

Central Asia and further east towards Han China. Gandhara-Buddhist art, often in the form of stone sculpture, spread also, and its influences can be detected as far away as Southeast Asia in Buddhist monuments such as Borobudur in central Java. By the fifth century CE, the region of Gandhara came under strong outside influence, Hinduism ascended in the region and, by the time of the Islamic conquests, Buddhism had gone into substantial decline; Taxila was in ruins and Buddhist monasteries were deserted.

As Rui observed in 2008, it is difficult to date Gandhara sculpture with a high degree of confidence; a mere five pieces have inscribed dates,

and scholars debate the precise dating of even these. Creating a chronology is particularly difficult, and is prevented largely by the lack of dependable evidence from either inscriptions or documentation relating to stratified excavations. Even the precise historical chronology of the region is a controversial issue among scholars. Problems with various attempts at specifying a chronology often ignore the fact that the greater Gandhara region had several subregional units, each existing side by side and producing its own unique pieces of sculpture.

Rui, in a scholarly, well-focussed article, stressed the importance of realizing that influences on

Figure 4.49 Buddhist sculpture, first to fourth century CE, Gandhara region (Victoria and Albert Museum)

Figure 4.50 Buddhist sculpture, first to fourth century CE, Gandhara region (Victoria and Albert Museum)

Figure 4.51 Buddhist sculpture, first to fourth century CE, Gandhara region (Victoria and Albert Museum)

Gandhara came from 'multiple sources and at multiple moments', and that such influences were 'continually mixed with pre-existing or other heterogeneous elements' (2008). As a step towards creating a chronology Rui identified five visual types, placed in loosely demarcated categories, among Gandhara Buddhist sculpture (particularly from the Peshawar area).

DISCUSSION OR ASSIGNMENT TOPICS

Symbolic Dragons

Using illustrative material of your choice, discuss the symbolism of dragon motifs in the context of dynastic China.

The Oxus Treasure

What is the Oxus Treasure? Which museums hold the relevant objects?

Steppe Art

Discuss the nature of steppe art, its main thematic focus and the types of motif used.

Gandhara Sculpture

Making reference to illustrative material of your choice (up to ten examples which you consider typical), describe the stylistic nature of Gandhara sculpture. From the illustrative material selected, identify and discuss possible stylistic influences which you consider had origins outside the region known as Gandhara.

---

further reading

Aruz, J., Farkas, A., Alekseev, A. and Korolkova, E. (2001). *The Golden Deer of Eurasia: Scythian and Sarmatian Treasures from the Russian Steppes*, The State Hermitage, Saint Petersburg, and the Archaeological Museum, Ufa. New York: Metropolitan Museum of Art.

Baumer, C. (2000). *Southern Silk Road: In the Footsteps of Sir Aurel Stein and Sven Hedin*, Bangkok: Orchid Press.

Berendt, K. A. (2007). *The Art of Gandhara in the Metropolitan Museum of Art,* New York: Metropolitan Museum of Art.

Christian, D. (2000). 'Silk Roads or Steppe Roads? The Silk Roads in World History', *Journal of World History*, 11 (1): 1–26.

Rhi, J. H. (1994). 'From Bodhisattva to Buddha: the Beginning of Iconic Representation in Buddhist Art', *Artibus Asiae*, 54: 207–25.

Rudenko, S. I. (1970). *Frozen Tombs of Siberia: The Pazyryk Burials of Iron Age Horsemen.* Tr. M. W. Thompson. Berkeley and Los Angeles: University of California Press.

Watt, J. C. (1990). 'The Arts of Ancient China', *The Metropolitan Museum of Art Bulletin*, New Series, 48 (1): 1, 2, 4–72.

Zwalf, V. (1985). *Buddhism: Art and Faith,* London: British Museum Press.

Zwalf, V. (1996). *A Catalogue of the Gandhara Sculpture in the British Museum,* vol. I and II, London: British Museum Press.

5

cultural interaction and exchange

As stressed on a number of occasions previously in this book, by the end of the first century BCE, there was substantial long-distance international trade, involving the Roman Empire, the Parthian Empire, the Kushan Empire, a confederation of Central Asian nomads and Han China. As noted in the introduction to Chapter 4, various trade routes developed, and terms such as Amber Route, Spice Route, and Incense Route, as well as Silk Route (or Silk Road) have been used to refer to geographically dispersed networks, each named in relatively modern times by reference to the main products traded. A common feature of these channels of exchange and commerce is that they were conduits for the transmission of cultural outlooks, including artistic styles and associated techniques. Baron Ferdinand von Richthofen, a nineteenth-century German explorer, coined the term *Silk Road*, which refers to a network of east-to-west routes or channels of trade that connected China to southern Europe and the Mediterranean region, a distance of around five thousand miles of often harsh and difficult terrain (Beach 2007). Christian (2000) used the plural form *Silk Roads*, rather than *Silk Road*, and argued that this was sensible when referring to a 'constantly shifting network'. The network of routes from east to west is the focus here. Silk and other woven goods were indeed transported, but so also were spices, porcelains, religious relics, precious stones, metals, jewellery

and other valuable items. Not so valuable, utilitarian items may have been exchanged also, but probably across shorter distances. Parallel with the transport of physical items, artistic methods and compositional rules, technological and other knowledge, motifs and symbols, styles of music, religions, languages and literature, philosophies and political ideologies spread from region to region, and probably involved the participation of migrant populations, groups or individuals, who brought with them the skills and know-how so that these non-tangible goods could be introduced and accepted in new environments. Rather alarmingly, various diseases also migrated along these routes (McNeill 1977).

networks

As noted in the introduction to Chapter 4, it is important to recognize that a network existed rather than a single road, and it is doubtful that many traders travelled the full distance; they likely exchanged goods at various locations between east and west. The most commonly identified key points along the routes from Chang'an (regarded invariably as the first or last staging post in China) were Lanzhou, the Gansu Corridor (between the Tibetan and Mongolian Plateaus), the Taklamakan Desert, Dunhuang, several routes which ultimately joined in Kashgar, the Pamir mountains, further routes into Central Asia or southwards into present-day Pakistan, India or Afghanistan, the Iranian Plateau, the Black Sea, the Sea of Marmara, through the Balkans to Venice or across the Black Sea to Georgia and then to Byzantium (present-day Istanbul, known as Constantinople from the early fourth century). Several sea routes also were operational.

This book stresses the importance of trade networks as pathways for cultural interaction, possible cultural change and the diffusion of motifs, patterns and styles up to the late first millennium CE. Numerous scholars have placed particular geographic focus on the network known as the Silk Road. Boulnois (1966), McNeill (1977), Curtin (1985), Franck and Brownstone (1986) and Bentley (1993, 1996) produced informative background publications.

textiles

Textiles, primarily because of their easy portability, are of importance when examining the development of visual art styles across the trade networks of the first millennium CE. Traders exchanged textiles in substantial quantities in both easterly and westerly directions. Styles or adaptations of motifs or symbols from elsewhere abound. For example, ranges of objects exhibiting stylistic features associated with Parthian, Sasanian, Gandaran and Central Asian visual traditions arrived in Tang China. Trade in silk (in yarn and fabric form) was well established by the middle of the first millennium BCE. Not until the second century BCE did Chinese powers send out military expeditions to further control and regulate trade in silk and to ensure that China benefitted from associated taxation (Feltham 2010: 9).

Raw silk (presumably in twisted continuous yarn form) was imported from China to both Persia and Byzantine Syria, where it was dyed and woven into twills and brocades, the latter by using a draw loom (inspired by Chinese technology though developed further by producers in Syria). Traders then sent these value-added items eastwards, back to China or beyond to Japan, or northwards to Byzantium and other parts of Europe (Feltham 2010: 17). As knowledge of textile processing spread and associated skills developed, designs were copied widely.

Trade in silk textiles produced largely in state-controlled Sasanian workshops ensured that, by the late eighth century, certain compositions, motifs and patterns became familiar across much of Asia and Europe, from Japan in the east to Byzantium in the west (Feltham 2010: 5). A common Persian textile design from the Sasanian period consists of repeating roundels, each with a border of pearl-necklace-like forms. Frequently, within each roundel, pairs of confronting animals, such as lions, griffins, peacocks or stags, are represented. Often these figures are positioned on either side of a tree. Hunting scenes, typically depicting a ruler confronting a wild beast of one type or another, are also common. No matter where the textiles were woven (Byzantium, Spain, Persia, Syria, China or Japan), motifs and compositional arrangements appear to have undergone little if any change when compared to the Sasanian prototypes. Feltham observed:

[T]he same design would be woven up from imported Chinese silk thread, or from locally produced silk from Nara to Samarqand, from Alexandria to Constantinople, from Baghdad to Andalusia, and would be prized both as decorative elements in the costumes of the wealthy and powerful and as wraps for religious treasures and relics. (2010: 22)

Designs on silver bowls, dishes and jugs produced in Sasanian Persia used a similar repertoire to that used in the production of silk textiles. These were also copied widely. Deer, lions, senmurvs and boar, as well as winged horses, were popular motifs on both silverware and textiles. As with textiles, Sasanian silver was traded as far as Japan, as well as throughout much of Central Asia. With the conquest of the Sasanian Empire by the forces of Islam in the seventh century, trade in silk continued and the luxurious nature of the products produced was maintained.

Byzantine silk textiles, inspired in their design by Sasanian prototypes, spread across Europe and, in Charlemagne's court at Aachen (Germany), they acted as inspiration for illuminated manuscript design and were held as treasured possessions in newly built cathedrals.

the Pazyryk Carpet (cs 10)

The Pazyryk Carpet was discovered in the late 1940s, during an archaeological dig in the Pazyryk Valley, amid the Altai Mountains in southern Siberia. Measuring 1.83 metres by 1.98 metres, the carpet was found in a *kurgan* (tomb or barrow). A production date of the third century BCE has been estimated (Hann 2011), based largely on the article 'Dendrochronological and Radiocarbon Dating of the Scythian Burial Place in the Pazyryk Valley in the Altai Mountains, South Siberia', in which Bonani and colleagues claimed that the carpet 'yielded a calibrated age (95 per cent

confidence limit) of BC 383–332 (25.4 per cent) or BC 328–200 (74.6 per cent). In combination with tree ring studies of wood samples from the different kurgans, an absolute age of BC 260–250 could be determined' (2001).

In addition to the renowned carpet, the Pazyryk digs yielded other, much smaller, carpet fragments, appliquéd felted fabrics, embroidered silks, looped textiles, kilim-woven fragments, musical instruments, mummified human and horse remains, decorated horse harnesses and bridles and a four-wheeled carriage or chariot made totally of birch wood. The intention of this case study is to present a brief description and a stylistic, thematic and structural analysis of the carpet.[1]

Stylistic, thematic and structural features of the carpet

The carpet features five principal borders, with a series of mini-borders separating these (Figure 5.1). The first border consists of a repeating series of lozenge-shaped medallions, each holding a griffin-like motif. The author has estimated that a total of ninety-four of these motifs was woven into the original item; at the time of examining the carpet (2007), one of the carpet's corners was in a severely deteriorated state.

The second border consists of successive images of horses and human figures (estimated at an original total of twenty-eight). Some of the human figures are depicted riding horses and others as grooms, each walking beside a horse. The images of horses and riders featured in the second border are the most remarkable decorative feature of the carpet. Each horse is of similar build and is depicted with a decorated saddle blanket and bridle. The designs on the blankets vary from horse to horse. Several horse blankets

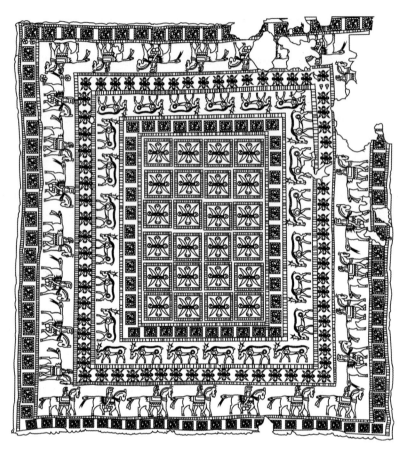

Figure 5.1 Outline drawing of Pazyryk Carpet (CW)

(or *shabraks*) of felted wool were found in the Pazyryk *kurgans*. Each horse depicted on the carpet has a braided tail. Horse tails wrapped in gold foil were also found in the Pazyryk *kurgans*. All horses face anti-clockwise around the carpet. Scholars generally agree that horses played a significant role in the nomadic life of the various Scytho-Siberian groups, providing means of transport, sources of food and items for trade. Rudenko commented: 'In the Altai the life of everybody, men and women, was so closely bound up with horses that these animals had to accompany the dead into the next world' (1953: 56).

The third border shows a repeating star-like shape, often referred to as the 'lotus border'; numbers here were estimated at sixty-nine motifs (sixteen in the lower component of the border; seventeen in the upper component; seventeen in the left component; nineteen in the right component). These motifs, though of smaller scale, are similar to the motifs repeated in the central field.

The fourth principal border depicts a repeating motif of a deer-like animal (twenty-four in total) all facing clockwise around the carpet. Consideration of the scale of the antlers relative to the body size suggests that the animal is a caribou, elk or reindeer. Such motifs are commonly depicted in the

Altai region, though generally as if in battle with some carnivore and not as sedately as on the carpet. Hubel maintained that the depiction of these animals called to mind images associated with the Achaemenid palaces of Darius at Susa and Persepolis (1970: 14).

The fifth border shows a series of medallions (forty-two in total), each containing a depiction of a griffin-like animal similar to that shown in border number one, though facing in the opposite direction.

The carpet has six separating mini-borders consisting of blocks, each with alternating colours following a repeating sequence from black to white, to red, to white. The central rectangular area of the carpet (known as the central field or ground) consists of a repeating arrangement of twenty-four star-like motifs, arranged in four columns of six motifs each. Each motif exhibits fourfold reflection symmetry and appears to be composed of two differently coloured, superimposed crosses, one turned through 45 degrees. Schurmann drew a link between these motifs and Neo-Assyrian pine cones (1982: 9). Hann (2011) previously discussed numerical and proportional relationships relating to the design composition of the carpet.

Both Rudenko and Schurmann maintained that the animal featured in the medallions in the first and fifth borders is a griffin (Rudenko 1953: 257; Schurmann 1982: 9). On balance the animal motif on the carpet appears similar to the Assyrian griffin. The possibility that it may have derived also from the senmurv or hippocampus should not be ignored. Both the griffin and the senmurv were deemed to exercise a protective force. Similar motifs are depicted on several items from the Pazyryk *kurgans*. Around each of the medallions appears a repeating series of black and white pearls

or dots, characteristic of Sasanian (224–624 CE) Persian textiles, but originating in the Achaemenid dynasty (557–330 BCE), a period prior to the carpet's manufacture. Hann (2011) previously presented a detailed structural appraisal of the carpet together with a debate on possible provenance.

Possible channels of diffusion

While the author accepts that the various felted textiles found in the same *kurgan* as the carpet may have been the outcome of local Pazyryk production, it seems unlikely that the Pazyryk Carpet and the range of other woven textiles found with the carpet were produced in the Pazyryk Valley. The precise means by which they were acquired is unknown. It does, however, seem reasonable to suggest that such textiles may have been kept as prized possessions (and thus included as grave goods buried with tribal chiefs and other high-ranking individuals) and that they were the outcome of exchange or gift, or were kept over or left over from quantities of other textiles traded in stages from east to west and north to south, between successive Scytho-Siberian groups and others. At some final stage, at locations close to the north-western, western and south-western extremities of Scytho-Siberian influence, the goods (e.g. Chinese silks) were given in exchange to Celts or Persians. The author believes the Pazyryk Carpet fell into the hands of the Pazyryks as a result of such trade and exchange, probably involving other Scytho-Siberians located closer to an area under Persian control. Such producers would have had an exceedingly well-developed carpet-weaving tradition and would also need to be familiar with caribou, elk or reindeer (not a possibility in the area covered by present-day Iran), as the motifs depicted confirm a first-hand visual familiarity with the animal rather than an impression gathered from hearsay, from second-hand images or through any form of oral or storytelling tradition.

The carpet's construction evinces sophisticated knowledge of geometrical composition. A large proportion of carpets produced in the modern era show clear bilateral symmetry (where left and right are precise reflections). This is not the case with the Pazyryk Carpet, yet a comfortable visual balance has been achieved.

Most scholars and researchers accept that the Silk Road (with its numerous tributaries) was the primary network, from east to west, for trade in silk and other goods (and also the potential channel for the diffusion of weaving techniques) from the Han dynasty onwards. The interaction between the Chinese and Scytho-Siberians is of importance. In the few centuries before the beginning of the Han dynasty, the Scytho-Siberians obtained quantities of decorated textiles (probably traded for horses, and some have been found in the various *kurgans*). It is hypothesized here that some of these items were kept and the remainder transported westwards, possibly as exchange goods or gifts between neighbouring Scytho-Siberian tribes. Traders or merchants perhaps transported the carpet to the Pazyryk Valley following a chain of exchange between traders associated with carpet weavers in an area under Persian control and the Pazyryk nomadic groups.

When the Pazyryk Carpet is compared to relatively modern carpets (say, Turkish or Persian carpets produced during the nineteenth or twentieth centuries), certain similarities and differences are obvious. The majority of modern carpets exhibit a series of main borders on all sides, separated with minor, relatively narrow borders; the Pazyryk Carpet shows the same feature. On most modern carpets, it appears that the dominant visual feature is placed in the central field; this is the focus

of attention. With the Pazyryk Carpet this does not seem to be the case; rather the circulating horses and grooms, as well as the deer-like animals, all placed in main borders, command the most attention. All in all a sedentary scene is created, which seems at odds with the war-like lifestyle assumed in much of the literature for these nomadic groups, a lifestyle that seems more attuned with some of the other artwork (held mainly in the State Hermitage Museum in Saint Petersburg) depicting wild animals attacking horses or other pasture animals. A further remarkable feature of the Pazyryk Carpet, when compared with carpets from the modern era, is that it shows only limited reflection symmetry. The star-type shape (or lotus) border and the central field both hold motifs with reflection symmetry, but overall the carpet does not show reflection down a central axis (as would be the case with the vast majority of carpets from modern times).

Hagia Sophia (cs 11)

Hagia Sophia (Church of Holy Wisdom or Sancta Sophia) is a former Byzantine basilica, later made a mosque and declared a museum in 1935 (Figures 5.2–5.11). A church was dedicated first on the site around the middle of the fourth century. This and a subsequent construction were destroyed during riots; the building still standing in the early twenty-first century was constructed in the second quarter of the sixth century on the instructions of Emperor Justinian. This third edifice served as the Eastern Orthodox seat of the Patriarchate of Constantinople and held this role until Ottoman Turks under Sultan Mehmed II conquered the city in the mid-fifteenth century. The Turks changed the city's name to Istanbul and converted Hagia

Figure 5.2 Hagia Sophia interior detail, Istanbul

Figure 5.3 Hagia Sophia interior detail, Istanbul

Figure 5.4 Hagia Sophia
interior detail, Istanbul

Figure 5.5 Hagia Sophia
interior detail, Istanbul

Figure 5.6 Hagia Sophia interior detail, Istanbul

Figure 5.7 Hagia Sophia interior detail, Istanbul

Figure 5.8 Hagia Sophia interior detail, Istanbul

Figure 5.9 Hagia Sophia interior detail, Istanbul

Figure 5.10 Hagia Sophia interior detail, Istanbul

Figure 5.11 Hagia Sophia interior detail, Istanbul (SN)

Sophia to a mosque; past Christian motifs and symbols were either removed or hidden from view, and a mihrab, a minbar and minarets were added. The building served as a model for many Ottoman mosques such as Sultan Ahmed Mosque (known as the Blue Mosque) and Suleymaniye Mosque, both in Istanbul.

Reliefs showing twelve lambs (representing twelve apostles), originally part of the front entrance of the second church, were discovered after the monument was declared a museum in the 1930s. In 2011, these lay in an excavation pit adjacent to the entrance. During the building of Hagia Sophia, Greek columns from the Temple of Artemis at Ephesus, stone from quarries in Egypt, green marble from Thessaly, black stone from the Bosporus region and yellow stone from Syria were acquired and used in the building's construction. Earthquakes in the mid-sixth century caused the main dome to collapse. This and damage in subsequent centuries were addressed and restoration work carried out.

the ship cloths of Sumatra (cs 12)

This chapter includes this case study because it highlights the importance of sea trade to many Asian nations throughout much of the first millennium CE, hundreds of years before the arrival of seafaring Europeans in search of the rare spices of South and Southeast Asia (particularly the islands of Indonesia). As stated previously in this book, land-based networks played a crucial role in cultural diffusion and exchange (manifested in the visual arts) between the Mediterranean and lands to the east during the first millennium, long before the arrival of European traders. The importance of parallel sea-based trading activities should also be recognized.

Ballard and colleagues observed that representations of ships 'have assumed an exceptional symbolic significance in Southeast Asian societies' (2003: 385). Manguin (1986) believed boats were a key metaphor for social organization throughout the region.

Many ancient communities of maritime Indonesia regarded the sea as a unifying element rather than a force of separation. This unification involved much inter-island trade and, in ancient times, the phrase *tanah air kita* (our land water) was used to refer to the islands constituting much of the archipelago known in more recent times as Indonesia. In many parts of Indonesia the roofs of traditional houses took the form of an upturned boat (Lewcock and Brans 1976; Barraud 1985; Manguin 1986: 190). Manguin (1986: 191) observed that high-ranking dignitaries in South Sumatra travelled to ceremonies on wheeled boats, and Crystal (1985: 142–3) noted carvings of boat prows reserved for the coffins of dignitaries among the Toraja of Sulawesi. Representations of boats have been found in the rock art of Borneo (Harrison 1958), Sulawesi (Kosasih 1991) and the eastern part of the Indonesian Archipelago (Ballard 1988; O'Connor 2003).

The ship or boat therefore holds deep symbolic significance throughout much of Southeast Asia, and this is particularly true in the island of Sumatra. In visual art form, various ships or boats were represented on textiles and other objects used in ceremonies such as birth, circumcision, tooth filing, marriages and funerals. The ship cloths of Sumatra are particularly renowned (Gittinger 1972: 202). These cloths were produced throughout much of the twentieth century and before, and depict a highly stylized boat as the central dominant

Figure 5.12 Sumatran ship cloth, early twentieth century (University of Leeds International Textiles Archive)

motif on each (Figures 5.12 and 5.13). This motif was associated with the transitions in life or life's journey, and represented the development of a person's soul when moving from one stage of life to another. The boat was the symbolic vehicle used to transport the soul through these various life cycle stages or rites of passage. Of course, initially, the boat was the tool that allowed communications between island-based communities and the diffusion of ideas, objects and religious beliefs.

Manguin (1986: 190) and Ballard and colleagues (2003) recognized the importance of ship imagery in the context of mortuary practice, and showed how many communities perceived ships as the principal vehicles for ferrying the souls of the dead to a place of afterlife.

Various forms of Sumatran ship cloths can be identified. The long ceremonial banners known as *palepai* were associated with clan nobility and used at weddings and funerals of local dignitaries. Such cloths were regarded as family heirlooms

Figure 5.13 Drawing of Sumatran ship cloth, by Hasri Direja, Bandung, Indonesia

and were passed from generation to generation, as symbols of hereditary leadership.

Possibly the best-known ship-cloth type is the *tampan*. Still considered a vital ritual accessory, these cloths were made by the women in small rural households and were more common than the larger *palepai* variety. The style and number of cloths in the possession of any family was a measure of its rank in society. Such cloths were exchanged at the time of marriages and also used in ceremonies such as those associated with the completion of a new building, or were used simply as a wrapper for ceremonial gifts (Ballard et al. 2003).

Tatibin are a variety of ship cloth, smaller and rarer than the *palepai* and *tampan* varieties. *Tatibin*

commonly decorate the seating platform used by the bride and groom during wedding ceremonies.

The representations on the ship cloths reflect historical, cultural and economic developments, practices and changes in the region, particularly changes associated with waves of trade and colonization. The central motif was modified as different types of seagoing vessels sailed and anchored in the region, including those from Indian, Arabic, Chinese and European sources.

The iconography on these cloths ranges from simple boat forms to complex scenes incorporating fabulous animal motifs, royal elephants and populous crew. Occasionally, human figures are highly stylized forms, reminiscent of the refined style of the Javanese shadow puppets (or

Wayang); these suggest the immigration to Sumatra of people from the neighbouring island of Java. Sometimes the central ship motif evokes a dragon boat, or occasionally it may resemble a European galleon with masts and flags. In a more recent phase, *tampan* cloths depicted highly stylized geometric forms of the central ship motif, a change possibly stimulated by the consolidation of Islamic influence and expansion throughout the region.

On the monument known as Borobudur (in Central Java, Indonesia), several representations of ships appear (an example is given in Figure 5.14). One particular variety is a double-outrigger sailed vessel. The outrigger functioned as a stabilizer for the vessel and was a feature both historically and in relatively modern times of many seagoing craft among seafarers, particularly island communities, across much of the Indian and Pacific oceans. The types of craft depicted on Borobudur were probably similar to those used in the period from the last few centuries of the first millennium CE and the early few centuries of the second millennium CE. Such crafts were probably used, many centuries ago, for trading cinnamon along a shipping route, with vessels sailing from Indonesian islands, across the Indian Ocean, to the Seychelles, Madagascar, South Africa and even further around the Cape of Good Hope to locations on the west coast of Africa. In the early years of the first decade of the twenty-first century, an expedition set sail from Jakarta in Indonesia, using a wooden ship built to specifications drawn up from examination of the Borobudur ship reliefs, and arrived via the Seychelles in Madagascar, thus verifying to some degree that the maritime technology available at the time of Borobudur had the potential of covering such distances and thus confirming the possibility of sea-trading links between Indonesia and East Africa as early as the last few centuries of the first millennium CE.

Figure 5.14 The depiction of a rigged ship, Borobudur, Java, Indonesia. Photograph by HC

Of some relevance to the theme explored here is the work of Ballard and colleagues (2003) who considered the visual culture of the South Scandinavian Bronze Age, making reference to rock carvings, decorated metalwork and above-ground monuments, and focussing on imagery showing boats, occasionally associated with burial and funerary rites, and compared these findings with boat imagery from Southeast Asia.

DISCUSSION OR ASSIGNMENT TOPICS

The Pazyryk Carpet

Identify the nature of archaeological material associated with the series of *kurgan* digs in the Pazyryk Valley in the twentieth century. Which museum currently holds the bulk of this archaeological material? Focussing particular attention on the so-called Pazyryk Carpet, describe its visual composition, noting the types of motifs used and their possible stylistic origins.

Hagia Sophia

Identify and discuss the principal architectural features of Hagia Sophia, noting also where it is located, when it was built and its changing function historically.

Ship Cloths of Sumatra

Using illustrative material of your choice, discuss the pictorial nature of the ship cloths of Sumatra.

Trade by Sea

Discuss the development of maritime trading networks during the first millennium CE. Which products and raw materials were of importance to this trade?

The Development of the so-called Silk Route

Trace the development of the so-called Silk Route, identifying the main participating settlements, oases, towns or cities forming part of the trade connection between the eastern Mediterranean and China. Discuss the nature of cultural change and diffusion (particularly expressed through changes or influences associated with the visual arts and their geometry which occurred as a direct result of activities along the routes). What role do you feel Alexander the Great may have played in laying a foundation from which trade could be developed centuries after his death? What was traded? What changes in culture can be associated with trade along the Route? Which empires, dynasties or rulers are of importance and which religions spread as a result of the opening up of the Route? Who were the following: Marco Polo, Ibn Battuta, Xuan Zang (or Hsuan Tang), Aurel Stein and Sven Hedin? In what way is each associated with either the Silk Route itself or with areas which held a key strategic position along the Route? When was the Han Dynasty? When was the T'ang Dynasty? Why are these dynasties of importance in the context of trade and stylistic change in the visual arts?

further reading

Albenda, P. (1978). 'Assyrian Carpets in Stone', *The Journal of the Ancient Near East Society*, 10: 1–34.

Ballard, C., Bradley, R., Nordenborg, M., Myhre, A. and Wilson, M. (2003). 'The Ship as Symbol in the Prehistory of Scandinavia and Southeast Asia', *World Archaeology*, 35 (3): 385–403.

Bauman, J. (1987). *Central Asian Carpets: Study Guide*, Islamabad: Asian Study Group.

Rudenko, S. I. (1970). *Frozen Tombs of Siberia: The Pazyryk Burials of Iron Age Horsemen*, Tr. M. W. Thompson. Berkeley and Los Angeles: University of California Press.

note

1. Technically, the carpet has a level surface (suggesting that it was cut postproduction) and an estimated 3,600 knots per decimetre (Bauman 1987: 14). It has a central field surrounded by several borders of differing dimensions. It is likely that an item of such technical sophistication and complexity was, first, part of a long-standing tradition of carpet weaving stretching back 'several centuries' previous to its production (Bauman 1987: 14) and, second, that this production was within a settled community, under conditions of political, economic and social stability. It appears that the population of the Altai region, at the time of the carpet's interment, consisted largely (if not entirely) of pastoral nomads. It seems highly unlikely, therefore, that a carpet of such manufacture, design and fineness could have been produced within the unsettled, nomadic environment of the time in the Pazyryk Valley, but instead was produced in lands to the west.

stupas and mandalas

The foundations for the development of Buddhism as a major world religion are traceable to the last few centuries BCE. The religion spread across much of present-day India and Pakistan to Southeast Asia, northwards to Central Asia and subsequently to East Asia, including China, Korea and Japan. Buddhism has evolved in association with national cultures to a bewildering extent, and several types of followers can be identified: for example, those who follow Theravada or Hinayana (lesser vehicle) Buddhism, dominant in Sri Lanka, Burma and Southeast Asia; those who follow Mahayana (great vehicle) Buddhism, prevalent throughout much of East Asia, Tibet and Nepal; those who follow Vajrayana (diamond vehicle) Buddhism, originally from Bengal and popular in Himalayan lands and Mongolia. Although the various perspectives or doctrines may be differentiated in theory as well as practice in the modern era, early forms of Buddhism combined elements of these and other perspectives (including, on occasion, elements of Hinduism, Taoism and Confucianism).

In ancient times in Asia, trade routes (both maritime and overland) were the channels of transport and communication for international travellers. Buddhism travelled along these routes from India, its home base, to the Himalayas, East Asia and Southeast Asia. The process of diffusion to different regions yielded different results as adaptation and local interpretation took place. The outcome of this was that the visual art in each region yielded pronounced stylistic variation, on the one hand, and commonalities with Indian Buddhist imagery on the other.

Buddhist stupas (cs 13)

A *stupa* is a mound-like construction containing Buddhist relics (often ashes of a deceased). The term *reliquary* is used occasionally (presumably after the Christian equivalent, though this is often a casket of some kind rather than a mound). Originally it was a simple mound of earth to cover relics of the Buddha; more sophisticated constructions were built as the centuries passed. Various types can be identified: the relic stupa, which holds the remains of the Buddha, his disciples or other notable individuals; the object stupa, which contains interred items, such as a begging bowl, a robe or an important piece of Buddhist scripture, believed to have been in the possession previously of the Buddha or one of his disciples; the commemorative stupa, built to celebrate events in the lives of the Buddha or his disciples; the votive stupa, which is like a supplementary stupa, used to gain additional spiritual benefits, and usually located in the close vicinity of a prominent renowned stupa. Important features include: the *torana* (the gateway or entrance to the stupa); *vedica* (a fence-like enclosure meant to protect the stupa); *hamica* (a square platform with railings built on top of the dome of the construction); a circumambulatory pathway to allow the pilgrim or worshipper to walk (or move) around the stupa. Various stupa types can be identified: the lotus-blossom stupa; the enlightenment stupa; the stupa of many doors; the stupa of descent from heaven; the stupa of great miracles; the stupa of reconciliation; the stupa of complete victory. Although the stupa initially functioned as a reliquary, an additional function as a devotional monument developed at an early stage.

The earliest archaeological evidence for Buddhist civilization/culture is in the form of stone carvings (mid-third century BCE). In the second century BCE, Buddhist monasteries were cut out of rock, and numerous stupas were built. Generally, stupas have five components: the square base which represents earth, the round dome representing water, the cone shape representing fire, the canopy representing air and the volume of the stupa representing space or void (various plans are given in Figures 6.1a–f).

India

Prior to his death, the Buddha gave instructions to cremate his body and to distribute the remains (ash and fragments of bone) among representatives from various regions. Ultimately these bodily relics played an important role in worship and were enshrined in stupas, with the earliest examples dating to the time of King Ashoka (c. 269–232 BCE), the third monarch of northern India's Maurya dynasty, who (legend has it) commissioned the building of 84,000 stupas throughout South and Southeast Asia, each housing a small portion of the original subdivided remains formerly accommodated in the original reliquaries (Cummings 2001: 14). Although it seems unlikely that this ambitious project reached fruition, it is certain that the Ashokan reign bequeathed various lasting works of architecture and art that have survived into modern times. Most notable among these is the Great Stupa at Sanchi (central India, forty-five kilometres outside Bhopal) (Cummings 2001: 16). Sanchi was constructed in the mid-third century BCE and served as a model for stupa design for the next seven centuries (Cummings 2001: 16). From a base of 36.5 metres in diameter, the stupa rises 16.5 metres (Cummings 2001: 16). The large dome (*anda*), constructed of blocks of stone, is 'surrounded by a circular stone balustrade . . . used to guide worshippers in their ritual and contemplative circumambulation of the stupa' (Cummings 2001: 14). Four stone gateways (*torana*) permit access through the balustrade to the dome's base. Both the gateways and balustrade are richly decorated with sculpted scenes from Buddhist legends and mythology. Many rock-carved, goblet-shaped stupas are found in cave temples, dating from the first century BCE to around 700 CE, in India, at Karli, Bedsa, Bhaja, Nasik, Ajanta and Ellora (Cummings 2001: 24).

Pakistan

After Sanchi, it seems that the region of Gandhara played an important role in stupa development as well as in other forms of Buddhist art. Gandhara was located around the modern city of Peshawar in Pakistan and was ruled by Greeks from Bactria (northern Afghanistan) at that time (third century BCE). Under the influence of Buddhist missionaries from northern India, rulers of the state of Gandhara

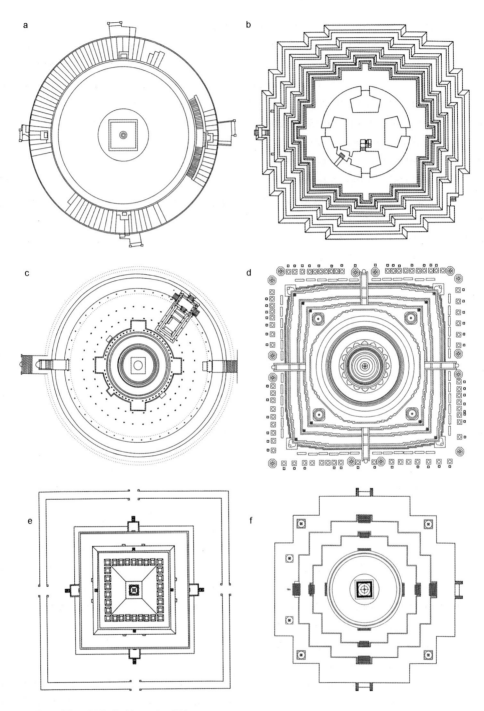

Figure 6.1a Plan of Sanchi, India (drawn by CW)
Figure 6.1b Plan of Gyantse Kumbum, Tibet (drawn by CW)
Figure 6.1c Plan of Thuparama Dagaba, Sri Lanka (drawn by CW)
Figure 6.1d Plan of Shwezigon Paya, Myanmar (drawn by CW)
Figure 6.1e Plan of Pha That Luang, Lao (drawn by CW)
Figure 6.1f Plan of Bodhnath Mahachaitya, Kathmandu (drawn by CW)

converted to Buddhism and, over the next 200 years, craftspeople in the region fused Buddhist thought and Greek art to produce unique sculpture (Cummings 2001: 20). Many stupas were also built. Although relatively large quantities of Buddhist sculpture survive from the Gandhara region and period, the most visible stupa remains in Pakistan are associated with a later period and are located at Taxila. These date from the second and first centuries BCE, long after Ashoka's reign in northern India. While the Sanchi Great Stupa is roughly hemispherical, domes associated with Taxila are more cylindrical with rounded tops and sit on square pediments. Relief sculptures chronicling the Buddha's life were applied directly to the pediments. Showing strong Greek influence, this school of sculpture extended roughly from 50 BCE to 500 CE and is commonly referred to as Greco-Buddhist or Gandharan.

Sri Lanka

Sri Lanka's oldest surviving stupa appears to be Thuparama Dagaba, reputed to contain a relic of the cremated remains of Buddha, brought to Sri Lanka from India by King Ashoka's son in the third century BCE (Cummings 2001: 32).

Indonesia

The most renowned of Indonesian Buddhist sites is Borobudur (in central Java), the largest Buddhist monument in the world and also the largest human-made construction in the southern hemisphere. Its main features are its carved relief panels, which number a few thousand and extend along several terraces. Archaeologists have estimated that construction began around 760 CE and may have been completed around 830 CE (Miksic 1990: 25). Further details are given in a later case study (cs 30) in Chapter 12.

Myanmar

One of Myanmar's most notable stupas is the eleventh-century conical Shwezigon Paya, with three diminishing terraces and various forms of floral decoration. According to Cummings (2001: 64), Shwezigon Paya is considered the prototype for all subsequent stupas in the region.

Cambodia

In Cambodia, from the mid-ninth century for the next 350 years under a succession of Khmer rulers, the style of Buddhist architecture 'evolved into the sophisticated . . . walled . . . complexes known collectively as Angkor' (Cummings 2001: 78), often including tapered towers and diminishing terraces reminiscent of Borobudur (in Indonesia).

Thailand

Cummings suggested that Thailand boasts the greatest variety of stupa styles in Asia, and that this is probably due to its location as an important commercial and relay point, criss-crossed by trade routes between India and Cambodia, and China and the Malay and Indonesian archipelago, and thus subjected to numerous cultural and religious influences (2001: 80). Thailand has numerous stupas. Wat Arun, with its eighty-two-metre tower-like stupa constructed in the first half of the nineteenth century, has a mosaic covering of broken, multicoloured Chinese porcelain (evidence of past trade when Chinese merchant ships used old porcelain as ballast).

Laos

Cummings notes that, although Laos boasts many fewer stupas than its neighbour Thailand, a uniquely Lao style of stupa was created between the fifteenth and eighteenth centuries. One of the most venerated in Laos is Pha That Luang (Great

Sacred Reliquary), built in 1566 (probably on the site of an old Khmer monastery of the eleventh to thirteenth centuries CE).

Korea

Tower stupas or pagodas are the norm in Korea. The most famous is the thirteen-metre-high, marble, ten-storey Gyeongcheonsa Pagoda, regarded as a Korean national treasure and housed (in 2012) in the National Museum of Korea in Seoul.

Japan

Tower stupas (or *to*) are also the norm in Japan. There are also smaller stone structures called *gorinto*, meaning literally five (*go*), element (*rin*) and pagoda (*to*), a reference to the assembly of the construction from five stones carved into shapes representing the five elements: earth (cube), water (sphere), fire (triangle/cone), air (hemisphere) and space (oval) (Cummings 2001: 168).

The publication by Cummings and Wassman (2001) provides a substantial and well-illustrated guide to the main stupas of Asia. This source played a key role in the development of the plan drawings presented with this case study.

Tibetan thangkas (cs 14)

Numerous countries have produced items which can be classified under the heading of Buddhist art or Buddhist visual arts. The objects and architecture created in Himalayan regions seem inspired largely by a Buddhist outlook or ideology. This is particularly true when considering the visual arts of Tibet from the eleventh century onwards. An important class of object, represented frequently in museums worldwide, is the *thangka*. The word *thangka* derives from the Tibetan language and denotes a visual record of some event. Thangkas are portable painted scrolls, mounted and framed with silk fabric (invariably figured brocade) depicting Buddhist themes. Traditionally, such objects were hung in temples and shrines to support prayer and other spiritual practice. Thangkas fall into two distinct categories: *gothang*, silken pictorial scrolls, and *trithang*, or painted cotton or silk scrolls. The latter type is the concern here. Subdivision of these painted scrolls is also possible. Broadly speaking two particular types can be identified: those that depict enlightened

Figure 6.2 Thangka, water-based pigment on cotton, possibly nineteenth century, Tibet (University of Leeds International Textiles Archive)

Figure 6.3 Thangka, water-based pigment on cotton, possibly nineteenth century, Tibet (University of Leeds International Textiles Archive)

Figure 6.4 Thangka, water-based pigment on cotton, possibly nineteenth century, Tibet (University of Leeds International Textiles Archive)

beings, Buddhas, *bodhisattvas*, gurus and guardians; those that depict mandalas. Rectangular in shape, the dimensions of painted scrolls vary from 30 by 20 centimetres to 3 metres by 2 metres (Figures 6.2–6.14).

Thangka painting was a family craft, passed from master craftsman (or father) to apprentice (or son). Thangka painting seems to have been an occupation reserved for males only. First a supporting cloth (often white, bleached linen, but occasionally silk) was stretched on a wooden frame, and the surface on one side primed with a base of chalk mixed with gum Arabic. The master craftsman made a free-hand sketch (using charcoal),

showing the outlines of the composition. These outlines were refined using black ink, and the intended disposition of colours was indicated. Apprentices (sons) added the colours to the outlines. A common form of thangka depicts a mandala (from Sanskrit meaning circle). In the sacred art of both Hinduism and Buddhism, a mandala is used as a spiritual teaching tool and as an aid to meditation. Mandalas may be in the form of painted scrolls or may be temporary creations; the latter are made from impermanent materials (such as coloured sand, rice or other grains) which are destroyed after a particular initiation or ceremony and poured into a nearby river or stream. The

Figure 6.5 Thangka, water-based pigment on cotton, possibly nineteenth century, Tibet (University of Leeds International Textiles Archive)

Figure 6.6 Detail of thangka, water-based pigment on cotton, possibly nineteenth century, Tibet (University of Leeds International Textiles Archive)

Figure 6.7 Detail of thangka, water-based pigment on cotton, possibly nineteenth century, Tibet (University of Leeds International Textiles Archive)

Figure 6.8 Detail of thangka, water-based pigment on cotton, possibly nineteenth century, Tibet (University of Leeds International Textiles Archive)

Figure 6.9 Detail of thangka, water-based pigment on cotton, possibly nineteenth century, Tibet (University of Leeds International Textiles Archive)

Figure 6.10 Detail of thangka, water-based pigment on cotton, possibly nineteenth century, Tibet (University of Leeds International Textiles Archive)

Figure 6.11 Detail of thangka, water-based pigment on cotton, possibly nineteenth century, Tibet (University of Leeds International Textiles Archive)

Figure 6.12 Detail of thangka, water-based pigment on cotton, possibly nineteenth century, Tibet (University of Leeds International Textiles Archive)

Figure 6.13 Detail of thangka, water-based pigment on cotton, possibly nineteenth century, Tibet (University of Leeds International Textiles Archive)

Figure 6.14 Detail of thangka, water-based pigment on cotton, possibly nineteenth century, Tibet (University of Leeds International Textiles Archive)

basic form is a square shape with representations of four gates containing a circle with a centre point. Each gate is T-shaped. Mandalas often show a concentric-type composition, with radial symmetry.

Structurally, the temporary mandalas, as well as the scroll-painted equivalents, consist of precise combinations of regular geometric figures, especially circles, squares and other regular polygons, and have five orientations, directions or locations corresponding to the four principal compass points and a centre, with each of the five associated with a colour (green, yellow, blue, red and white), an element (air, earth, water, fire and void) and a means of transport (mythical bird, horse, elephant, peacock and lion). Various symbols (such as the diamond, the bell, the wheel and the lotus) might be included as graphic elements, as might depictions of various Buddha-like figures, as well as representations of *bodhisattvas* (human beings who let themselves be born again to act as spiritual guides to other living creatures). Typically mandalas feature four gateways leading inwards to three or more concentric levels. Invariably a main deity is represented towards the centre and often surrounded by other deities at each of the concentric levels.

Buddhist symbols and other imagery (cs 15)

Buddhist imagery is readily recognizable and remarkably similar from region to region and from period to period. This may be because descriptions provided in Indian texts prescribed to the craftsperson details of what the object or image should look like, including posture and gesture of figures as well as colour, style and thematic content of associated motifs and symbols. As these instructions were from the geographic source or homeland of the religion, they probably held much sway and authority. While it may be tempting to suggest that artists working outside India imitated the imagery associated with Indian Buddhism and blindly followed instructions, this would be an oversimplification as there appears to be much distinctiveness from region to region. Also, it appears to be the case that, while much of the imagery across the Buddhist world is similar, certain peculiarities persist from region to region. Figures 6.15–6.21 present relevant illustrations.

Important symbols include the eight-spoked *dharma* wheel (*dharmachakra*), which symbolizes the wheel of the law or truth. The eight spokes symbolize the eightfold path or path of destiny, and the three segments at the centre symbolize the Buddha, dharma (the teachings) and *sangha* (the spiritual community of monks and nuns). The wheel can also be divided into three components, each symbolizing an aspect of Buddhist practice: the rim (concentration); the spokes (wisdom); the hub (discipline). The Buddha is also considered as a wheel turner who sets a new cycle of teachings in motion and in so doing changes the course of destiny. Often, at the centre of the wheel, a motif with three whirling segments is depicted.

Buddhist imagery, particularly on textiles or other forms of surface design, especially when produced in China, may include portraits of the Buddha and representations of the so-called Buddhist eight precious things. These are commonly explained as follows: the wheel, which symbolizes the law (at times a bell takes the place of the wheel); the conch shell, which calls the faithful to prayer; the canopy, which indicates victory; the

Figure 6.15 Buddhist initiation cards, possibly fifteenth century, Tibet (originals in Art Institute, Chicago) (EC and KL)

umbrella, which is associated with nobility; the endless knot, or knot of destiny, which suggests the path that leads to happiness; the lotus, which represents purity; the pair of fish, which symbolizes the union of happiness and utility; the vase, believed to contain the elixir of heaven, which denotes enduring peace. Buddhism utilizes many symbols in addition to the eight precious things. The most common are identified next.

The throne is a symbol which refers to the royal ancestry of Siddharta Gautama (the founder of Buddhism). Sometimes the base of the throne is decorated with other symbols such as lions and deer (both associated with the Buddha's

Figure 6.16 Small Buddha, coastal resort, Hong Kong

teachings). The lion is associated with regality, strength and power. Where deer are represented, this is a reference to the Buddha's first teaching in the Deer Park. Footprints of the Buddha, the begging bowl, the mountain symbol and the swastika are sometimes represented. The Bodhi tree refers to the tree under which the Buddha achieved enlightenment and, as a result, the Bodhi tree and leaf motifs are regarded as devotional symbols. Carvings may show the dharmachakra and the Bodhi tree on top of a throne. Buddha's footprints represent the physical presence of the Buddha as it is believed that prior to his death the Buddha left an imprint of his foot on a stone near Kusinara, a reminder of his presence on earth. A later development is the depiction of the Buddha's eyes (often on stupas) frequently seen in Nepal. They look in four directions, representing the omniscient mind of a Buddha.

Figure 6.17 Big Buddha, Lan Tau Peak, Hong Kong

Figure 6.18 Buddhist precious objects: wheel and endless knot (University of Leeds International Textiles Archive)

Figure 6.19 Buddhist precious objects: vase and parasol (University of Leeds International Textiles Archive)

Figure 6.20 Buddhist precious objects: fish and lotus (University of Leeds International Textiles Archive)

Figure 6.21 Buddhist precious objects: conch shell and canopy (University of Leeds International Textiles Archive)

DISCUSSION OR ASSIGNMENT TOPICS

Stupas

What is the function of a stupa? Identify and describe the main physical features of stupas. Select five important stupas located in the continent of Asia and compare and contrast their forms.

Stupa Symmetry

Select three floor plan illustrations from those provided in this chapter. Compare and contrast the symmetry characteristics of your selections.

Thangkas

Using illustrative material of your choice, describe the pictorial nature of Tibetan thangkas, focussing particular attention on their underlying geometric structure.

Symbolism in Buddhist Visual Arts

Using appropriate illustrative material, discuss the role of symbolism in Buddhist visual arts from a geographical location of your choice.

The Spread of Buddhism

Trace the spread of Buddhism via established trade routes from its origins in North India, identifying and explaining the nature of different schools of Buddhist thought and, in particular, the characteristics of the visual arts and architecture, sculpture and cave paintings associated with notable Buddhist centres, areas or countries. Focus particular attention on the importance of geometry in the design of objects and buildings. Your response should make mention of the acceptance of Buddhism outside India and its diffusion to Nepal, China and Southeast Asia. Which countries in particular? Which branch of Buddhism? Identify oases towns such as Khotan, Kucha, Turfan and Dunhuang. Where are these towns? Where are the important cave complexes (with paintings and/or sculptures)? Which visual symbols are associated with Buddhism and with Buddhist visual arts? What does each symbolize? What is a mandala?

further reading

Bochert, H. and Gombrich, R. (1984). *The World of Buddhism*, London: Thames and Hudson.

Cummings, J. and Wassman, B. (2001). *Buddhist Stupas in Asia: The Shape of Perfection*, with foreword by A. F. Thurman, London: Lonely Planet Publications.

Foltz, R. C. (2010). *Religions of the Silk Road: Premodern Patterns of Globalization*, New York: Macmillan.

Lee, S. (2003). *A History of Far Eastern Art*, 5th ed., New York: Prentice Hall.

Miksic, J. (1990). *Borobudur: Golden Tales of Buddhas*, Singapore: Periplis Editions (HK) Ltd.

Scarre, C. (ed.) (1991). *Past Worlds: The Times Atlas of Archaeology*, London: Times Books Limited.

7

---

mosques and minarets

Within one century of the death of the prophet Muhammad in 632 CE, Islam had become firmly established in much of the former Eastern Roman Empire, Persia, North Africa and some parts of Asia and Europe. Islamic civilization flourished in Jerusalem, Damascus, Alexandria, Fez, Tunis, Cairo, Cordoba and Baghdad, and stimulated notable advances in science, engineering, mathematics, philosophy, medicine, literature, the visual arts and architecture. This chapter concerns developments in the visual arts and architecture. In the context of this book, the term *Islamic visual art* (and architecture) is used to refer to visual art or architecture produced in countries under Islamic rule or control, though it should be recognized that precise definition is difficult. Oleg Grabar (a notable authority) debated the use of relevant terminology in his publication *The Formation of Islamic Art* (1973: 1–18).

Islamic visual arts and architecture are best considered by reference to various periods or dynasties. Centres of control (or what could loosely be called capitals) shifted over time. Much overlap is also apparent. Consideration is given briefly to the characteristics of the visual arts associated with the following notable periods or dynasties: the Umayyad Period (661–750 CE); the Abbasid Period (750–1258 CE); the Fatimid Period (909–1171 CE); the Seljuqs of Iran (1040–1157 CE); the Ayyubid Period (1171–1260 CE); the Ilkhanid

Period (1256–1353 CE); the Mamluk Period (1250–1517 CE); the Timurid Period (1370–1507 CE). This list is by no means exhaustive, as a number of additional sub-periods are associated with particular regions or cultures. This chapter reviews the main developments of relevance to the visual art and architecture in each of the selected periods, and also presents two case studies of relevance to Islamic achievements in the visual arts. Note that attention is focussed elsewhere in the book on developments in southern Spain (711–1031 CE) as well as in Turkey under the Ottomans, Persia under the Safavids and Indian and Pakistan (then united as components of a larger geographic entity) under the Mughals.

the Umayyad origins of Islamic visual arts

The Umayyad period or dynasty (661–750 CE) is the first in Islamic chronology, with the city of Damascus (Syria) as its capital. Although Islam became the foremost religion across an extensive region, artists continued to work in ways established previously under different religious regimes. This was reflected especially in metalwork and textiles, and in the use of animal, plant and figural motifs. As the dynasty progressed, new visual art conventions were used. In architecture, the new religion influenced a new approach to the use of space, but this also necessitated making reference to past forms and styles.

It is readily apparent that architectural and visual art styles practised across the empire were enriched by ideas, traditions and building practices from elsewhere. Umayyad control stretched from southern Europe in the west to the Indus valley in the east, with Damascus as a central control point. Syria was strategically placed geographically to draw inspiration from various cultures or societies newly combined within the Islamic empire. So Greco-Roman, Babylonian, Neo-Assyrian, Parthian and Sasanian sources were influential (Hillenbrand 1999: 14). The Umayyad practice of conscripting craftspeople and raw materials from other Islamic provinces as well as from outside the Islamic world, including from the remainder of the Eastern Roman Empire, further discouraged parochialism (Hillenbrand 1999: 13–14).

Relatively small numbers of decorated objects such as pottery, metalwork, carpets and textiles have survived into the twenty-first century. However, the importance of outside influences and the intrinsic nature of developments in visual art and architectural styles are discernible from a number of important buildings. Two in particular should be identified: the Dome of the Rock (Jerusalem) and the Great Mosque of Damascus. Each shows reference to a Greco-Roman heritage and, at the same time, indicates the use of a newly developing stylistic language. The Dome of the Rock (Jerusalem), completed in 691 CE, is the earliest major Islamic monument to survive into the twenty-first century. This domed, octagon-shaped building has clear Islamic functions, with a double interior ambulatory encircling the rock located centrally. Stylistically the building has certain Greco-Roman

components, including wall mosaics used on the interior and exterior of the building. The Great Mosque of Damascus (705–15 CE) was built on a rectangular site, with the covered mosque itself taking up around one half of the area and extending the length of the rectangle. The remaining area was devoted to an open courtyard with a surrounding arcade. The Great Mosque of Damascus was to become the prototype for many subsequent large mosque-building projects. The building style is strongly reminiscent of a typical Christian basilica (Hillenbrand 1999: 25), though this resemblance is lessened to some degree by the later addition of minarets. Hillenbrand highlights various features of both the Dome of the Rock and the Great Mosque of Damascus, which draw on Christian and other building heritages (1999: 25–8).

During the Umayyad and subsequent periods, connections between distant peoples (Iberians, North Africans, Persians, Turks, Egyptians, Arabic peoples, some Central Asians and Indians) increased, and efficient dissemination of knowledge relating to the visual arts and architecture was an important feature. Islamic scholars were quick to absorb Greek mathematics and philosophical perspectives. The work of Euclid and work ascribed to Pythagoras or his followers were among the first scholarly works translated into Arabic. The study of geometrical principles was integral to the understanding of astronomy. Such principles were also of immense value to the developments in tiling geometry, an area of patterning in which Islamic craftspeople excelled. Developments in tiling geometry may have also been stimulated by the discouragement of figural representation (especially humans). Hillenbrand identified three 'consistent characteristics' which typified Umayyad art and architecture: it was eclectic, experimental and propagandist (1999: 34). It was eclectic because (as mentioned earlier) it was open to many influences, including those from Egypt and Armenia, as well as Mesopotamia, Sasanian Iran, Central Asia and India (Hillenbrand 1999: 34). Its experimental nature was influenced by the 'virtually limitless' funds set aside for architectural projects (Hillenbrand 1999: 34). In other words, with ample resources available there was scope for experimentation with new styles, materials and techniques. The propagandist aspect was influenced by the significant patronage provided by the ruling powers and this, according to Hillenbrand, gave a 'political and proclamatory dimension' to all building projects (1999: 36).

The Umayyads were influential in establishing the foundations for Islamic control of much of the Iberian peninsula (excluding a few provinces in the north). The area of Iberia controlled by the Umayyads coincided with much of present-day Spain and was known as al-Andalus; the city of Cordoba was its administrative, intellectual and cultural capital. Major achievements from the viewpoint of the visual arts and architecture are evident in the Great Mosque of Cordoba and the Alhambra Palace complex in Granada, as well as large quantities of luxury objects, including figured silks and ceramics, metalwork and ivory. These achievements are the focus of attention in the next chapter.

relevant periods, caliphates and dynasties

During the Abbasid Period (750–1258), the political and cultural capital shifted from Syria to Iraq, where Baghdad (the circular city of peace) was founded in 762. Baghdad became an intellectual centre with a strong influence from Persia, especially in the early years. Its location in proximity to two great rivers—the Tigris and the Euphrates—allowed seagoing trade to develop, and its strategic geographical location also allowed trade by land to increase. By the late eighth and early ninth centuries, Baghdad was absorbing ideas and influences from not only Iran, but also from India, China, Africa and Central Asia, and then producing and exporting products across the Islamic world (Hillenbrand 1999: 40).

New techniques associated with the visual arts were introduced, and these spread throughout the empire. The use of abstract plant forms led to the development of what has become known as the *arabesque* (used in wall decoration, pottery, metalwork and wood). Large quantities of luxury goods were produced, including plates, bowls and ewers, often from metal alloys such as brass or bronze, or sometimes from silver and occasionally gold. A strong Sasanian influence appears in the iconography, involving fabulous beasts and hunting scenes, and with increased trade strong Central Asian, Turkish and Chinese influences, including motifs, techniques and themes, became evident (Hillenbrand 1999: 58). Large quantities of Chinese pottery were imported overland via Persia or by sea via India; these items seem to have had a strong influence on the nature of Abbasid pottery (Hillenbrand 1999: 51). Hillenbrand observed that Abbasid pottery had been found in Samarqand, Sind (present-day Pakistan), Egypt, Spain and Tunisia. Abbasid lustre tiles were used to tile the mihrab of the Great Mosques of Qairawan in Tunisia (1999: 54). Monumental minarets with structures reminiscent of Greco-Roman lighthouses or ancient Mesopotamian ziggurats or temple towers were a feature (Hillenbrand 1999: 46). Government-run workshops, known as *tiraz*, produced large quantities of high-quality textiles (also known as *tiraz*).

Present-day Algeria, Tunisia, Egypt and Syria as well as Sicily were under the control of the Fatimid dynasty (909–1171). Cairo emerged as the cultural centre and as the new administrative capital. Developments were evident in metalwork (especially gold), wood carving, figured silk weaving (particularly tiraz fabrics), pottery and glass production. Developments in architecture included elaborate funerary structures and shrines, notable mosques, and secular buildings and centres for higher learning. According to Hillenbrand, however, the small quantity of Fatimid architecture preserved does not permit reliable generalization (1999: 72), and what was actually typical architecturally is not readily discernible. Some of the surviving mosques from the period lack contemporary minarets and others have towers as corner features (Hillenbrand 1999: 72). From lustre wares (i.e. pottery), it seems that the number and variety of motifs used and themes depicted expanded substantially. Eastern Roman themes were probably stimulated by the Coptic minority in Egypt. The design of many pieces showed a strong Chinese influence. According to Hillenbrand, Fatimid ceramics were used to decorate church walls in Italy (Rome, Pisa and Ravenna), France and Greece (1999: 82).

The Seljuqs (1040–1157) were of Central Asian nomadic origin and, by 1055, they controlled Baghdad; within fifty years they had created a vast empire which included all of Iran, Iraq and the bulk of Anatolia (much of present-day Turkey). By the end of the eleventh century, control of the empire was split and different branches of the dynasty governed separate regions, with the Great Seljuqs retaining control of Iran, which subsequently witnessed a time of cultural prosperity. Seljuq art combines Persian and Central Asiatic and Turkic elements with a clear Islamic tradition. Of note are inlaid bronze and brass objects, the use of copper, silver and gold, decoration using Arabic calligraphy and ceramics (with the development of new techniques). Building activity was prolific, with large numbers of madrasas (schools) being built. Although they were ethnic Turks, the Seljuqs (or Seljuks) adopted aspects of Persian culture.

The Ayyubid period (1171–1260) was established under the leadership of Salah al-Din (known to many Europeans of the day as Saladin). Of particular note in the visual arts are the inlaid metalwork, ceramic production, enamelled glass and carved wood. Egypt and Syria also experienced great architectural development.

Mongol forces began incursions into the Islamic world in 1221, and by 1250 controlled most of west Asia, including Iran, Khorasan, the Caucasus, Iraq and parts of Asia Minor. The time span of resultant Mongol control was around 100 years and was known as the Ilkhanid Period (1256–1353). Power was centred in north-west Iran, and an environment of extensive cultural exchange and artistic development was characteristic. There was much absorption, adoption and adaptation of art styles, motifs and patterns. Textiles, pottery, metalwork and jewellery continued to develop during the period. Illuminated manuscripts, both religious and secular in focus, received much attention, and Baghdad again became an important centre. Chinese-sourced motifs, including cloud bands, phoenixes, dragons, peonies and lotuses, were in widespread use. Well-known secular works such as the Shahnama (Book of Kings) were popular. Many mosques and shrines were built in cities across Iran.

During the Mamluk Period (1250–1517), Cairo became the artistic centre of the Islamic world. Much prosperity was evident, primarily resulting from international trade. Refugee craftspeople from east and west contributed to developments in the visual arts (particularly textiles, woodworking, inlaid metalwork and enamelled glass). The influence of Mamluk glassware on Venetian glass is mentioned often in the relevant literature. There was much building work also, including mosques, hospitals, minarets and madrasas. Commercial activity and trade were of importance during the period.

The Timurid period (1370–1507) was the last dynasty to emerge from Central Asia. Under the leadership of Timur (known also as Tamerlane), a Turko-Mongol who had settled in Transoxiana, Samarqand was established as the capital. Within a few decades, much of Central Asia, Iran, Iraq, parts of southern Russia and India were under Timurid control. To the west, Timurid forces conquered Mamluk Syria in the early 1400s. Timur died in 1405, and the empire was greatly weakened because of internal conflict. From the viewpoint of the visual arts the Timurid period is recognized as one that witnessed great developments and the blending of styles from sources as far as Anatolia and India. The eastern Islamic world rose in importance culturally with Herat as an important centre. Manuscript illumination was of particular note, as were metalwork and the carving of jade. Shrines, madrasas, mosques, and khanqahs (convents) were built. Typical architectural characteristics or features include minarets, polychrome tilings and substantial double-dome structures. Three non-Arab dynasties or empires carried forward the developments initiated by the Timurids: the Safavids, the Ottomans and the Mughals (each introduced later in this book). Each made a substantial contribution to the diffusion of Islamic culture, as well as to developments in what can be referred to as Islamic art and design. Further to this, note that important developments in the visual arts are also associated with the region known as the Maghrib, mainly lands to the west of Egypt, including the coastline of North Africa and much of the Iberian Peninsula.

motifs, symbols and patterns

In earlier periods, plant motifs and patterns were drawn largely from pre-existing Eastern Roman and Sasanian sources. By around the tenth century, a more characteristic Islamic style had begun to emerge, and this included widespread use of arabesque-type designs (though the term *arabesque* was not used until the nineteenth century). Geometric motifs and patterns formed major compositional elements in all Islamic art. Geometric tilings were used extensively on the interior and (often) exterior of mosques and also secular buildings, and the related geometry was applied to smaller, portable objects. A new visual art style emerged which mirrored the intellectual contributions of Islamic scientists, mathematicians and astronomers. Often underpinned with simple geometric figures (circles, squares and other regular polygons), tilings were created through intricate combinations of geometric figures which were duplicated, overlapped and interlaced.

Islamic star tilings (cs 16)

Tilings and mosaics can be found in numerous cultural and historical contexts, including ancient Rome and the Sasanian Empire. In the Islamic context, such forms of surface design were elaborated to impressive heights of complexity across many Islamic cultures. In the design of tiling constructions, use was made of the pair of compasses and the straight edge, though further practical aids such as stencils and set squares were also used (Hann 2012: 58). The underpinning geometrical elements included circles and various regular grids (especially those which featured equilateral triangles, squares or hexagons). Invariably,

Figure 7.1a–f Stars from overlapping polygons (CW)

designs tiled the plane without gaps or overlaps. Some designs showed repeating elements and some were nonrepeating compositions. Generally designs were non-representational, but there was occasional use of floral motifs of various kinds and arabesques. Often, calligraphy and interlacing effects were incorporated. In all cases there was a strict adherence to an underlying geometric structure, explored previously by Hann (2012: 58–62). Owen Jones (1856) provided early recognition of the aesthetic value of Islamic designs in *The Grammar of Ornament*. This work stimulated further interest among scholars, and there were many attempts to discover the procedures used by ancient Islamic craftspeople. Of note is the work of Broug (2008), who presented detailed instructions on procedures suited to constructing designs associated with various well-known Islamic buildings and monuments. Abas and Salman commented that 'the most striking characteristic of Islamic geometric patterns is the prominence of symmetric shapes which resemble stars and constellations' (1995: 4). These star tiling designs can be found with five, six, eight, ten, twelve or sixteen points, and orders of seven and nine are rare though not unknown. Hann observed that higher orders, generally in multiples of eight up to ninety-six, were also possible (2012: 59). Star tiling designs are the focus of the following case study. Hann previously discussed the most convenient means of constructing star-type motifs

(2012: 60–2). A brief summarized version is given below.

Star-type motif construction involves drawing lines connecting predetermined points on a circle or the overlapping of regular polygons within a circle (Figures 7.1a–f). The stages of construction involved in creating the outline for an eight-point star are shown in Figure 7.2. It is important to realize that several construction methods could conceivably be employed with the same outcome. Following procedures suggested by Field (2004), various twelve-point motif constructions are shown in Figures 7.3a–e. Figures 7.4–7.11 give examples of relevant Islamic tilings.

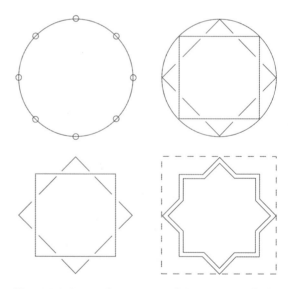

Figure 7.2 Stages of construction of eight-point star (CW)

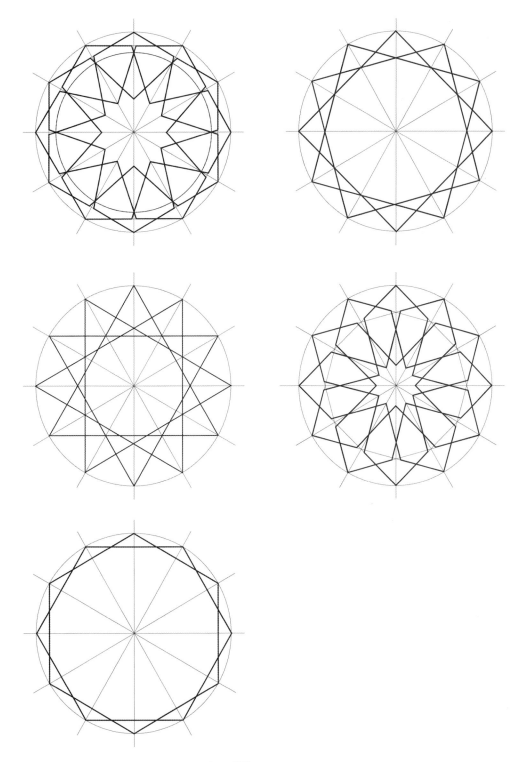

Figure 7.3a–e Various twelve-point star constructions (CW)

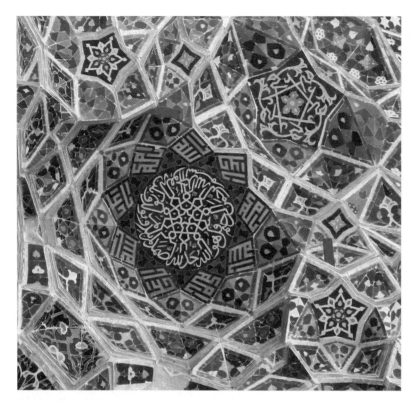

Figure 7.4 Islamic tiling (MV)

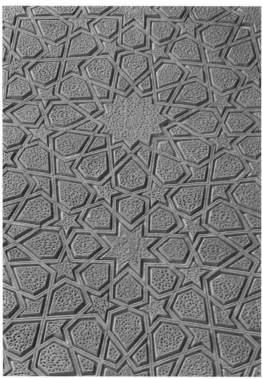

Figure 7.5 Islamic tiling (MV)

Figure 7.6 Islamic tiling (JC)

Figure 7.7 Islamic tiling (JC)

Figure 7.8 Islamic tiling (JC)

Figure 7.9 Islamic tiling (JC)

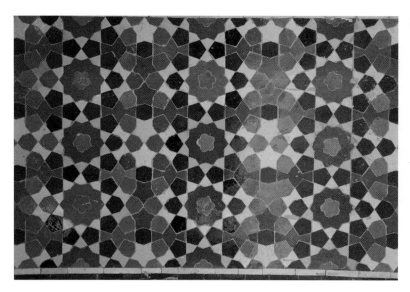

Figure 7.10 Islamic tiling (MV)

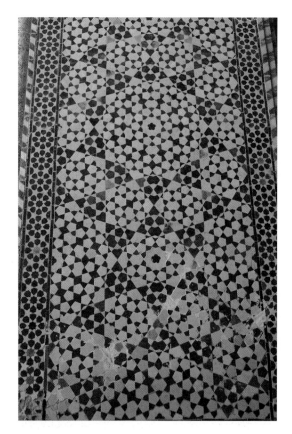

Figure 7.11 Islamic tiling (MV)

mosque tilings of Shiraz (cs 17)

The city of Shiraz has been celebrated as a cultural hub for many centuries. It was the Iranian capital during the Zand dynasty (1749–79), when many of the historic buildings were built. This case study presents a review of a selection of tiling designs from a small number of buildings in Shiraz. These include two mosques, Vakil and Nasir al-Mulk, both recognized internationally as important historical monuments.

Built between 1751 and 1773, during the Zand dynasty, the Vakil Mosque is located in the city of Shiraz in south Iran (Figures 7.12–7.16). The mosque fell into disrepair and was restored in the nineteenth century. *Vakil* means *regent*, a title adopted by Karim Khan, founder of the Zand dynasty. The building is tiled extensively with complex tilings, characteristic of Shiraz in the latter half of the eighteenth century. The mosque has a prayer hall with a substantial series of pillars carved with

Figure 7.12 Vakil Mosque, Shiraz, Iran (MV)

Figure 7.13 Vakil Mosque, Shiraz, Iran (MV)

Figure 7.14 Vakil Mosque, Shiraz, Iran (MV)

Figure 7.15 Vakil Mosque, Shiraz, Iran (MV)

Figure 7.16 Vakil Mosque, Shiraz, Iran (MV)

Figure 7.17 Nasir-al-Mulk Mosque, Shiraz, Iran (MV)

Figure 7.18 Nasir-al-Mulk Mosque, Shiraz, Iran (MV)

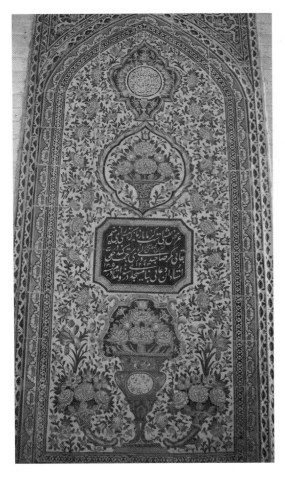

Figure 7.19 Nasir-al-Mulk Mosque, Shiraz, Iran (MV)

Figure 7.20 Nasir-al-Mulk Mosque, Shiraz, Iran (MV)

Figure 7.22 Nasir-al-Mulk Mosque, Shiraz, Iran (MV)

Figure 7.21 Nasir-al-Mulk Mosque, Shiraz, Iran (MV)

Figure 7.23 Nasir-al-Mulk
Mosque, Shiraz, Iran (MV)

Figure 7.24 Nasir-al-Mulk Mosque, Shiraz, Iran (MV)

Figure 7.25 Nasir-al-Mulk Mosque, Shiraz, Iran (MV)

Figure 7.26 Nasir-al-Mulk Mosque, Shiraz, Iran (MV)

Figure 7.27 Nasir-al-Mulk Mosque, Shiraz, Iran (MV)

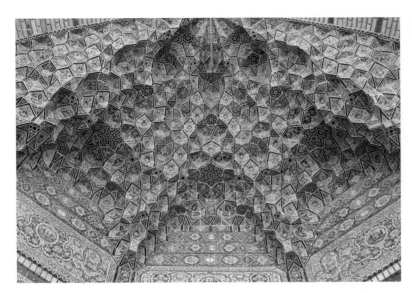

Figure 7.28 Nasir-al-Mulk
Mosque, Shiraz, Iran (MV)

spirals. Each pillar has an acanthus-leaf capital. A further notable feature, in addition to the exuberant floral tiling, is a minbar (which has a similar function to a pulpit) cut from solid green marble. Other notable buildings in the vicinity include bathhouses and a bazaar.

A further mosque located in Shiraz is Nasir al-Mulk, built between 1876 and 1888 (Figures 7.17–7.28). An important feature of this building, which still operates as a working mosque, is the exquisite tiling on both interior and exterior walls and the main entrance.

DISCUSSION OR ASSIGNMENT TOPICS

Tiling Symmetry

Using original illustrative material (either your own drawings or photographs), discuss symmetry in Islamic star tilings.

Mosque Tilings

Citing examples from relevant historical monuments, and using illustrative material of your choice, discuss the structural geometry of mosque tilings.

Islamic Visual Arts and Architecture

Write brief notes on the nature of Islamic visual arts and architecture (focussing particular attention on the role played by geometry) during each of the following periods: the Umayyad Period (661–750 CE); the Abbasid Period (750–1258 CE); the Fatimid Period (909–1171 CE); the Seljuqs of Iran (1040–1157 CE); the Ayyubid Period (1171–1260 CE); the Ilkhanid Period (1256–1353 CE); the Mamluk Period (1250–1517 CE); the Timurid Period (1370–1507 CE); the Safavid Period (1501–1722 CE). In each case note where the centre of power was located. Your response should focus on the nature of the visual arts (metalwork, woodwork, furniture, tilings, textiles, costumes or carpet production. Where appropriate, mention architecture, including notable monuments and other buildings. Your response should identify which visual arts were of particular importance in each period. What types of motifs or symbols were used? Are particular production techniques (e.g. in pottery or metalwork) or the use of particular raw materials (e.g. silk or silver) worth mentioning? Which visual arts do you deem of importance in each period? Can you recognize any continuum from one period to the next? You should briefly explain the nature of Islamic architecture and note how it evolved over the centuries. What are the unique features? What is the nature of mosque architecture? Does Early Islamic (particularly mosque) architecture show any apparent similarities to previous (e.g. Byzantine) architecture?

---

further reading

Abas, S. J. and Salman, A. S. (1995). *Symmetries of Islamic Geometrical Patterns*, London: World Scientific.

Broug, E. (2008). *Islamic Geometric Patterns*, London: Thames and Hudson.

Field, R. (2004). *Geometric Patterns from Islamic Art and Architecture*, Norfolk (UK): Tarquin Publications.

Grabar, O. (1973). *The Formation of Islamic Art*, New Haven, CT and London: Yale University Press.

Grabar, O. (1992). *The Mediation of Ornament*, Princeton, NJ: Princeton University Press.

Hann, M. A. (2012). *Structure and Form in Design: Critical Ideas for Creative Practice*, London and New York: Berg.

Hillenbrand, R. (1999). *Islamic Art and Architecture*, London: Thames and Hudson.

8

Islamic Spain

The part of the Islamic world west of Egypt was known as the Maghrib (sometimes spelled Maghreb) and included present-day Morocco, Algeria, Tunisia and much of the Iberian Peninsula. The region was largely isolated from the rest of the Muslim world (in a very real sense because of the restrictions imposed by the deserts of western Egypt and Libya). Also, maritime links with lands to the east were restricted or not dependable as they were often subject to hostilities from the Christian powers dominant on the north side of the Mediterranean. So, for cultures located in the western part of the Islamic world, it was difficult to avoid focussing inward. There were, however, significant developments in the visual arts and architecture, particularly in the region known as al-Andalus. The objective in this chapter is to briefly review developments in the visual arts and architecture in al-Andalus during the period from around the late eighth century CE to the mid-fifteenth century CE.

Umayyad origins

Boone and Benco (1999) observed: 'Aside from the Balkan region of south-eastern Europe and Sicily and southern Italy, the Iberian Peninsula is the only region of the European subcontinent where Islamic social, political, and cultural dominance was established for any length of time.' In 711 CE much of the Iberian Peninsula came under Islamic control, and some time later, the first dynasty was established under an Umayyad prince by the name of Abd-al-Rahman, a fugitive from Syria, where the Abbasids had taken control. In Iberia the Umayyads made Cordoba their capital and, by the tenth century, this had become a thriving centre for culture, manufacture and trade. The Umayyad Arabs held sway in al-Andalus until the early eleventh century CE. Thereafter, political control of the area became fragmented and passed to around forty minor states (or *taifas*). Important subsequent dynasties included the Almoravids and the Almohads (Hillenbrand 1999: 184). After the dissolution of the Almohad Empire, the kingdoms of the south were combined under the control of the Nasrids. For much of the period under consideration, Cordoba was an important seat of learning and culture, highly regarded throughout the Mediterranean region in general and in the Islamic world in particular. Other important cities were Seville and Toledo. In the final centuries, before the Christian conquest of the total peninsula, the city of Granada rose in importance and became the capital of the Nasrid dynasty. The fall of Granada to Christian forces in the late fifteenth century marked the end of Islamic rule in the Iberian Peninsula.

Boone and Benco (1999), in their review of a wide range of archaeological research associated with developments in North Africa and the Iberian Peninsula from the seventh century to the Late Middle Ages, gave an appraisal of the contribution of several centuries of Islamic settlement in Spain and its cultural and political significance. This chapter is principally concerned with developments in the visual arts and architecture.

Throughout much of its history al-Andalus seems to have existed under a constant state of siege, due largely to threats looming from the Christian kingdoms to the north. There were also occasions of internal conflict among Arab factions within Al-Andalus itself, as well as sporadic aggressive intentions expressed from kingdoms in North Africa. Under these circumstances, and considering its geographical isolation, developments in the visual arts and architecture as well as in mathematics, astronomy, medicine and engineering seem all the more remarkable.

Major achievements, from the viewpoint of the visual and architectural arts, were the Great Mosque of Cordoba and the Alhambra palace complex (Granada). Luxuries included figured silks and numerous portable objects of silver and ivory. There were notable developments associated with ceramic production. Some of these are considered briefly in this chapter.

As De Montequin (1987: 162) observed, by the late eighth century certain aesthetic rules and norms were already being established. These drew from the legacy of ancient Mediterranean and medieval European sources, which converged with a rich Persian inheritance. Three categories of motif and pattern were employed: vegetal, geometric and calligraphic. De Montequin (1987: 162) identified one particular category of

embellishment which dominated the characteristic architecture of Cordoba and elsewhere, a sort of vegetal arabesque (referred to by De Montequin as *ataurique*), often used in conjunction with geometric and calligraphic motifs, patterns or additions (1987: 162). De Montequin maintained that the *ataurique* was the outcome of a process of visual development with origins in the Assyrian palmette which fused with 'the botanical forms of the acanthus and grape leaf of classical antiquity' (1987: 162). Key monuments exhibiting the relevant form of decoration include the Great Mosque of Cordoba (built 786–991) and the palace complex known as Madinat al-Zahra (936–1010). De Montequin noted further developments in the motif later, in the eleventh and twelfth centuries, associated with its use in North Africa (1987: 162).

achievements in various visual arts (manuscripts, textiles, ceramics, metal and wood)

A distinctive style of Qur'anic illumination developed alongside the continued use of vellum up to the fourteenth century, by which time the rest of the Islamic world had long since switched to paper (Hillenbrand 1999: 176). Ivory carving, principally on caskets, cosmetics cases and pyxides, was of importance. Textiles were produced in abundance over the centuries, with *tiraz* factories established in Seville and Cordoba, as well as Almeria and Malaga. Raw silk was obtained locally, fed from Malaga's mulberry groves. Motifs and decoration on textiles in general proclaimed Islamic origins, often with Arabic inscriptions glorifying the sultan. Two ceramic techniques were introduced and developed: glazing with an opaque white tin-based glaze, and lustre ware (imitative of metallic finishes and giving iridescent effects). Lustre ware was often made for Christian patrons, and included coats of arms and Christian inscriptions such as 'Ave Maria' (Hillenbrand 1999: 192).

Motifs included griffins, double-headed eagles, basilisks, harpies and sphinxes, lions, antelopes and various birds. A common theme was the power of royalty, expressed through symbols or inscriptions. Hillenbrand observed: 'the architectural vocabulary of Andalusia—horseshoe arches, roll mouldings, rib vaults, interlacing arcades— infiltrated the Christian architecture of the north and even crossed the Pyrenees leaving its mark on the Romanesque churches of south-western France in particular' (1999: 182).

After the Christian conquest of Spain, many notable scholarly works, across many subject areas, were translated into Latin and made accessible to much of Europe. Indeed it seems that the fall of Islamic Spain in 1492, and the increased awareness of its achievements, acted as a stimulus for an intellectual renaissance in Europe. The architecture and visual arts of the Moors and Andalusians who remained in the peninsula after the Christian conquest but did not convert to Christianity is called mudéjar. This style is largely assumed to have resulted from Jewish, Christian and Muslim craftspeople living and working side by side. The style developed between the twelfth and sixteenth centuries and was commissioned mainly by Christians. Further explanation of mudéjar contributions to the visual arts and architecture in the peninsula is given briefly in the following section.

mudéjar visual arts

The word mudéjar, derived from the Arabic mudajjin (domesticated), is used either to refer to the

Muslims permitted to remain domiciled in Iberia after the Christian conquest but subject to strictly imposed laws, or to describe the style of architecture and decorative arts of the Moors who remained in the peninsula after the Christian conquest. mudéjar can thus be used to refer to a style of visual arts or architecture associated with non-Muslim Iberia, but influenced by the styles of al-Andalus.

Mudéjar visual art and architecture can be regarded as the link between the Islamic and Christian artistic traditions of the Iberian peninsula; the equivalent term Hispano-Moresque is sometimes used. The technical expertise exhibited is of importance. The mudéjar craftspeople excelled in trades associated with buildings and construction (brickwork, plasterwork and carpentry), as well as in ceramic and textile production and many other crafts. A pronounced geometric character emerged in mudéjar tilework, brickwork, plaster carving and in ornamental metal and woodwork, as well as in many architectural details.

Great Mosque of Cordoba (cs 18)

In the mid-eighth century, a power struggle, instigated (with success) by the Abbasids of Persia, led to the removal from power of the Umayyads. One survivor of the coup, Abd al-Rahman, fled to Spain and, breaking the link with Baghdad (the new religious, cultural and political capital under the Abbasids), created an independent Umayyad inspired Islamic nation. Under his leadership the building of the Great Mosque of Cordoba was initiated (Figures 8.1–8.12). Also known as the Mezquita, the work began in the 780s and continued over the next two centuries. With four expansions in less than three centuries, the Great Mosque of Cordoba 'grew to become one of the largest mosques of all' (Hillenbrand 1999: 172).

Figure 8.1 Exterior portal, Great Mosque of Cordoba (MV)

Figure 8.2 Interior details, Great Mosque of Cordoba (JC)

As Khoury observed, the Great Mosque of Cordoba is recognized universally 'as one of the most singular monuments of medieval architecture' (1996: 80).

In 756 CE, the ancient city of Cordoba was selected as the Umayyad capital in al-Andalus. Subsequently, many Syrian refugees settled in Cordoba and brought with them various intel-lectual perspectives and knowledge embracing a wide range of disciplines and subjects. Their ideas relating to mosque architecture mirrored the stylistic characteristics associated with their native Syria, and these were manifested in the early built stages of the Great Mosque of Cordoba, which used horseshoe-shaped arches and two-tiered arcades, as well as a minaret with a square base

Figure 8.3 Interior details, Great Mosque of Cordoba (JC)

(similar to that in the Damascus mosque of the time and differing from forms of Islamic architecture developing elsewhere).

By the ninth century, Cordoba had risen to become a well-organized and powerful city-state characterized by a cultural diversity and religious tolerance absent from states across much of the Mediterranean region at the time. Many scholars fled to al-Andalus from other parts of the Islamic world (e.g. from Abbasid-controlled Baghdad), bringing with them skills, talents and knowledge, as well as a wide cultural vision which embraced both Eastern and Western outlooks. Cordoba became the centre of a sophisticated, cosmopolitan society and, together with other cities such as Toledo, became associated with blossoming intellectual developments in many areas including the visual arts and architecture. In terms of social amenities, Cordoba had no equal in Europe. Hillenbrand commented: 'Its houses were bountifully supplied with hot and cold running water, its

Figure 8.4 Interior details, Great Mosque of Cordoba (JC)

Figure 8.5 Interior details, Great Mosque of Cordoba (JC)

Figure 8.6 Interior details, Great Mosque of Cordoba (JC)

Figure 8.7 Interior details, Great Mosque of Cordoba (JC)

Figure 8.8 Interior details,
Great Mosque of Cordoba (JC)

Figure 8.9 Exterior details,
Great Mosque of Cordoba

Figure 8.10 Exterior details, Great Mosque of Cordoba

streets were lit at night, its royal library—if one may trust the chroniclers—had 400,000 volumes at the time when the major libraries in western Europe scarcely reached a thousand' (1999: 175). Often noted is the largely harmonious coexistence of Muslims, Christians and Jews. Occasionally noted is the apparent prominence given to women as scribes, librarians, poets and musicians, while the rest of the Islamic world, as well as the non-Islamic European societies of the day, were largely male-dominated (Hillenbrand 1999: 175). Following the Christian-led conquest of Toledo in the late eleventh century, many scholarly works were translated from Arabic to Latin and were passed to other parts of Europe, where they stimulated further intellectual developments.

Located in the Spanish city of Cordoba in southern Spain, the Great Mosque of Cordoba was used formerly as a mosque during Islamic times, but since 1236 has been used as a Catholic

Figure 8.11 Exterior details, Great Mosque of Cordoba

Figure 8.12 Exterior details, Great Mosque of Cordoba

cathedral. In its role as a mosque the building acted as a focal point for the Islamic population of al-Andalus for over three centuries.

Considering the Umayyad roots of early developments in Al-Andalus, it is not surprising that the Umayyad architecture (of Syria) was copied to some degree; as noted above important examples include the square minaret associated traditionally with Syrian mosque architecture, as well as horseshoe-shaped arches and two-tiered arcades characteristic of the Great Mosque of Cordoba (Hillenbrand 1999: 171). As stated previously, Spanish Islamic decorative art and architecture is referred to often as *Moorish* or *Hispano-Moresque*. In comparison to other parts of Europe, much architectural innovation is evident, including 'interlacing multi-foil arches' and 'ribbed domes of great variety and complexity' (Hillenbrand 1999: 174). The architecture of the Great Mosque of Cordoba was thus (in its initial stages) developed from a style characteristic of Syria but, through four extensions in a period extending over a few hundred years, the Great Mosque developed its own distinctive visual and architectural vocabulary.

The monument is most noted for its arcaded area with a forest of 856 columns, predominantly of onyx marble and granite, many taken from the Roman temple which had occupied the site previously as well as from other Roman ruins in the vicinity. Double arches permitted higher ceilings. A centrally located, honeycombed dome featuring blue tiles decorated with stars and richly gilded prayer niches are further features. The large rectangular prayer hall has aisles arranged in the same axial direction as the *qibla* (the direction of prayer). Inspiration for the architectural style can be detected from Greco-Roman, Syrian, Islamic Abbasid, Persian and local Visigothic sources.

Various key-type patterns, in red and white brickwork, are depicted in the exterior doorways and arches of the Great Mosque of Cordoba. The symmetry properties of these designs have been assessed and are reported briefly below. From a total of eighteen key-type frieze patterns, all eighteen showed reflection properties: thirteen with two-direction reflection symmetry; five with one-direction reflection symmetry in association with

Plate 1 Detail of nineteenth-century Qing dynasty embroidery

Plate 2 Detail of Javanese batik

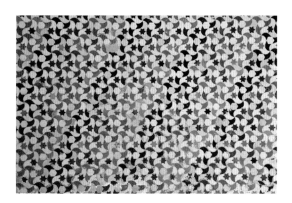

Plate 3 Wall tiling, Alhambra palace complex, Granada

Plate 4 Detail of processional lion, Ishtar Gate reconstruction, Staatliche Museen zu Berlin

Plate 5 Alhambra palace complex, Granada

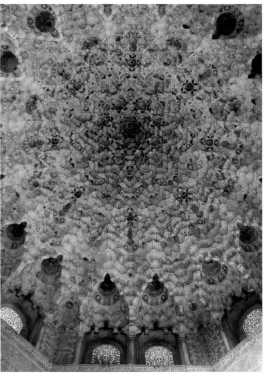

Plate 6 Alhambra palace complex, Granada

Plate 7 Alhambra palace complex, Granada

Plate 8 Great Mosque of Cordoba

Plate 9 Great Mosque of Cordoba

Plate 10 Alcazar, Seville

Plate 11 Nasir-al-Molk Mosque, Shiraz, Iran

Plate 12 Nasir-al-Molk Mosque, Shiraz, Iran

Plate 13 Hagia Sophia, Istanbul

Plate 14 'Big Buddha', Lan Tau Peak, Hong Kong

Plate 15 The 'Blue Mosque', Istanbul

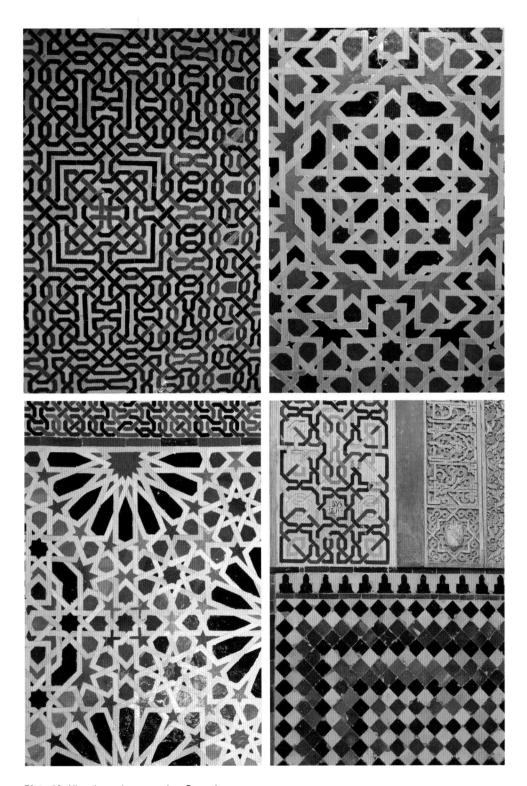

Plate 16 Alhambra palace complex, Granada

Plate 17 Tiling details, Moshir Mosque, Shiraz, Iran

Plate 18 Detail of Tibetan thangka, water-based pigment on cotton, probably nineteenth century

Plate 19 Detail of Tibetan thangka, water-based pigment on cotton, probably nineteenth century

Plate 20 Pair of Qing dynasty snuff bottles

Plate 21 Detail of a griffin-headed bracelet (one of a pair)

Plate 22 Detail of embroidered textile, eighteenth century, Gujarat, India

Plate 23 Four princesses playing polo, ink, opaque water colour and gold on paper

Plate 24 Taj Mahal, India

Plate 25 Detail of nineteenth-century Qing dynasty embroidered silk

Plate 26 Detail of nineteenth-century Qing dynasty embroidered silk

Plate 27 Detail of nineteenth-century Qing dynasty embroidered silk

Plate 28 Detail of nineteenth-century Qing dynasty tapestry-woven silk fabric

Plate 29 Detail of nineteenth-century Qing dynasty embroidered silk

Plate 30 Detail of nineteenth-century Qing dynasty embroidered dragon-robe fabric

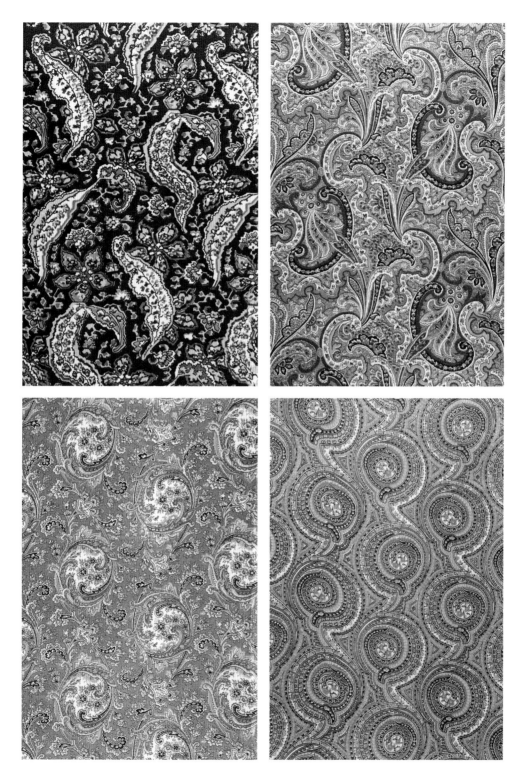

Plate 31 Early twentieth-century engraved copper roller printed textiles

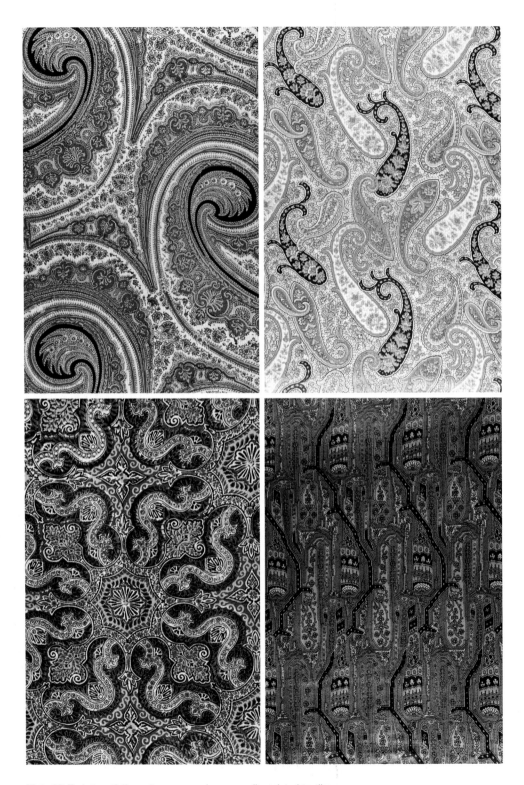

Plate 32 Early twentieth-century engraved copper roller printed textiles

other symmetry characteristics. From a total of thirteen key-type all-over patterns, six showed reflection symmetry of some kind; various other symmetry characteristics were evident in the thirteen, but none of these showed as high an incidence as reflection symmetry. Overall, it can be seen that from a total of thirty-one patterns (eighteen frieze patterns and thirteen all-over patterns) twenty-four displayed reflection symmetry to varying degrees. Not surprisingly, the predominance of reflection symmetry can be seen readily in many exterior and interior architectural features: doorways, arches, mihrab shapes, ceilings and floor plans. This predominance is also noted in many other visual arts of al-Andalus, especially in textiles and wall tilings.

does not seem to have followed a clear structural scheme. The majority of buildings in the complex are quadrangular in plan, with each room opening on to a central court. Over the years the complex was extended by different rulers, each following the theme of creating a paradise-type environment with columned arches, water fountains and pools. Patterning includes stiff foliage, Arabic inscriptions and numerous painted geometric tilings often acting as panelling to walls.

Set on a mountainous outcrop overlooking Granada, the complex remained a seat of Muslim power until the Christian conquest. Much damage and destruction were done and ill-thought-out additions were made to the complex subsequently,

Alhambra palace complex (cs 19)

The Alhambra is a complex of palaces, built in the tenth century, located in Granada in southern Spain and consisting of various living quarters, courtyards, gardens, fountains, streams, towers and a mosque. This was the fortified city of the rulers of Granada, and was the last bastion of Muslim rule in Spain. After the Christian conquest, the Christian rulers used some parts of the complex, and, in the first half of the sixteenth century, the palace of Charles V was added to the site, but in subsequent centuries the Alhambra fell into disrepair and was subjected to wilful vandalism until the cause for conservation and repair was taken up by nineteenth-century scholars and travellers from other parts of Europe. During the course of the twentieth century, the complex became a major tourist attraction; this has continued into the early twenty-first century (Figures 8.13–8.29).

The complex underwent several phases of construction and extension, but the overall layout

Figure 8.13 Alhambra palace complex, Granada (RD)

Figure 8.14 Alhambra palace complex, Granada (RD)

and for many centuries the Alhambra was neglected. Following restoration work in the late nineteenth century, and a continuous restoration programme in the twentieth century, the complex became the most visited historic site of medieval Europe by the early twenty-first century. The constituent palaces are renowned for their rich interior patterning, especially the glazed tile surfaces, Arabic inscriptions, carved woodwork and arabesque-type foliage. The exterior walls are largely plain, and primary blue, red and golden yellow were employed in the interiors.

Important parts of the palace complex include: the Court of the Myrtles; the Hall of the Ambassadors; the Court of the Lions; the Hall of the Abencerrajes; the Hall of the Two Sisters. Each is described briefly below.

The Court of the Myrtles, also called the Court of the Blessing or Court of the Pond, was built in the first half of the fourteenth century, and is

Figure 8.15 Alhambra palace complex, Granada (JC)

Figure 8.16 Alhambra palace complex, Granada (JC)

Figure 8.17 Alhambra palace complex, Granada (JC)

Figure 8.18 Alhambra palace complex, Granada (JC)

Figure 8.19 Alhambra palace complex, Granada (JC)

Figure 8.20 Alhambra palace complex, Granada (JC)

forty-two metres by twenty-two metres with a large pond set centrally and galleries on the north and south sides. The Hall of the Ambassadors is a square room with sides of twelve metres, and a dome rising to twenty-three metres. The building projects from the palace complex, and has a total of nine windows, which permit light to enter on three sides. This area functioned as the grand reception area, with the throne of the sultan placed facing the entrance. Walls are tiled to a height of around a metre, with added oval medallions and inscriptions interwoven with floral decoration. The ceiling has blue, white and gold inlays, circular

and star-and-crown shaped. The Court of the Lions, built in the latter half of the fourteenth century, is oblong (around 35 metres by 20 metres), and surrounded by a low gallery supported on 124 white marble columns. Pavilions with filigree walls project into the courtyard at each of the two lengthway extremities. Located centrally in the courtyard is the Fountain of Lions, an alabaster basin supported by one dozen sculpted white marble lions (not executed in a realistic fashion, but probably added to symbolize power and sovereignty). The Hall of the Abencerrajes is a square room with a dome and trellised windows. The Hall of the Two Sisters, which is opposite the Hall of the Abencerrajes, is so called because of the two

Figure 8.21 Alhambra palace complex, Granada (JC)

Figure 8.22 Alhambra palace complex, Granada (JC)

Figure 8.23 Alhambra palace complex, Granada (JC)

Figure 8.24 Alhambra palace complex, Granada (JC)

Figure 8.25 Alhambra palace complex, Granada (JC)

white marble slabs (each 50 by 22 centimetres) which form part of the pavement. A fountain is located in the middle of the hall and the domed honeycomb-like vaulted ceiling, composed of numerous (around five thousand) decorative cells, is a characteristic feature. Other architectural features include the Hall of the Kings; the Hall of Justice; the Court of the Vestibule; the Queen's Robing Room.

The Alhambra palace complex has acted as an inspirational stimulus to numerous poets, musicians and artists. It is often claimed that M. C. Escher's visit in 1922, and his study of the use of symmetry in the Alhambra tilings, inspired his subsequent work which made regular divisions of the plane. Many mathematical observers have recorded and classified the tiling types exhibited at various points throughout the complex. It is readily evident that a large proportion of all-over symmetry classes (from the seventeen classes possible) are represented to varying degrees (this author has detected fifteen classes). The tile work and other patterned surfaces certainly show a preponderance of one-direction, two-direction and four-direction reflection symmetry. The present-day floor plan, with its several additions over the centuries, does not exhibit any clear symmetry characteristics worth noting. Not surprisingly, ceilings, doorways, window frames and several other architectural features show clear reflection-symmetry characteristics.

Figure 8.26 Alhambra palace complex, Granada (JC)

Figure 8.27 Alhambra palace complex, Granada (JC)

Figure 8.28 Alhambra palace complex, Granada (JC)

Figure 8.29 Alhambra palace complex, Granada (JC)

DISCUSSION OR ASSIGNMENT TOPICS

The Great Mosque of Cordoba

Describe the Great Mosque of Cordoba and identify and discuss its principal architectural features. Gather illustrative material which shows a broad range of tilings or other designs featured on the walls or other surfaces of the monument. Classify these designs with respect to their geometric symmetry. Which types of symmetry are predominant? Why could this be the case?

Alhambra Surface Patterning

Making reference to illustrative material of your choice, describe the symmetry characteristics of the various forms of surface patterning associated with the buildings within the Alhambra palace complex.

The Visual Arts and Architecture of Al-Andalus

Review and discuss the nature of the visual arts and architecture associated with al-Andalus, during the period from around the late eighth century CE to the mid-fifteenth century CE. Your response should focus on architecture and the visual arts (metalwork, tilings, textiles, work in ivory, or the production of any other item that you think of significance). Where appropriate, give examples of notable objects or buildings. What are the important features of these? What types of motifs or symbols were used? What distinguishes the decorative arts of al-Andalus from the visual arts from elsewhere?

---

further reading

Ecker, H. (2004). *Caliphs and Kings: The Art and Influence of Islamic Spain*, Washington, DC: Arthur M. Sackler Gallery and Smithsonian Institute.

Grabar, O. (1992). *The Mediation of Ornament*, Princeton, NJ: Princeton University Press.

Hillenbrand, R. (1999). *Islamic Art and Architecture*, London: Thames and Hudson. (Chapter 7 in particular)

9

Safavid Persia

Although Safavid roots can be traced to fourteenth-century Azerbaijan, the dynasty rose to power in Persia during the early sixteenth century and remained influential until the early eighteenth century. Important cities, from the viewpoint of the visual arts and architecture during the Safavid dynasty and subsequently, included Tabriz, Ardabil, Kashan, Kirman, Shiraz and Isfahan. During the reign of Shah Abbas, the most renowned Safavid ruler, Isfahan was selected as the newly designated capital and seat of government, and a newly built city was commissioned there (built beside the old city), with the centrepiece being the Maidan-i Shah (or royal area). Stylistically, Safavid visual arts were strongly influenced by Turkoman culture, as well as Chinese, Ottoman, and Western European sources.

The most notable achievements in the visual arts were in miniature painting and manuscript illumination, textile manufacture, and carpet and ceramic production—all of these were of importance in the development of international trade. A new Safavid style of painting developed. One of the most important manuscripts illuminated during the period was the Shahnama epic. Large quantities of high-quality carpets and other textiles were produced, including block-printed cottons, various woven silks, brocades using silver and gold metallic yarns, as well as embroideries and velvets. Much also occurred in architecture, with numerous mosques, mausoleums and palace complexes commissioned.

architecture

Important associated building projects in Isfahan included the Qaysarieh or grand bazaar, the Mosque of Sheikh Lutfallah, the Shah Mosque and the Allaverdikhan Bridge. Tilings associated with mosque architecture were particularly innovative, as was the use of *muquarnas* (stalactite-type tiling arrangements built in three dimensions as parts of ceilings or alcoves). As Hillenbrand observed, 'The muqarnas or honeycomb vault has many functions in Islamic architecture: it articulates a curved space, dissolves surfaces, bridges contrasting spaces, and creates a frame for related discrete motifs'(1999: 230).

manuscripts

Under the Safavids, Persian miniature painting, associated in particular with book production, became an important driving force for the visual arts in general. The royal workshops were very influential and much of their work was copied further, especially in provincial centres such as Shiraz. A range of books was copied, illuminated, and bound, including Korans and other religious works as well as renowned pieces of Persian literature, such as the Shahnamah, and various scientific treatises associated with Sufism. Paper, a Chinese invention, was introduced in Persia in the thirteenth century. In the time of Shah Abbas's reign in the late sixteenth and early seventeenth centuries, painting continued to flourish, though the emphasis was, by then, on single-page drawings and paintings rather than whole manuscripts. Interestingly, various forms of visual arts had similar rules of composition (e.g., calligraphy and painting). Illumination and tapestry weaving developed in parallel and had similar compositional templates.

carpets

For many centuries, Persia was renowned as an important area for carpet (or rug) manufacture. During the Safavid period and subsequently, carpet production achieved the status of an important national industry and, as Hillenbrand remarked, the Safavid period was the first to offer a 'critical mass of physical evidence' of carpet manufacture to permit a dependable history and chronology from 1500 to 1700 (1999: 246). Carpets were worked in various fibrous raw materials including silk, wool, cotton, and metallic threads of silver or gold. Techniques included flat weaves (*zilus* and *kilims*) and both coarse and very fine pile-woven pieces. Hillenbrand remarks on a closely woven piece composed of 800 knots per square inch (1999: 246). Irrespective of the design type, red, yellow, blue and white were the dominant colours. Many of the decorative themes and motifs used also appear in other visual arts, including tilings, metalwork and manuscript illumination (1999: 246). Hillenbrand

commented: 'The strongly pictorial character of so many Safavid carpets plainly owes much to Safavid book painting, a borrowing which extends even to the concept of pictorial space, as in the adoption of the high horizon and stepped planes and the plethora of small-scale detail' (1999: 249). The use of Chinese motifs in Safavid carpets is strikingly common, and includes representations of clouds, phoenixes, dragons, peonies and lotuses.

Many categories of design can be identified: hunting scenes, garden scenes, animal rugs, medallion and vase carpets, floral rugs and prayer rugs. Important manufacturing locations included Tabriz, Qazvin, Kashan, Isfahan and Kerman. Stone observed: 'Kashan is thought to be the source of fine silk hunting carpets and Isfahan was probably the source of Polonaise carpets. Large medallion carpets are attributed to Tabriz and vase carpets have been attributed to Kerman' (1997: 194). Decoration was similar to that used in book bindings and illumination. The majority of carpets in the sixteenth century were medallion carpets which included a large central multi-lobed medallion with quarter medallions in the corners. Probably the most famous museum-held medallion carpets are the so-called Ardabil carpets (one held in the Victoria and Albert Museum, London, and the other, a substantial fragment, held in the Los Angeles County Museum); these originated in the second quarter of the sixteenth century.

Around the beginning of the seventeenth century, vase carpet production became common (with a central vase shape with sprigs of flowers). Garden carpets (divided into rectangular sections, in imitation of a planned garden) were common by the late seventeenth century. Carpets depicting hunting scenes were also common. Carpet-weaving villages and towns throughout Persia had their own individual specialisms. For example Kashan produced relatively small carpets of 100 per cent silk, with a red or blue background as the setting for fights between animals, often borrowed from Chinese mythology.

other textiles

Prior to the Safavid dynasty, the Persian textile industry was already well established and proficient in the production of various textiles, including 'printed cotton, silk shorn velvet, reversible brocades in gold and silver thread, and embroidery' (Hillenbrand 1999: 250). Hillenbrand commented further: 'Architecture, painting and carpets may fairly claim to represent the principal achievements of the Safavids in the visual arts, but this was a productive period in many other media too.'

Persian silk textiles of the period are particularly noted for their delicate and fine quality. Increased state control of the silk trade developed in the seventeenth century, especially in the Caspian provinces, the principal source for the nation's fibrous silk. Compound weave structures, using gold and silver strips and wrapper metallic yarns, were common, as were silk velvets, with either continuous pile areas or voided effects (created by presenting flat woven areas against adjacent pile areas). Colour combinations were innovative, and included combinations such as pistachio green, salmon pink, alizarin, cream and ochre. State-sponsored textile workshops in Isfahan, Kashan and Kirman ensured high quality.

ceramics

The study and dating of Persian ceramics are prone to difficulties, as few pieces are dated and indications of the place of manufacture are rare. Many workshop locations have been identified, but with little certainty. Safavid potters developed new types of Chinese-inspired blue-and-white wares. Motifs were numerous and, as was the case with carpet manufacture, many motifs were drawn from Chinese sources and included cloud bands, cranes, phoenixes, dragons, lotuses and peonies. This is hardly surprising when one realizes that Shah Abbas invited 300 Chinese potters and their families to settle in Iran (Hillenbrand 1999: 250).

Iconography drawn from Islamic sources included the Islamic zodiac and arabesques, and from the Ottoman world the honeysuckle (a commonly used Turkish motif). In the second half of the seventeenth century, access to the Chinese market was restricted and demand for Safavid ceramics increased. This led to even wider use of Chinese iconography and would occasionally include false marks of Chinese workshops (thus suggesting Chinese production), all in response to the strong European demand for Chinoiserie pottery. Indeed some of the vases produced in Kirman were passable as Chinese ware (Hillenbrand 1999: 250). Lustre ware was produced in large quantities, but, according to Hillenbrand, Persian lustre ware had a 'brassy sheen', and patterning was restricted largely to vegetal motifs (1999: 250–1).

a Safavid prayer rug cartoon (cs 20)

An unlabelled package discovered among a quantity of unsorted textile fragments at the University of Leeds International Textiles Archive (ULITA) contained a cartoon for a silk prayer rug together with a handwritten copy of an accompanying letter (dated 28 July 1900) from Sidney J. A. Churchill of the British consulate in Naples. The text of the letter is reproduced here.

Copy

British Consulate, Naples.
July 28.1900.

Dear Sir,

I am in receipt of your letter of July 23. Owing to the necessity of having to leave Palermo hurriedly in order to take charge here, temporarily, I omitted to write to you acquainting you fully with the contents to which I had added the full working design for a silk prayer rug. The design has been carried out. The silk is to show the woman weaving the rug exactly what tints and dyes are to be used.

In packing up some of my things in order to change houses in Palermo I found it amongst much else. This design is valuable, and its gift shows you how much I am interested in doing anything to further the progress of textile education in England.

In Persia somewhere I must still have a fragment of a magnificent ancient carpet. I will see if I can get it.

Bardini of Florence has a Persian silk rug, very much patched, but I think it is the more valuable thus, educationally, because it holds more designs than it would have done if complete. I had hoped to induce the Edinburgh [missing word or words] Branch to buy but the death of Sir R. M. Smith has upset my plans.

Yours faithfully
Sidney J. A. Churchill

The cartoon was drawn on squared, cloth-backed paper with a fine brush and coloured with a water-based pigment (Figure 9.1–9.6). Swatches of dyed silk are attached at several places across the drawing. The design includes parts of a mihrab shape and is curvilinear with arabesques and flower heads (lotus, peony, chrysanthemum and magnolia).

In the late twentieth century, N. L. Kirby, a dissertation student at the University of Leeds working under the direction of the present author,

Figure 9.1 Silk prayer rug cartoon (University of Leeds International Textiles Archive)

Figure 9.2 Silk prayer rug cartoon detail (University of Leeds International Textiles Archive)

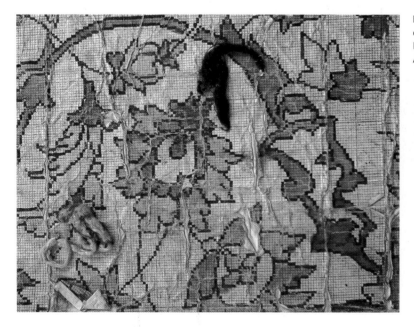

Figure 9.3 Silk prayer rug cartoon detail (University of Leeds International Textiles Archive)

Figure 9.4 Silk prayer rug cartoon detail (University of Leeds International Textiles Archive)

Figure 9.5 Silk prayer rug cartoon detail (University of Leeds International Textiles Archive)

consulted with various experts (affiliated with the National Museums of Scotland, the Victoria and Albert Museum and Christies of London) to develop an understanding of Persian rug manufacture in general as well as the possible role played by the cartoon in the production of the silk prayer rug mentioned in Churchill's letter.

This case study briefly discusses the contents of the letter, outlines the characteristics of typical prayer rugs, comments on the likely provenance (identified by different experts as Kirman, Isfahan or Kashan) and focuses particular attention on the stylistic aspects of the design presented on the cartoon. Brief biographical details are given of

Figure 9.6 Silk prayer rug cartoon detail (University of Leeds International Textiles Archive)

Sidney J. A. Churchill, Sir R. M. Smith, and Bardini of Florence. Where appropriate, reference is made to the unpublished dissertation of N. L. Kirby (1992).

A prayer rug, prayer carpet or prayer mat is a textile (generally woven, with or without a pile surface) used by Muslims as a portable, clean area on which to pray, facing Mecca, five times over the course of a day. Prayer rugs may vary in size, but need to cover enough area for worshippers to kneel at one end and, when bending during prayer, to place their heads on the other end. Dimensions of around a metre by three-quarters of a metre seem typical of a portable prayer rug. Invariably the design of prayer rugs includes a representation of a mihrab (an arch-shaped

prayer niche, often tiled, found in the interior of a mosque, positioned to indicate to the worshipper the direction of Mecca). In the majority of cases the space within the mihrab shape on a prayer rug is devoid of all-over patterning, though this does not seem to be the case with the cartoon design here.

The cartoon is drawn on a square grid (on paper backed with linen or glazed cotton). This grid is divided into blocks of ten by ten squares (thirteen millimetres by thirteen millimetres average), and these blocks, in turn are grouped in fours, thus providing larger squares of twenty divisions by twenty divisions (twenty-six millimetres by twenty-six millimetres). Most authorities agree that components of the design are typical of carpet designs from Safavid times, although the cartoon may well have been produced in subsequent years. The design style is certainly in sympathy with decoration on Safavid ceramics. It is envisaged that the single corner decoration shown in the cartoon would have been repeated at each corner of the carpet and that the portion of border shown in the cartoon would have been continued around the rectangular piece. Also, it is envisaged further that the central half-mihrab shape would have been reflected across a vertical axis to produce the full intended mihrab shape. It seems likely that the carpet, if made to the exact 1:1 scale of the cartoon, with each of the smallest squares of the grid representing one knot, would have resulted in a carpet with a knot density of just over seven knots per centimetre, in both weft and warp directions (though this does not make an allowance for dividing wefts placed between knots to hold them secure). Allowing for the addition of weft threads to hold knots secure, this would equate to around seven knots centimetre (weft ways) by around three knots per centimetre (warp ways) or around twenty-one knots per square centimetre.

Although the letter claims that the cartoon is a full working design for a silk prayer rug, it may be the case that parts have been removed since receipt of the parcel in Leeds in 1900. There is certainly a gap where it is believed a mosque lamp or vase may have been represented within the prayer niche or mihrab. It is assumed also from the documentation accompanying the cartoon that the design is indeed for a single upright mihrab prayer rug (which is most common). A reflected (double) mihrab shape (obtained by reflecting the full mihrab across an axis horizontal to the lower part of the mihrab) producing a large oval-shaped central field, is another possibility, though this would have led to a much longer carpet than envisaged currently. Also it is unknown whether the cartoon was at one time part of a larger entity. Maybe the craftsperson who sold the item had a more substantial portion (which could be used to weave further carpets). Also, Churchill stated that the design had been carried out; it is unknown however if he had actually seen the finished article.

The curvilinear and arabesque design features suggested to various experts that the design may have been produced in Kirman or Isfahan or Kashan, all important carpet-weaving locations. Scholars agree the design was produced in a settled workshop environment and was not the product of nomadic rug weaving. There are conflicting views on when the cartoon was produced, with one expert suggesting the sixteenth or seventeenth century and another the mid-nineteenth century, although there seems to be a consensus that the design was Persian and also that it was strongly influenced by Safavid decoration. Palmettes and flower heads of various kinds can be identified, and all of these are typical of Safavid decoration, which was in turn influenced by Ming dynasty porcelain. The strong structural arabesque shapes in the spandrel area (the area between the mihrab and upper border) suggest an architectural influence, possibly from tilings or similar forms of wall decoration.

The blue background given in the corner was probably intended as a background colour across not only all corners but all borders as well. However, it is unknown whether the intention was to use the same colour as a background colour within the mihrab field.

By way of summary, note that the promised high quality of the final result (in silk) would suggest that the carpet was produced in Isfahan. It may well have been commissioned by a high-ranking individual. It was probably woven on a vertical loom, and the silk used was probably imported (though this is by no means certain). The curvilinear design confirms that the final carpet would have been woven in an established workshop (probably with some aristocratic association) rather than by nomadic or village producers.

Sidney J. A. Churchill was a career diplomat who collected Persian, Arabic, Turkish and Hebrew manuscripts for the British Museum and also acquired carpets for the Victoria and Albert Museum. Robert M. Smith was a career soldier (reaching the rank of major general) and archaeologist and was awarded a knighthood (Knight Commander of St Michael and St George) in 1888 for services in Persia. He became the director of the Museum of Science and Art in Edinburgh. Stefano Bardini was a painter, restorer and antique collector. The author has been unable to identify other items mentioned in the letter: the 'fragment of a magnificent ancient carpet' or the 'much patched Persian silk rug'.

the Ardabil Carpet (Victoria and Albert Museum) (cs 21)

The Ardabil Carpet held in the Victoria and Albert Museum (London) is one of a pair of carpets, with the other of the pair held in the Los Angeles County Museum of Art. The carpet held in London is the most complete, as sections from that held in Los Angeles have been used in the restoration of the London carpet. The London carpet, which measures 10.5 metres by 5.3 metres, has a warp and weft foundation of silk and a knotted pile of wool. It was woven in three shades of blue, three shades of red, and yellow, green, black and white. The carpet was completed during the reign of the Safavid Shah Tahmasp I in the mid-sixteenth century. Some scholars believe that the object was initially housed in a large shrine in Ardabil, though this is by no means certain. The place of production was probably Tabriz or Kashan (Figure 9.7).

The carpet was displayed for several decades, hanging vertically against a wall in the Victoria and Albert Museum (London). In the first decade of the twenty-first century the carpet was instead shown flat in a special glass pavilion and placed centrally in the Islamic gallery. Here, the lighting is kept to an absolute minimum (though it is increased slightly for a few minutes each hour during museum opening times) to ensure a favourable conservation environment for the carpet.

The carpet has four borders, each differing in terms of content and design structure. The outer border has an arabesque-type floral-based motif, with twisting buds and tendrils. Mason (2002: 215) detected an axis of reflection at right angles to the border's edge (or directional orientation). The second border is the widest of the

Figure 9.7 Ardabil Carpet, Victoria and Albert Museum (Source: Wikipedia)

four borders and holds motifs which bear some resemblance to those in the central field of the carpet. Two differently sized medallions, containing floral elements of various kinds, are repeated around the carpet. Mason (2002: 216) detected two-direction reflection symmetry (operating both in parallel and perpendicularly to the border's sides). The third border consists of a repeating design of vegetal buds and tendrils. In this case Mason detected a few symmetries, including one-direction reflection, two-fold rotation and glide reflection of motifs (2002: 216). The fourth border depicts flower buds with associated foliage and tendrils. Mason (2002: 217) detected a glide reflection axis in this border. The central field, or main body, of the carpet contained within the successive borders forms the main focus for viewers (and presumably past users) of the carpet. Curling floral buds and tendrils are the overall feature of the central field, but dominant is a large central medallion with an associated depiction of two hanging mosque lamps. The central medallion has sixteen equally distributed radiating petals. This central medallion exhibits eightfold reflection symmetry and can be classified as a d8 motif using the symmetry classification system proposed in Chapter 2. The central medallion is the basis of four corner designs also placed in the central field. Each corner design consists of one quarter of the central medallion and its associated petals.

Wearden observed that the central field design consists of layers, including a design of thick stems with blossoms and leaves superimposed on another design of thinner stems bearing only blossoms. She commented further that the carpet exhibits reflection symmetry along its vertical axis (1995: 61).

A notable feature is the relative physical sizes of the two lamps flanking the central medallion: one is obviously smaller than the other when the carpet is viewed across its width; one lamp appears to be long and thin and the other lamp shorter and fatter. When the carpet is viewed along its length, however, the difference is not readily apparent. It is well known that objects in the distance appear to be smaller than equally sized objects positioned closer to the viewer. So the difference in size of the lamps may have resulted from a deliberate attempt by the designer to ensure that the lamps appeared to be the same size when viewed along the length of the carpet.

Shiraz tiling façades (cs 22)

Shiraz is a city of ancient origin, celebrated as a cultural centre for many centuries. It was the designated Persian capital during the Zand dynasty (1749–79), when many of the historic buildings of the city were constructed. This case study considers a small collection of photographs of building façades, taken by Marjan Vazirian in her work on the older part of the city of Shiraz in the first decade of the twenty-first century. The present author has been informed (2012) that the buildings depicted have either undergone radical refurbishment (removing the tiling façades) or have been demolished (Figures 9.8–9.11).

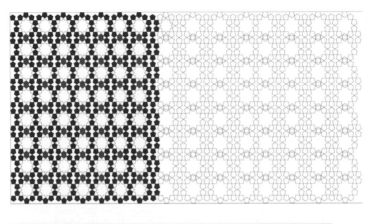

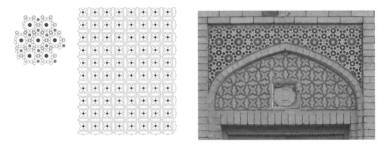

Figure 9.8 Shiraz façade photographs and redrawn component designs (MV)

Figure 9.9 Shiraz façade photograph and redrawn component designs (MV)

Figure 9.10 Shiraz façade photograph and redrawn component designs (MV)

Figure 9.11 Shiraz façade photograph and redrawn component designs (MV)

 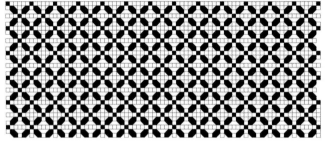

The tiling façades depicted in the photographs were probably designed by architects or other designers involved in mosque building or refurbishment projects during the late nineteenth or early twentieth centuries. The tiling designs are not radically different, in some instances, from those found on mosques in the city. The working methods, materials used, colour combinations and individual tile dimensions also appear to be similar.

This case study provides a structural analysis of a selection of tiling designs taken from a small number of façade photographs and reproduces these in graphic form. Based on this visual analysis, steps are taken towards the creation of a fresh collection of tiling designs (Figures 9.12–9.15).

Figure 9.12 Development of original design from Shiraz façade (MV)

Figure 9.13 Development of original design from Shiraz façade (MV)

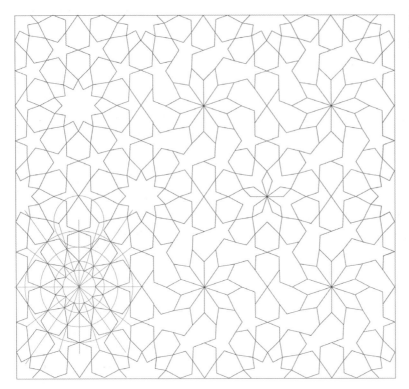

Figure 9.14 Development of original design from Shiraz façade (MV)

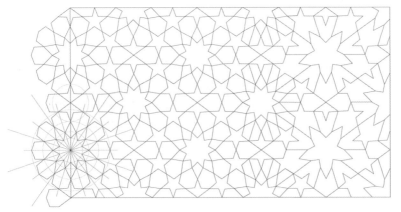

Figure 9.15 Development of original design from Shiraz façade (MV)

DISCUSSION OR ASSIGNMENT TOPICS

Prayer Rugs

Describe the function of, and identify the main stylistic features of, prayer rugs.

The Ardabil Carpet (V&A)

Making reference to its historical background, discuss the structural geometry of the Ardabil carpet held in the Victoria and Albert Museum.

Safavid Persia

Select an historic city in Persia which was of national importance during the Safavid period. Gather visual representations of tilings and other surface designs featured in domestic, social or religious contexts. Create a collage of the images selected and conduct a visual analysis of the surface designs depicted. Building on this visual analysis, create a fresh collection of six original designs, coloured with a palette which you consider commercially valid for an end use of your choice.

Safavid Visual Arts and Architecture

Review the nature of the visual arts and architecture of Safavid Persia. Make reference to manuscript production, carpet and textile manufacture, metalwork, tilings (and the production of any other patterned item that you think appropriate) and architecture. Identify which visual arts were of particular importance. What types of motifs or symbols were used? Which types of production techniques (e.g. in pottery or metalwork) were of importance? Identify important raw materials (e.g. silk or silver) and their potential sources. What and where are the main sites/buildings? What were the principal influences and developments? Did developments in the visual arts and architecture contribute to or influence changes elsewhere?

---

further reading

Bennett, I. (1972). *Book of Oriental Carpets and Rugs*, London: Hamlyn.

Bennett, I. (1978). *Rugs and Carpets of the World*, London: Quarto Publishing.

Hillenbrand, R. (1999). *Islamic Art and Architecture*, London: Thames and Hudson.

Wearden, J. (1995). 'The Surprising Geometry of the Ardabil Carpet', *Ars Textrina*, 24: 61–6.

10

Ottoman Turkey

As indicated elsewhere in this book, for much of the second half of the first millennium CE the ultimate westwards destination of traded goods across the Eurasian trading network was the Eastern Roman Empire, with its capital at Constantinople (present-day Istanbul). As the second millennium progressed, the city failed to compete successfully with the Genoese and Venetians who dominated the bulk of trade into the Mediterranean region. The city's population was severely hit by the Black Death in the mid-fourteenth century, and in the fifteenth century the city was conquered by the Ottoman Turks, who renamed it Istanbul and made it the designated capital of their expanding empire. Prior to the fall of Constantinople, Iznik and Bursa had acted as successive capitals. Both are of importance in the context of the visual arts: Iznik for pottery production and Bursa for silk production.

The Ottomans brought renewed prosperity to Constantinople, introduced a major building and repair programme and greatly expanded trade. Due largely to the city's strategic position and to Ottoman control of numerous seaports, the Ottomans exercised dominance over much of the Mediterranean basin and were ideally located to benefit from the trade interaction between Asia, the Middle East and Europe. Ultimately Ottoman control extended from Anatolia (much of present-day Turkey) and the Caucasus to the coastal regions of North Africa, Syria, Arabia and Iraq.

The visual arts were of immense importance in terms of trade. State-controlled workshops produced carpets and other textiles, calligraphy and manuscript painting, tiles and metalwork. Persian stylistic traditions were a strong influence on the decorative arts in general, and stylistic characteristics emerged in architecture, especially mosque architecture, which drew heavily from past Greco-Roman structures (especially the renowned church of Hagia Sophia).

As noted previously, Hagia Sophia was built in the second quarter of the sixth century under the orders of Emperor Justinian. Highly complex structurally, the building has a system of domes, semi-domes and vaults. The characteristic great dome is an impressive technical achievement, and the interior decoration is predominantly of marble and stone inlays. After the conquest of the city, the church was converted to a mosque and became known more commonly as Ayasofya Mosque. The building remained as the Great Mosque of the Ottoman capital until it was secularized and converted to a museum under the Turkish Republic in the second quarter of the twentieth century.

Hillenbrand commented that 'Ottoman architecture is unique in the Islamic world for its unswerving fidelity to a single central idea—that of the domed square [cubic] unit . . . It is the spinal cord running through the body of Ottoman architecture' (1999: 257). A dominant basic architectural feature is thus a cubic form with a dome placed on top. Other important features include domed buttresses, semi-domes, porticoes, domed cloisters, courtyards, minarets and fountains. All in all, hundreds of public buildings were designed and constructed during Ottoman times, including theological schools, hospitals, baths and mosques.

Mimar Sinan—the most renowned architect of the day, chief of the Corps of Royal Architects and in service to successive sultans Selim I, Süleyman, Selim II and Murod III—designed many mosques and other buildings during the sixteenth century. Süleyman, often referred to as 'the Magnificent', reigned for almost five decades, a period many regard as a golden age with much cultural, artistic and commercial activity. Not only did he initiate a substantial building and repair programme across Istanbul and other parts of Turkey, but he also ensured maintenance of and improvements to important monuments outside Turkey, including several additions to sites associated with the holy Islamic cities of Mecca and Medina.

Notable buildings and building complexes include the mosque complexes of Süleymaniye (Istanbul) and Selimiye (Edirne), both considered among the great architectural achievements of Mimar Sinan. The mosque of Ahmed I (Istanbul) was built in the first quarter of the seventeenth century, and is popularly known (mainly by tourists) as the Blue Mosque because of a component colour of its interior tiling. The external appearance, particularly the dominant central dome, as well as the scale, proportion and elegance, were strongly inspired by Hagia Sophia. Six minarets are a recognizable feature.

Topkapi Palace, the imperial palace and administrative centre of the Ottoman sultans from the late fifteenth century to the mid-nineteenth century, consists of scores of buildings intended for residential, educational and administrative use, together forming a small royal city arranged across a garden landscape and overlooking the Straits of Bosporus and the Golden Horn (the peninsula of Constantinople).

The Grand Bazaar has been in operation since the fifteenth century, and here traders have continued the tradition of ancient times and have, over the centuries, dealt in all manner of produce, including gold, silver, ceramics, and precious jewels and stones, carpets and other valuable textiles, glass and numerous other objects for various uses, as well as spices, herbs and a wide range of foodstuffs.

calligraphy and manuscript painting and binding

In the field of book painting or illumination, substantial quantities of religious images were created. However the bulk of illuminated manuscripts during Ottoman times focussed on secular use and depicted sieges and battles or illustrated prose histories of entire reigns. As Hillenbrand observed, 'Several Ottoman sultans were bibliophiles: it was a tradition for members of the élite to have libraries, and respect for knowledge found expression in luxuriously appointed manuscripts with fine bindings. Ottoman scholars wrote copiously if not originally on many topics' (1999: 176).

Turkish book bindings of the late fifteenth and early sixteenth centuries are characterized by empty space and the precise placing of decorative medallions or cartouches centrally, with four corner elements, often on coloured leather.

Hillenbrand commented: 'Perhaps this instinctively satisfying placement of decorative features is the result of mathematical calculation—it may have been governed by proportional ratios of the kind seen in so much Islamic architecture and book painting' (1999: 276).

carpets

The words *carpet* and *rug* are often used interchangeably (as is the case in this book). Occasional differentiation is introduced by allowing the word *carpet* to refer to a larger-scale item and the word *rug* to refer to a smaller item (say to a maximum of 125 centimetres by 75 centimetres), which would fit lengthways against a modest twentieth- or twenty-first-century domestic fire surround in a typical UK urban living room. Carpets may be pile- or flat-woven, both with decorative elements created through the weaving process. The word *pile* refers to a raised surface created by the addition of a series of knots of thread, tied around warp threads, introduced during the weaving process. Flat-woven items may be produced by various techniques (including a tapestry-type technique and a brocading technique), and the finished item will not exhibit a pile structure.

The earliest Ottoman carpets date to around the beginning of the fifteenth century and were strongly influenced by Chinese forms. The making of Turkish carpets, knotted or flat-woven (*kilim, soumak, cicim, zili*), is a long-established craft among Central Asian and Turkic or Turkoman peoples living to the east of Anatolia. Any reference to carpet-weaving regions will invariably make mention of production in Turkestan (an ill-defined region which stretches from the Caspian Sea eastwards, for around three thousand miles or more, across Turkmenistan, Uzbekistan, Kazakhstan, Kyrgyzstan, Tajikistan to Sinkiang (in the western part of China) (Bennett 1972: 34). During the late nineteenth and twentieth centuries, essentially nomadic Turkoman tribal peoples, who resisted settling under various authoritarian regimes, fled to Persia, Afghanistan and Pakistan (Bennett 1972: 34), seemingly in pursuit of the maintenance of their nomadic lifestyle.

In modern times, the term *Turkish carpet* tends to cover not just items produced in the territory of Turkey, but also those produced by Turkic people living to the east of Anatolia. When reference is made to Turkish carpets in this book, however, the concern is not with the vast area indicated earlier, but rather it is with the region encompassed by present-day Turkey and adjacent border areas. In particular the intention is simply to underline the importance of carpet manufacture throughout Ottoman times and to give a brief explanation of the nature of the composition on a few carpet types.

The Turkish carpet, like the Persian carpet, evolved from a simple tribal handicraft product of everyday practical use to a sophisticated and highly desirable luxury object. Initially produced largely by nomadic peoples as a practical, portable, domestic object, the carpet was adopted within the settled urban environment, promoted as an export item, and manufactured under state patronage, with high-ranking state officials ensuring quality. During Ottoman times, state-controlled workshops manufactured large quantities (for court use or for export). Nomadic peoples, as well as small communities settled in villages and towns across much of Anatolia, continued to produce items of variable quality, fineness and consistency.

Many textbooks when introducing early Ottoman carpets mention a particular carpet, measuring around 172 centimetres by 90 centimetres, with one lengthways decorated border and two widthways decorated borders, and the remainder divided horizontally into two approximate squares, each depicting a highly stylized dragon and phoenix in combat, both in indigo blue, outlined in red and against a yellow background. This carpet, held in the Islamische Museum, Berlin, in the early twenty-first century, is an important piece of evidence suggesting a strong Chinese influence on early Ottoman production in terms of the motifs, colour palette and other compositional details.

Village and nomadic rugs usually depicted inherited (or traditional) motifs and compositional structures. In many cases the motifs used were mutated forms with their original significance long forgotten, reproduced largely from memory or by reference to a previously made piece, and following the guidelines introduced by a parent or grandparent.

Carpets manufactured in state-controlled workshops contrasted greatly with these village rugs. Such workshops assured homogeneity in the articles produced, and homogeneity was what the export markets demanded. Regarded over the centuries by international markets as more sophisticated than the village-made alternatives, these state-controlled workshop products often included curvilinear compositional elements, and were manufactured under strict quality-control standards; so, for example, the number of knots per inch would be consistent throughout the piece, motifs were to a precise size and in the designated location in the composition, in exact colours and in the precise raw material type. State-controlled products were invariably woven by reference to a cartoon, made of squared paper (mounted on a cloth background),

depicting one quarter of the whole design, with one square representing one knot, and samples of dyed yarn attached to the cartoon indicating the precise colour to be used in each area.

During Ottoman times, the production of prayer rugs was of particular importance and was associated principally with village weaving, in particular with the towns (and surrounding areas) of Ghiordes, Ladik and Bergama. Ghiordes, in western Anatolia, gave its name to a notable type of prayer rug woven in villages in the region. Two distinct subtypes can be identified. The first has what is often described as a horseshoe-shaped arch with a plain red mihrab from which is attached a depiction of a mosque lamp. In some examples, columns (with no apparent suggested architectural function) sit at each side of the mihrab shape (Bennett 1972: 197). The second rug subtype, regarded by some reputable scholars as firmly outside the mainstream of Turkish carpet design (see Bennett 1972: 199), typically has a straight-sided, part-rectangle shape with a shoulder and v-shaped arch (like a child's drawing of the side view of a house), using dark blue, red, buff, cream or white, surrounded by elaborate floral borders each with a greater width than the mihrab itself (Bennett 1972: 199). Bennett (1999) and Schurman (1982) gave good appraisals of these and many other carpet types.

Ladik prayer rugs often depict a triple-arched mihrab. Bergama prayer rugs often have double-ended mihrabs, containing one of two designs: either an angular arabesque of stems with large flowers with stylized mosque lamp at either end or a large central medallion. In each case the double-ended mihrab itself is usually buff, red or cream and the main borders contain square and rectangular star shapes, the former containing further eight-point star shapes and the latter 'open medallions, arabesques and flower heads related to the design found in the mihrabs' (Bennett 1972: 205).

There are of course numerous variations, and designs and compositional characteristics noted earlier in this chapter are by no means unique to the regions mentioned. As Bennett noted, to make assured and accurate attribution requires considerable accumulated experience and knowledge of motifs, compositional rules, yarn types, dyestuffs, colour palettes and construction techniques. Numerous further distinctive groups of late Ottoman carpets produced in state-controlled workshops by craftspeople settled in towns across Anatolia, as well as by various nomadic groups, can be identified. Publications such as that by Bennett (1972 and 1978) give further classifications together with numerous illustrated examples and hints on identification and attribution.

other textiles (including embroidery)

Ottoman textiles from the sixteenth and seventeenth centuries have survived in large numbers, often in the form of clothing. By the early twenty-first century, substantial quantities were held in national museums worldwide. The collection held in Topkapi Palace Museum is particularly impressive. Hillenbrand commented that over 2,500 items were held with 1,000 of them in the form of kafkans (1999: 277). The Topkapi Palace also held substantial quantities of embroidered items, many with constituent golden metallic threads made by specialist teams working in the palace. Other types of embroidery were made by women in their own homes, possibly under commission to the palace.

In early Ottoman times, when Bursa was still the designated capital, the activities of the textile industry, including the import of raw materials, levels of production and pricing, were tightly controlled by the government. Since it was believed that high-quality products would ensure healthy levels of exports, particular focus was placed on ensuring that high-quality standards were maintained. Textile and clothing workers were organized in guilds and their wages were fixed by the governmental bureaucracy of the day (Hillenbrand 1999: 278).

ceramics

The factories at Iznik had achieved prominence by the start of the sixteenth century, when the Ottoman government began to oversee production, and influenced the widening of the range of designs together with improvements in the overall quality and increases in the quantity of output. The colour palette, though rather limited, was modified consistently, most notably with the introduction of a brilliant tomato red in the third quarter of the sixteenth century (Hillenbrand 1999: 270). Popular motifs included roses, carnations, tulips, hyacinths, ships, and various birds. Occasionally, Qur'anic inscriptions were the dominant feature. Further explanation of the nature of Iznik pottery is given in cs 24, later in this chapter.

motifs and symbols from Ottoman times (cs 23)

The range of motifs and patterns used in the visual arts of Turkey during Ottoman times is extensive and includes geometric forms such as circles, squares, triangles and hexagonal shapes; natural phenomena such as the sun, stars, serpents, fish, flowers and water; man-made objects such as cups, vases and various weapons; products of the human imagination including dragons, mermaids and other mythological creatures. The following section introduces and considers dominant motifs (many used outside the courts of power and instead found commonly in village crafts such as embroidery).

The symbolic significance of many motifs may vary from culture to culture and may on occasion change with the passage of time (Munro 1970: 51–2). A circular shape, for example, may lend itself to various interpretations: as the wheel of the law, or as the cyclical recurrence of the seasons, or simply as a representation of the sun. Combinations of symbols often have cumulative meanings; this is a common aspect, for example, of traditional Chinese embroidery (Hann, Thomson and Zhong 1990: 4). Goddess figures, together with various related symbols, are commonly depicted and often associated with concepts of fertility, life, death or cosmic creation, depending on the region or culture. Likewise, fertility may be symbolized by a goddess figure in one culture or region and by a tree of life in another (Paine 1990: 65–6).

Across the Mediterranean, including much of present-day Turkey, earth-goddess figures have featured in the surface design on many artefacts. The figure may appear in various forms including, for example, as part tree or bird (Paine 1990: 66). Its use can be detected in Mediterranean regions and across much of Europe. It has, for example, been depicted on a fourth-century BCE felt fabric found in a kurgan in the Pazyryk Valley in southern Siberia (Paine 1990: 66, 67). Derivations of the goddess figure are commonly also depicted on embroideries and other domestic crafts throughout much of Asia.

In some cases, figurative motifs originated from Christian biblical sources or from engravings or prints, rather than from ancient mythology (Paine 1990: 67). Throughout the regions where Islam became the dominant religion, figurative motifs were not as common; where they were present, they were probably not easily recognizable because of the high degree of stylization. The *sahmeran*, for example, which in original form is half woman and half snake, is sometimes depicted in highly stylized form on Turkish folk embroideries (Senturk 1993: 151), even during Ottoman times.

Water, fish and ships are common motifs, especially with seafaring nations across much of Asia. Water usually symbolizes the mystery of life, having a life-giving power related to waters of birth. The fish motif is common in Turkish, Tunisian, Indian and Pakistani visual arts. Occasionally a fish is interpreted as the emblem of the soul, a spiritual searcher or as the preserver of life (Paine 1990: 119–20). Traditionally, in China, a pair of fish was deemed Buddhist in origin and was considered to symbolize marriage and unity (Zhong 1989: 38). In the context of Turkish visual arts, the fish motif is a symbol of fertility, good fortune or prosperity (Dural 1979). In Bengal, the motif is also used as a fertility symbol. Pomegranate, grape and melon motifs are also common symbols of fertility; this is the case in Turkish, Syrian and Balkan visual arts as well as in the Qing dynasty Chinese context (Paine 1990: 70).

Across the full range of the visual arts, in many cultural contexts, the tree of life is a common motif and shows many versions and varieties. Generally, it consists of a symmetrical plant shape, often flanked by front-facing birds, beasts, demons or worshippers. This composition has persisted since ancient times and is found across much of Asia. Various interpretations of the motif have been offered, including that of the cosmic tree sustaining the universe and linking the earth to the heavens or, alternatively, as relating to the change of the seasons and symbolizing life itself. The animals flanking the tree vary: peacocks or roosters are common as are dragons or griffins and similar fabled creatures of ancient origin (Paine 1990: 71–3).

Since ancient times, a sun disc or simple circle represented the sun, appearing in visual arts of numerous cultures. It has been featured as the innermost of five concentric circles (each representing a planet) on pottery, dating to around the first century CE, in various parts of the Mediterranean (Gombrich 1979: 221). Other forms include a circle with a central dot, a circle with rays emanating from its outer circumference and a circle with a cross within its boundaries. The swastika is often considered a solar symbol and is also related to the concepts of movement and change, as are other motifs such as the Maltese cross and star shapes. Representations of the moon are common as this is deemed to hold a mystical relationship with the menstrual cycle (Paine 1990: 80). In some Asian countries, swastikas, stars and circles were depicted in the visual arts, often in association with spirals and triangles. In Turkish embroideries, the whirl (or pin wheel) motif, triangles and stars were common; in India and Pakistan sun discs, stars and circles were used; in traditional Chinese embroidery, circles and swastikas were depicted frequently.

Bird motifs appeared often on Ottoman embroidery design, commonly associated with the tree of life as well as with floral motifs and solar symbols. Eagles, peacocks and roosters were the bird motifs most commonly featured in Turkey as well as across much of Asia; these could be interpreted either as symbols of good luck or as messengers from heaven (Paine 1990: 79–80).

In Qing dynasty Chinese embroidery, pairs of birds symbolized harmonious relations between people whereas, in Turkish embroideries, flying birds represented forthcoming good news or happiness.

Floral and plant motifs have been used worldwide on embroidery and other home-produced items. In the Turkish context, the carnation, the rose, the tulip, the hyacinth, the pomegranate, and pine and cypress trees are characteristic (Palotay 1953–5: 3662). Such motifs also appear in the visual arts from areas where Turkish influence remained strong until the twentieth century; examples include Hungary, the coastal Adriatic region, the northern Greek islands and northern Syria, although the degree of stylization differs from region to region.

Stylized flower heads or flower sprays with bent or encircling stems and serrated leaves and hooked stem ends are all typical of Turkish ceramics and embroideries (Wace 1935: 5). Similar motifs were used in Morocco (Wace 1935: 7, 8). In India, Pakistan and Turkestan, floral motifs were usually stylized into simple circular forms. In Persia and Algeria, flower and leaf forms appeared on arabesque frameworks. In China, common floral motifs included the lotus, the peony, the chrysanthemum, the plum flower and the crabapple flower, and common fruit motifs included the pomegranate and the fingered citron (Zhong 1989: 47).

Motifs consisting of three circles (known as *chintamani*), as well as cloud bands are common on Turkish ceramics, textiles and embroideries from the sixteenth century onwards. Similar motifs are also found on Chinese embroideries, in which case they are attributed a Buddhist origin (Paine 1990: 115).

A typical Turkish pattern (especially on embroideries) is the mosque and cypress tree pattern, which consists of a series of houses or mosque-like buildings in association with tree-and-flower motifs. This scenic composition is typical of eighteenth- and nineteenth-century embroideries from Istanbul and Bursa (Wace 1935: 6). Similar patterns can be found also in the south of Turkey. Narrow border patterns, with a mosque-like building motif alternating with a single cypress tree motif, are characteristically Turkish, but are also found on embroideries from parts of the present-day Russian Federation (Wace 1935: 5). The pomegranate or artichoke motif is common in Turkish embroidery and textiles and is also found occasionally on ceramics. According to Wace the design may have originated in Asia Minor (1935: 11). Figures 10.1–10.10 depict a range of designs from Ottoman times.

Figure 10.1 Detail of Ottoman embroidery, nineteenth century (University of Leeds International Textiles Archive)

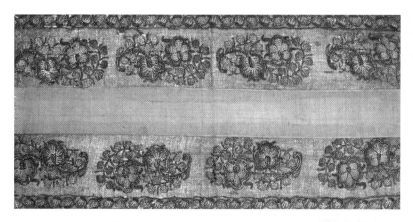

Figure 10.2 Detail of Ottoman embroidery, nineteenth century (University of Leeds International Textiles Archive)

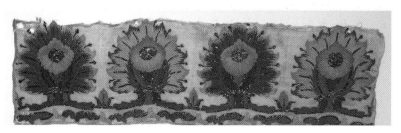

Figure 10.3 Detail of Ottoman embroidery, nineteenth century (University of Leeds International Textiles Archive)

Figure 10.4 Detail of Ottoman embroidery, nineteenth century (University of Leeds International Textiles Archive)

Figure 10.5 Detail of Ottoman embroidery, nineteenth century (University of Leeds International Textiles Archive)

Figure 10.6 Detail of Ottoman embroidery, nineteenth century (University of Leeds International Textiles Archive)

Figure 10.7 Detail of Ottoman embroidery, nineteenth century (University of Leeds International Textiles Archive)

Figure 10.8 Detail of Ottoman embroidery, nineteenth century (University of Leeds International Textiles Archive)

Figure 10.9 Detail of Ottoman embroidery, nineteenth century (University of Leeds International Textiles Archive)

Figure 10.10 Detail of Ottoman embroidery, nineteenth century (University of Leeds International Textiles Archive)

Iznik pottery (cs 24)

Iznik pottery is named after a town in Anatolia and was produced from the last quarter of the fifteenth century until the end of the seventeenth century. Early examples show the use of cobalt blue under a colourless glaze. Typically, Iznik pottery combined Ottoman arabesque designs with Chinese motifs (inspired by Chinese blue-and-white porcelain, which was highly prized by the Ottomans). It seems that this Chinese inspiration gave the initial impetus for production, though the Ottoman craftspeople were unable to make porcelain (Figures 10.11–10.20).

Other colours were introduced during the sixteenth century, initially turquoise combined with a dark shade of cobalt blue, and then sage green and pale purple. In the mid-sixteenth century characteristic red replaced the purple and a bright emerald green replaced the sage green. By the late sixteenth century, there was a deterioration of quality (with shapes, colours and glaze not as precise as previously), but production continued into the seventeenth century.

In the early twenty-first century many surviving Iznik pieces were kept in museums worldwide. Numerous further examples, particularly in the form of tiles, can be seen in mosques, tombs, libraries and palace buildings in Istanbul, Bursa, Edirne and Adana. Note that other important places were known for Turkish pottery production, but identifying the place of manufacture of pottery produced in Ottoman times is not easy. For example, it appears that similar designs, materials and techniques were used in Kütahya. The imperial workshops in Istanbul were also of importance.

One of the most famous Iznik design types is the tugra-style spiral decoration which was inspired by the scroll-like decoration associated with the imperial monogram (*tugra*) of Süleyman the Magnificent. In ceramics decorated with this effect, fine spiral-like scrolls bearing tiny floral motifs and tiny s-shaped tendrils, generally painted in cobalt blue on white, are typical.

symmetry analysis of motifs and patterns (cs 25)

The purpose of this case study is to give some indication of the basis on which a symmetry analysis project can be conducted. Data are presented from a project which examined the symmetry characteristics of several varieties of hand-knotted carpets (Mason 2002).

Mason (2002) conducted symmetry analysis on a randomly selected sample of 500 Turkish carpet images, selected from a range of

Figure 10.11 Turkish ceramics from Iznik, sixteenth century (Victoria and Albert Museum)

Figure 10.12 Turkish ceramics from Iznik, sixteenth century (British Museum)

Figure 10.13 Turkish ceramics from Iznik, sixteenth century (Victoria and Albert Museum)

Figure 10.14 Turkish ceramics from Iznik, sixteenth century (Victoria and Albert Museum)

Figure 10.15 Turkish ceramics from Iznik, sixteenth century (Victoria and Albert Museum)

Figure 10.16 Turkish ceramics from Iznik, sixteenth century (Victoria and Albert Museum)

Figure 10.17 Turkish ceramics from Iznik, sixteenth century (Victoria and Albert Museum)

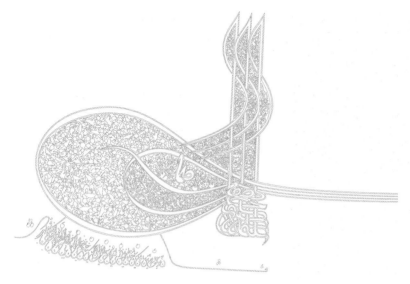

Figure 10.18 Tugra of Süleyman the Magnificent (drawn by Septia Andin, ITB, Indonesia)

Figure 10.19 Turkish ceramics from Iznik, sixteenth century (Victoria and Albert Museum)

authoritative sources: Bennett (1972); Campana (1969); Cecil-Edwards (1983); Eiland and Eiland (1998); Gans-Ruedin (1971); Gantzhorn (1998); Harris (1977); Kendrick and Tattersall (1922); Milhofer (1976); Reed (1972); Zipper and Fritzsche (1989). The field design for each of the 500 was analysed and classified, making reference to its symmetry characteristics. A non-random distribution resulted, and there was a clear predominance of reflection symmetry: nearly 40 per cent of the total sample of field designs showed one-direction reflection symmetry; nearly 25 per cent

Figure 10.20 Turkish ceramics from Iznik, sixteenth century (Victoria and Albert Museum)

characteristics (nearly 15 per cent). Single-direction reflection symmetry was shown in 10 per cent of the sample.[2]

In a later, though related, project the present author gave consideration to the symmetry characteristics of motifs and symbols in a range of carpets from different sources. A predominant motif known as a *gul*, which, in many guises, is found on carpets from numerous sources, is predominant on Turkoman carpets. The area known as Turkestan historically was strongly influenced by Turkish culture. In the Turkoman context, varieties of the gul motif were used to symbolize tribal membership. The motif may appear as a single motif or, more commonly, in repeating pattern form and woven in parallel rows. Consideration of the symmetry characteristics

of the total sample showed two-direction reflection symmetry; nearly 17 per cent of the total sample showed four-direction reflection symmetry. With prayer rugs, one-direction reflection symmetry is almost always present, since the central mihrab shape displays this characteristic (Figure 10.21).[1] Many of the carpet designs selected had multiple borders. A total of 2,270 borders were counted from the selected 500 items. These were classified into various symmetry classes and a preference was shown for: twofold rotation symmetry (nearly 18 per cent), two-direction reflection symmetry (nearly 16 per cent) and simple translation or repetition without further symmetry

Figure 10.21 Turkish prayer rug drawing (CW)

of single-gul motifs from a sample of 100 carpets (taken from the authoritative sources listed earlier), it was found that 65 per cent of motifs showed one-direction reflection symmetry (d1 motifs) and 60 per cent of gul-based repeating patterns yielded one-direction reflection symmetry (p1m1) (Figures 10.22a–h). Two-direction reflection symmetry (d2 motifs) was another important feature (around 25 per cent of motifs).

By way of conclusion, it is clear there is an overall predominance of one-direction reflection symmetry in the designs from the sample of Turkish carpets, and two-direction reflection symmetry is the next most significant feature.

Figure 10.22a–h Turkish or Turkoman motifs showing one- or two-direction reflection symmetry (CW)

DISCUSSION OR ASSIGNMENT TOPICS

Symmetry in Visual Arts of Ottoman Turkey

Assemble up to twenty images of motifs, patterns, buildings or building details, tilings, textiles or objects of metal, wood or ceramic, from Ottoman Turkey. Making reference to this illustrative material, discuss the symmetry characteristics of the visual arts and architecture of Ottoman Turkey.

Iznik Pottery

What is Iznik pottery? What are its principal characteristics (including motifs and colours used)? Why was this category of pottery successful and in demand?

Turkish Carpets

Using illustrative material of your choice (drawn, traced or photographed), identify important motifs used in Turkish or Turkoman carpets. In all cases, discuss the probable origins and symbolism of the motifs identified.

A Review of Ottoman Visual Arts

Review the nature of the visual arts and architecture of the Ottoman Empire. Make reference to manuscript production, carpet and textile manufacture, metalwork, tilings (and the production of any other decorated item that you think appropriate) and architecture. Identify which visual arts were of particular importance. What types of motifs or symbols were used? Which types of production technique (e.g. in pottery or metalwork) were of importance? Identify important raw materials (e.g. silk or silver) and their potential sources. What and where are the main sites/buildings? What were the principal influences and developments? Did developments in the visual arts and architecture contribute to or influence changes elsewhere?

further reading

Bauman, J. (1987). *Central Asian Carpets. Study Guide*, Islamabad: Asian Study Group.

Bennett, I. (1972). *Book of Oriental Carpets and Rugs*, London: Hamlyn.

Bennett, I. (1978). *Rugs and Carpets of the World*, London: Quarto Publishing.

Campana, M. (1969). *Oriental Carpets,* London: Hamlyn.

Gombrich, E. H. (1979). *The Sense of Order*, London: Phaidon.

Munro, T. (1970). *Form and Style in the Arts: An Introduction to Aesthetic Morphology*, Cleveland, OH: Case Western Reserve University Press.

notes

1. Symmetry analysis of field designs from a random sample of 500 Turkish carpets:

   Top three results: Class pm accounted for 39.6 per cent of field designs; class pmm accounted for 24.8 per cent of field designs; class p4m accounted for 16.6 per cent of field designs.

2. Symmetry analysis of 2,270 border designs from a random sample of 500 Turkish carpets:

   Top four results: Class p112 accounted for 17.8 per cent of border patterns; class pmm2 accounted for 15.9 per cent of border patterns; class p111 accounted for 14.5 per cent of border patterns; class p1m1 accounted for 10.1 per cent of border patterns.

11

India and Pakistan

From the viewpoint of the visual arts and architecture, the Mughal Empire stands clearly as the most important contributor to prolonged development in South Asia during the second millennium CE. The geographical scope of the Mughal Empire, founded in the early decades of the sixteenth century, covered much of the northern and central parts of the South Asian subcontinent, located between the Safavid Persian empire to the west and Ming China to the east. Important cities were Agra, Delhi and Lahore. Control over Gujarat provided access to the Arabian Sea and thus permitted participation in the lucrative sea trade of the time. Zebrowski commented: 'They [the Mughal rulers] replaced the upper structure of Hindu governmental institutions with an Islamic framework, mainly based on an Iranian example. They imported a literary culture in Arabic and Persian and a visual aesthetic that derived its standards from the eastern Islamic world. But the conquerors employed Indian craftsmen, and Islamic tastes were soon conditioned by their practice' (1981: 177). Various European sources, especially the Dutch, French and British trading centres, further influenced the visual arts and architecture during Mughal times.

Akbar I, whose reign extended from around the mid-sixteenth century to the early seventeenth century, was a strong patron of the arts and commissioned many architectural projects, including the building of the new city of Fatehpur Sikri near Agra. Many forts, palaces, religious buildings and imperial tombs were constructed. In the visual arts, he employed Persian as well as Indian Muslim and Hindu craftspeople, and helped to develop a specifically Mughal style. Many paintings and books were commissioned during his time.

Akbar's son Jahangir (who reigned during much of the first quarter of the seventeenth century) was also a strong patron of the arts and commissioned many paintings and literary works. He was a central figure in the development of the Mughal garden. Jahangir's successor, Shah Jahan (who reigned for around three decades up to the mid-seventeenth century), is famous for one particular architectural commission: the Taj Mahal located at Agra on the banks of the River Jumna. On the death of Shah Jahan, one of his sons, Aurangzeb, took the reins of power. He was regarded as a controversial figure (apparently because of his attempts to introduce Sharia law); his contribution to the maintenance of an apparently tolerant multireligious nation and to further developments in the visual arts and architecture was limited and deterioration of the empire followed. By the nineteenth century, although the Mughals were nominally emperors of India, in reality they were simply held in place under the protection of the British, probably with the intention of ensuring political stability.

architecture

The Taj Mahal, built from marble rather than sandstone, was a tomb dedicated to the memory of Shah Jahan's wife, Mumtaz Mahal, who died after giving birth to the couple's fourteenth child. During Shah Jahan's reign, Delhi was selected as the designated capital. Another important achievement was the building of a new city (Shahjahanabad). The Red Fort (Delhi) is also an important building complex. In Lahore, Shalimar Gardens (mid-seventeenth century) are one of the most important architectural achievements. Gray (1981) identified and illustrated numerous further examples of notable Mughal architectural achievements.

miniature paintings and manuscripts

A new style of painting, inspired by Persian, Chinese and European art as well as the indigenous tradition, was developed at the Mughal court. Like the Safavids, the Mughals commissioned numerous illuminated manuscripts, including many Turkish, Arabic and Persian classics, as well as new original works by Mughal authors. Fresh editions of the Hindu epics, the Mahabharata and the Ramayana, were also produced. Many of the painters involved in these projects were Hindus, mainly from western India. Mughal painting reached high levels of sophistication and realism, with naturalistic depiction of human, animal and plant forms. A full range of moods, emotions, messages or compositional types was covered. Court scenes were common, and European influence can be detected in the gradual introduction of the European rules of linear perspective. Mughal patronage of the arts declined after Shah Jahan's rule was terminated forcibly by his son just after the mid-seventeenth century. Many of the artists associated with the Mughal workshops found work elsewhere, either in provincial Muslim courts (e.g. Lucknow, Murshidabad, Faizabad and Furrukhabad) or at the Hindu-controlled Rajasthani courts (at Bundi, Kota). The late-Mughal era saw increased patronage of the arts from Maharaja Jai Singh, who founded the city of Jaipur in the first half of the eighteenth century.

textiles

For many centuries the South Asian subcontinent was renowned as a source of patterned textiles. In fact textile producers in South Asia, during much of the second millennium CE, had an impressively wide variety of traditional textile types and designs, produced using an equally impressive range of fibre production techniques and colour palettes, unrivalled in their sophistication. Certain textile types attracted the attention of various European traders, not because of their intrinsic aesthetic value, at least initially, but rather because they functioned as a medium of exchange in the quest for spices such as pepper, cloves, nutmeg and mace, sourced elsewhere in Asia. Painted and printed cottons (often referred to as *chintz*), with a colour brilliance and fastness unknown elsewhere, were produced in many regions and used as wall hangings, coverlets, clothing, floor coverings, and other everyday items; textiles such as these were the focus of traders. Silver and gold coinage was used to obtain patterned textiles, and these textiles were traded for spices which were then shipped elsewhere in Asia or back to Europe. Guy, when considering the activities of the various European trading companies during the eighteenth century, noted that a recurring feature was the 'pivotal role played by Indian cloth' (1998: 7). However, Europeans were not the initiators of such trade. According to Guy (1998: 14), long before the arrival of European traders in the early sixteenth century, trade in textiles was part of a well-established Asian exchange mechanism, involving Arab, Indian, Malay and Javanese merchants. Even after the arrival of European trading ships, abundant evidence exists 'to suggest that the greater volume was carried by Asian merchants in Asian vessels' (Guy 1998: 7).

In addition to chintz, other (more rare) textiles were prized as trade goods. An important example is *patola* (singular *patolu*), a class of silk textile, probably more highly prized than any other group of textiles produced in the South Asian subcontinent. These are double-ikat cloths, in which both sets of threads, the weft threads and the warp threads, are coloured separately (generally in different dye baths) using a resist-dyeing technique involving covering (or tying) bundles of parallel sets of threads in a predetermined sequence prior to dyeing and subsequent weaving. The principal intended use was as sari fabrics. The region of Gujarat was for many centuries the main location for production. Intricate geometric, grid-based patterns, occasionally with associated figurative and floral motifs, were typical; within Gujarat itself were characteristic patterning differences from village to village and workshop to workshop. Colours were mainly primary red and yellow, mid-green, white and

maroon. Chapter 12 highlights the high value ascribed to these cloths in Indonesia.

Another form of decorated South Asian textile, produced in Orissa, was known as *bandas*, a type of textile that combined brocaded woven bands with ikat forms of decoration. Bandas were intended as sari fabrics; their decoration consisted of feather-like edges to motifs (which included various fish, birds and animals, shells, stars, architectural forms and trellis-type arrangements). Occasionally, depending on the workshop of production, fabrics were decorated using a combination of cotton threads and silk threads (generally with one fibre type as warp threads and the other as weft threads). Otherwise, bandas were wholly of silk threads, decorated with warp ikat, with occasional end pieces in weft ikat. A wide colour palette included primary reds, yellows and blues, as well as greens and purples was common, as were rows of floral, geometric or figurative forms in bands.

other visual arts

Because of the drastic variations in climatic conditions from season to season and the detrimental effect that this has on perishable items of wood or fibers, a detailed chronology of achievements in the visual arts is not readily possible. However, a large quantity of items has survived from late-Mughal times, including travelling chests, caskets and writing cabinets of teak, often inlaid with mother of pearl or ivory, wooden trays inlaid with brass and silver, gilded glass objects, wine cups in materials such as jade, crystal bowls, agate cameos; enamelled items of various kinds, painted and printed cottons used as wall hangings, coverlets, clothing and floor coverings, hand-knotted carpets and lacquered papier-mâché caskets. Floral forms of patterning were common, as was the use of arabesques and palm forms (found also in pre-Mughal times in mosque patterning in Gujarat, for example). Often the focus was on manufacture to be exported to the Ottoman Turkish market. The dating of South Asian decorative art is at best tentative and based to a large degree on comparisons with other items or with examples depicted in datable miniature paintings (Zebrowski 1981: 183).

the temple cloth of the mother goddess (cs 26)

The temple cloth of the mother goddess (or *mātā ni pachedi*) is a block-printed, mordant-dyed cotton cloth used generally as a ceiling or wall cloth and associated with religious worship. The production is exceedingly labour-intensive and requires several complicated stages, associated with the preparation of the fabric surface, the application of colour and the range of finishing, washing and drying processes. When the cloth is finished, strong

red and black on a white background are invariably the dominant colours. Erikson observed that during the finishing processes great care was taken to ensure that the object was treated with reverence: 'for no foot of man or animal may be placed on these cloths which are sacred to the great mother goddess' (1968: 14). The cloth selected as part of this case study is one such cloth, produced close to the city of Ahmedabad on the banks of the Sub-armati River and now held in the textiles archive at the University of Leeds (Figures 11.1–11.15).

The cloth examined as part of this case study measures 183.7 centimetres by 466 centimetres (around 72 inches by 183 inches). The cloth is significantly larger than the standard sizes produced in the latter half of the twentieth century. Measurements of 54 inches by 72 inches or 42 inches by 72 inches are the most common (Erikson 1968: x).

The cloth is block-printed with human-like figures (most dressed in Mughal-style garments) and other design elements, including animals and floral, architectural and abstract geometric motifs. Across the fabric several scenes appear,

Figure 11.1 Detail of temple cloth of the mother goddess, block-printed on cotton, early twentieth century (University of Leeds International Textiles Archive)

Figure 11.2 Detail of temple cloth of the mother goddess, block-printed on cotton, early twentieth century (University of Leeds International Textiles Archive)

Figure 11.3 Detail of temple cloth of the mother goddess, block-printed on cotton, early twentieth century (University of Leeds International Textiles Archive)

Figure 11.4 Detail of temple cloth of the mother goddess, block-printed on cotton, early twentieth century (University of Leeds International Textiles Archive)

Figure 11.5 Detail of temple cloth of the mother goddess, block-printed on cotton, early twentieth century (University of Leeds International Textiles Archive)

Figure 11.6 Detail of temple cloth of the mother goddess, block-printed on cotton, early twentieth century (University of Leeds International Textiles Archive)

Figure 11.7 Detail of temple cloth of the mother goddess, block-printed on cotton, early twentieth century (University of Leeds International Textiles Archive)

contained within rectangular spaces separated by block-printed, arabesque-type borders. The master printer determined the size of each rectangular section and the content of the composition itself, and each *pachedi* differs from others.

Relatively large-scale female figures occupy some of the rectangular spaces. Dominant, in separate boxes, are two figures (presumably goddess representations), each seated on a *howdah* (a saddle seat used commonly with a camel or elephant), placed on a depiction of a black bullock decorated with garlands and wearing a foot bell. Two further goddess figures are depicted seated (maybe on a throne) and placed separately within differently shaped arched spaces. Three additional relatively large-scale female figures appear to be carrying floral tributes. With only minor variation, each of the six-handed-goddess figures is depicted holding

relevant attributes (sword, dagger, incense bowl, and trident), suggesting an association with the goddess Kulagotar. A whisk and a bottle are further attributes, though not represented here. The group of attributes and even the perceived numbers of possible goddesses differ across India. Several of the rectangular areas are topped by dome structures and decorated with flags. Remarking on the nature of the typical composition, Erikson observed: 'the pattern form is always the same—the commanding figure of the goddess is centred—austere, stern, many armed and powerful. Under her is her mount or vehicle and around her in procession are her attendant gods and worshippers' (1968: 14). This description is a good fit for the cloth under consideration.

Over fifty further smaller-scale figures (predominantly, though not entirely, female) are depicted. A few of these are goddess figures, and a few,

Figure 11.8 Detail of temple cloth of the mother goddess, block-printed on cotton, early twentieth century (University of Leeds International Textiles Archive)

such as Ganesha (the elephant-like deity used as a symbol of wisdom), come from Hindu mythology. Some of the female figures hold pots on their heads, probably intended as tributes. Several seated male figures can be identified by curly moustaches. A few smaller rectangles are dominated by representations of black bullocks, each garlanded with flowers and with a foot bell. Numerous floral and bird motifs (including peacocks) are depicted. Several goats appear to be destined for sacrifice. Buglers and drummers are included in a few rectangles. Seventeen fish are presented alone in one bordered area, and what might be representations of grain or other agricultural crops are presented in an adjacent truncated triangular area; these additions may be expressions of the desire for a bountiful harvest or a plentiful catch of fish (but more profound religious symbolism may be intended).

The two goddess figures (each seated on a howdah) appear almost androgynous and wear male trousers and what appears to be chest armour. The goddess figures also wear heavily

Figure 11.9 Detail of temple cloth of the mother goddess, block-printed on cotton, early twentieth century (University of Leeds International Textiles Archive)

Figure 11.10 Detail of temple cloth of the mother goddess, block-printed on cotton, early twentieth century (University of Leeds International Textiles Archive)

Figure 11.11 Detail of temple cloth of the mother goddess, block-printed on cotton, early twentieth century (University of Leeds International Textiles Archive)

bejewelled headdresses. These and all other female figures wear earrings, nose rings, necklaces, arm and wrist bracelets, finger rings and anklets. Each of the other female figures wears a short blouse (*choli*), a skirt (*ghagra*) and a covering for head and chest (known as *orhni*), a style of female dress still witnessed in rural India during the early twenty-first century.

Figure 11.12 Detail of temple cloth of the mother goddess, block-printed on cotton, early twentieth century (University of Leeds International Textiles Archive)

Figure 11.13 Detail of temple cloth of the mother goddess, block-printed on cotton, early twentieth century (University of Leeds International Textiles Archive)

Figure 11.14 Detail of temple cloth of the mother goddess, block-printed on cotton, early twentieth century (University of Leeds International Textiles Archive)

Figure 11.15 Detail of temple cloth of the mother goddess, block-printed on cotton, early twentieth century (University of Leeds International Textiles Archive)

Kashmiri shawl motifs (cs 27)

During the eighteenth and early nineteenth centuries, numerous workshops in the Kashmir Valley in northern India manufactured shawls, with final products destined to meet the demands of an expanding European market. This trade provided the stimulus for far-reaching developments in European textile design and manufacture, centred on possibly the most widespread class of motifs to be applied as ornamentation on textile products: a device, with numerous variations, known as the *boteh* or Paisley motif (Figures 11.16–11.30). It is well known that this motif type influenced design in several parts of Europe, and also that it underwent several stages of development in parallel largely with changing European tastes. This particular class of motif is the focus of attention in this case study.[1]

Kashmir's association with shawls began during early Mughal times in the seventeenth century.[2]

Figure 11.16 Kashmir shawl detail (University of Leeds International Textiles Archive)

Figure 11.17 Kashmir shawl detail (University of Leeds International Textiles Archive)

Initially, patterned elements used on shawls consisted of naturalistic representations of fragile flowering plants, depicted in a formal repeating manner, in broad borders at the narrower ends of large rectangular (white or off-white) woollen cloths, typically of dimensions of 120 centimetres in width and 290 centimetres in length. Note that substantial variations occur and occasionally shawls deviate outside these dimensions. After the Afghan invasion of the mid-eighteenth century, restraint in design and composition appears to have been relaxed and the *boteh* began to lose track of its naturalistic floral origins and, instead, by the late eighteenth and early nineteenth centuries, in the wake of increased European influence, evolved into a cone shape with a slight twist on top, a form that became closely associated with

shawls produced in various European centres, including Paisley in Scotland. With the passage of the eighteenth and the first half of the nineteenth centuries, the motif became increasingly abstract and elongated and was used in complex polychromic compositions (produced in Kashmir as well as various European manufacturing locations). Ultimately the vagaries of European fashion-driven demand took their toll, with a resultant slump in demand for Kashmir products; this

Figure 11.18 Kashmir shawl detail (University of Leeds International Textiles Archive)

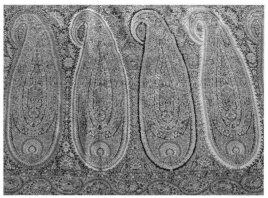

Figure 11.20 Kashmir shawl detail (University of Leeds International Textiles Archive)

Figure 11.21 Kashmir shawl detail (University of Leeds International Textiles Archive)

Figure 11.19 Kashmir shawl detail (University of Leeds International Textiles Archive)

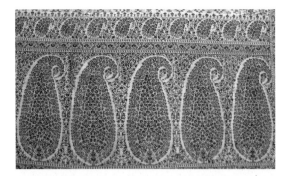

Figure 11.22 Kashmir shawl detail (University of Leeds International Textiles Archive)

Figure 11.23 Kashmir shawl detail (University of Leeds International Textiles Archive)

Figure 11.24 Kashmir shawl detail (University of Leeds International Textiles Archive)

slump was also driven partly by the availability of cheaper European substitutes. Decimating famine in the mid-1870s delivered a final blow to the fortunes of Kashmiri producers, and the Kashmir shawl passed (unnoticed at the time) into the domain of legend.

To place a shawl within a particular historical period requires consideration of a range of issues, especially the visual appearance of the constituent motifs and patterns, as well as an assessment of the structural characteristics of the fabric pieces and the construction of the shawl itself.

Comparison with authoritatively dated shawls in well-known collections is especially helpful. Irwin (1973) proposed a chronological pictorial development of the characteristic motif in the 1970s. This is still of value as an aid to classifying shawls within a series of eight periods, with each period typified by a particular motif form. However we should not assume that later developments necessarily displaced the use of earlier versions of the motif. Also some types of motif seem to fall between the proposed successive versions or may not fit clearly with any of the versions Irwin proposed.

Figure 11.25 Kashmir shawl detail (University of Leeds International Textiles Archive)

Figure 11.27 Kashmir shawl detail (University of Leeds International Textiles Archive)

Figure 11.26 Kashmir shawl detail (University of Leeds International Textiles Archive)

Figure 11.28 Kashmir shawl detail (University of Leeds International Textiles Archive)

Figure 11.29 Kashmir shawl detail (University of Leeds International Textiles Archive)

Figure 11.30 Open page of sample book used by nineteenth-century European producers (University of Leeds International Textiles Archive)

Shalimar Gardens (cs 28)

Shalimar Gardens, located on the outskirts of Lahore (in present-day Pakistan), were built (1641–2) following instructions from members of the court of Shah Jahan, the Mughal emperor.

The site is associated with five geographical sources of inspiration: Kashmir, the Punjab, the Delhi sultanate, Persia and Central Asia (Figures 11.31–11.37).

The gardens are laid out in three descending terraces within a rectangle provided by a high

Figure 11.31 Shalimar Gardens, Lahore, Pakistan

Figure 11.32 Tiling detail, Shalimar Gardens complex, Lahore, Pakistan

brick wall. Each terrace is deemed to express a different mood (or blessing): the upper terrace bears the title *farah baksh* (meaning refreshing); the middle terrace bears the title *faiz baksh* (meaning goodness and grace); the lower terrace bears the title *hayat baksh* (meaning life-giving). A central canal, fed from the Ravi river close by, intersects the gardens (at a central basin) and provides irrigation. A few hundred fountains distributed over the three terraces were designed to help cool the surrounding air in the garden. When built initially, various fragrant

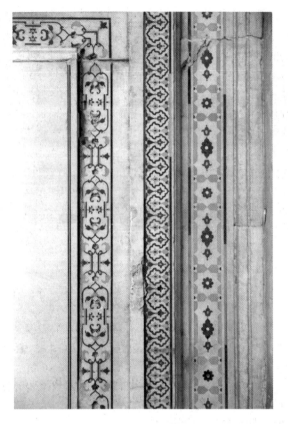

trees and shrubs were planted, including al-
mond, mulberry, mango, cherry, apricot, plum,
peach, orange and apple. Buildings within the
complex included pavilions, a royal bath, sleep-
ing quarters, resting chambers, a grand hall,
minarets and various further structures for the
exclusive use of the emperor and his immediate family. From the viewpoint of the visual arts,
a wide range of tiling designs can be detected,
though the site underwent severe deterioration
until being declared an UNESCO World Heritage
site (along with Lahore Fort) in 1981.

Figure 11.33 Tiling detail, Shalimar Gardens complex,
Lahore, Pakistan

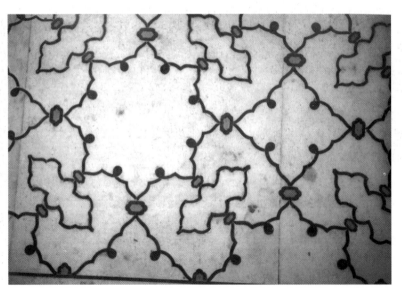

Figure 11.34 Tiling detail,
Shalimar Gardens complex,
Lahore, Pakistan

Figure 11.35 Tiling detail, Shalimar Gardens complex, Lahore, Pakistan

Figure 11.36 Tiling detail, Shalimar Gardens complex, Lahore, Pakistan

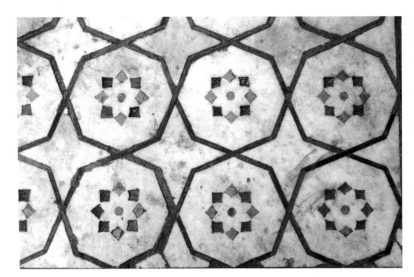

Figure 11.37 Tiling detail, Shalimar Gardens complex, Lahore, Pakistan

Sindhi ajraks (cs 29)

Ajrak is a term referring to a form of block-printed textile produced in Pakistan. Ajraks preserve one of the most ancient of textile-patterning techniques associated with the Indus Valley (examples are given in Figures 11.38–11.46). Askari and Crill commented: 'Although historical records for the production of ajrak are sparse, we have evidence of a medieval trade in similarly printed cotton textiles from the north-west of India to the Mediterranean along the trade routes of the Indian Ocean' (1997: 59). Towards the end of the twentieth century, ajraks became a strong symbol of Sindhi tradition and identity, used predominantly by men as a shoulder mantle or shawl, a turban or cummerbund.[3]

By the late twentieth century, the bulk of production took place in the province of Sindh (in Pakistan). Sindh province (which consists largely of the alluvial plain and delta of the River Indus) has been associated with block printing, in

particular with the use of mordants (those substances which allow dyes to adhere to, and thus colour, the cloth's surface), for the better part of three and a half thousand years. This suggests that a technique related to that associated with ajrak production may have been in use during the later stages of the Indus Valley civilization, at Mohenjo-daro, in the first quarter of the second millennium BCE. The ajrak process seems certainly to be of ancient origin, but whether traditional ajrak designs are of similarly remote origin it is not known.

Structurally ajraks consist of a series of borders surrounded by a central all-over pattern field. In the late twentieth century the author made a survey of traditional Sindhi ajraks and reported on the symmetry characteristics of a sample of designs (Hann 1992b). A representative sample of seventy-one designs was analysed and each design classified according to its symmetry class. From this sample, only five of the seventeen all-over pattern classes were represented to varying degrees.

Figure 11.38 Sindhi ajrak with typical design (University of Leeds International Textiles Archive)

Figure 11.39 Block-printed cotton with ajrak-type designs (University of Leeds International Textiles Archive)

Figure 11.40 Block-printed cotton with ajrak-type designs (University of Leeds International Textiles Archive)

Figure 11.41 Block-printed cotton with ajrak-type designs (University of Leeds International Textiles Archive)

By far the dominant class was four-direction reflection symmetry (class p4mm), evident in 60 per cent of the total sample. Further reflection symmetry (in the form of p2mm, p1m1 and c2mm patterns) accounted for a further 26 per cent of the total. Purely rotational classes (p211, p311, p411 and p611) were totally absent from the sample, as were all forms of glide reflection.

Simple statistical analysis confirmed a non-random distribution and showed that a definite preference was expressed towards a small number of symmetry classes, particularly those with reflectional symmetry. On the assumption that data were representative of traditional Sindhi ajrak patterns in general, the classification indicated a general consensus among ajrak producers in the predominant use of reflection symmetry. An awareness of purely rotational symmetry and glide-reflection symmetry was not evident.

Sindh province is also renowned for the production of patterned tiles (an activity also of apparent ancient origin in the region). During the

Figure 11.42 Block-printed cotton with ajrak-type designs (University of Leeds International Textiles Archive)

Figure 11.43 Block-printed cotton with ajrak-type designs (University of Leeds International Textiles Archive)

Figure 11.44 Block-printed cotton with ajrak-type designs (University of Leeds International Textiles Archive)

course of the field study reported previously (Hann 1992b) and outlined earlier, the author visited the cultural museum Lok Versa in Islamabad and reviewed a few published sources. The impression gained was that ajrak designs and patterned tiling designs were very similar in terms of dominant structural characteristics as well as colour. As was the case with the ajrak sample, the dominant symmetry class among groups of Sindhi tilings appeared to be the symmetry class with four-direction reflection symmetry (p4mm in all-over patterns and d4 in motifs).

Figure 11.45 Block-printed cotton with ajrak-type designs (University of Leeds International Textiles Archive)

Figure 11.46 Block-printed cotton with ajrak-type designs (University of Leeds International Textiles Archive)

DISCUSSION OR ASSIGNMENT TOPICS

Kashmiri Motif Chronology

Identify and assemble up to fifty images of typical Kashmiri shawl motifs (from the eighteenth and nineteenth centuries). Draw outlines of each and assemble these in what you believe is a valid chronological sequence. Compare with the dates given in reputable publications and museum websites and, from this comparison, adjust your sequence accordingly. Present a written discussion of your results (around 500 words).

Making reference to the drawings you assembled, present a chronological framework which you believe could be of value to museum curators or others seeking to attribute periods of production to Kashmiri-produced shawl fabrics.

Printed Textiles

Discuss the nature of motifs and patterns typically featured on a category of printed textiles produced in a country of your choice in South Asia.

Mughal Visual Arts

Review the nature of the visual arts and architecture of Mughal India. Make reference to manuscript production, carpet and textile manufacture, metalwork, tilings (or the production of any other decorated item that you think appropriate) and architecture. What types of motif or symbol were used? Which types of production technique (e.g. in pottery or metalwork) were of importance? Identify important raw materials (e.g. silk or silver) and their potential sources. What and where are the main sites/buildings? What were the principal influences and developments? Did developments in the visual arts and architecture contribute to or influence changes elsewhere?

---

further reading

Ames, F. (1986). *The Kashmir Shawl*, Woodbridge, Suffolk (UK): Antique Collectors' Club.

Davies, P. (1989). *The Penguin Guide to the Monuments of India*, vol. II. London: Viking.

Gray, B. (ed.) (1981). *The Arts of India*, Oxford: Phaidon Press.

Guy, J. (1998). *Woven Cargoes: Indian Textiles in the East*, London: Thames and Hudson.

Irwin, J. (1955). *Shawls: A Study of Indo European Influence*, London: HMSO.

Irwin, J. (1973). *The Kashmir Shawl*, London: HMSO.

notes

1. The fibrous raw material used in the production of the finer shawls came from the silky fleece of the Tibetan mountain goat (*capra lincus*). Known as *cashmere*, much of what was used in shawl manufacture in Kashmir was imported from Himalayan regions. In the raw state, the fibre was known as *pashm* and in the processed state as *pashmina*. The finest grades of shawls gave rise to anecdotes of the so-called ring shawls (woven so fine that they were capable of being pulled with ease through a wedding ring). By the mid-nineteenth century, supplies of the fleece could not meet demand, and this led to the adulteration with coarser wool types and,

as a consequence, finer qualities of shawls became increasingly rare.

2. Patterning on shawls in Kashmir was achieved generally through weaving or embroidery. Various block-printed imitations were produced in India and elsewhere. During the nineteenth century, the term *kani* referred to a particular pattern-weaving technique involving the manipulation of small wooden spools (known as *tojis*), each holding a different coloured thread. Each spool was inserted between warps (the lengthways threads on a loom) when that particular colour was required and, after weaving, was pulled out from between the warp threads when not required. As a result the patterned areas of a woven Kashmir shawl show coloured threads which do not travel the full width of the cloth, from selvedge to selvedge, as is the case with conventionally woven cloths. Instead, similarities can be seen with European tapestry weaving (though the Kashmir case is much finer and relies on a twill-woven foundation rather than the European plain-woven foundation). The woven structure used in Kashmiri shawl patterning became known to European and North American textile historians as interlocking-twill tapestry. A further feature resulting from the use of the Kashmiri technique was that the pattern was visible on both sides of the shawl fabric after weaving, but on the reverse side fine ridges outlining each pattern shape could be detected, and criss-crosses of weft from the spools could be discerned. With the *kani* technique, patterning became an integral component of the fabric structure. With an embroidered (or *amli*) shawl, needlework was applied independently of the ground woven structure. Occasionally the two patterning techniques were employed together in the manufacture of a shawl.

3. Ajrak printing is a combination of mordant and resist block printing/dyeing. Mordants allow dyes to adhere to the cloth, and 'resists' prevent dyes from reaching the cloth surface. Prior to the development of colour on the cloth's surface, the ajrak process involves three stages of printing, using hand-held wooden printing blocks. First, a resist mixture of chalk and gum is applied by block to predetermined areas of the cloth's surface; this prevents later colouration of these relevant areas. Second, a mordant paste containing iron sulphate is applied to predetermined areas, and third, a further mordant paste containing alum is applied. Each mordant attracts a particular dyestuff and ensures colouration and fixation of dye to relevant areas. Subsequently, the treated cloth is dipped into a cold dye bath of indigo, and exposed areas (with neither resist nor mordant) pick up a blue colour. After drying, the cloth is dyed in a simmering madder dye bath, where the chalk and gum areas of the cloth resist dye pick-up and thus remain white, the iron-sulphate-mordant areas are dyed black, and the alum-mordant areas are dyed red. The historic evolution of Sindhi ajrak printing and the precise details of the process remain largely unreported in the relevant literature. Yacopino (1987: 84–9) provided a brief, though highly ambiguous, account. Bilgrami (1990) gave details of the practicalities of the numerous preparatory and finishing processes as well as the many intricacies of production, including detailed recipes of processing materials used. In this latter publication, sixty-four master craftsmen and numerous ancillary workers were consulted and comments were also provided on the structural characteristics of several design types. Askari and Crill (1997) provided a good, concise explanation of the process and the nature of the product.

12

unity in diversity: the visual arts of Indonesia

Because of its geographic position along ancient sea-trade routes between eastern and western Asia, the Indonesian archipelago has been a port of call for countless foreign traders, adventurers, colonizers and missionaries. Before the arrival of the Portuguese, the Dutch and the British, all in search of rare spices and other precious commodities of Southeast Asia, Chinese, Indian and Arab traders had already left their cultural mark on parts of the archipelago. Buddhism and Hinduism appear to have coexisted in Java (the most populous island) for many centuries until Hinduism became dominant in the thirteenth century (Hann and Thomson 1993: 5). Islam became widely accepted by the sixteenth century, having spread gradually from various trading ports in Sumatra, Java and other islands where Arab and possibly also Indian traders had introduced the religion some centuries previously. Subsequently, European colonizers brought Christianity, which found particular acceptance in the islands in the eastern part of the archipelago. Multiple foreign influences have thus interacted with indigenous cultures across much of the archipelago for at least two millennia. Various cultural changes came in the wake of these successive waves of outside influence. In the visual arts, especially textiles, a rich catalogue of motifs, symbols and patterns developed, retained from ancient indigenous animistic beliefs and adopted from Buddhism, Hinduism and Islam, as well as various European, Indian, Chinese and other Asian sources. Certain islands or island groups, exposed to these outside influences, developed their own unique iconography, often adapting the new to fit or blend with the old in their own ways. Significant differences thus developed across the archipelago, and certain categories of motif, pattern and other stylistic features can be associated with particular islands or island groups. In the early twenty-first century, the use of a rich mixture of motifs and patterns from these various sources can still be detected, especially in categories of handcrafted products, above all textiles. At the same time, certain indigenous people, located on the more remote islands, remain largely unaffected and so retain associated forms of decoration more ancient in origin (Coleman 2008: 31–9).

monuments

Important early influences which form part of the cultural legacy of the archipelago, especially on the island of Java, are Buddhism and Hinduism. Various monuments testify to their dominance. The collapse of the Han dynasty disrupted overland trade between China and lands to the west.

From the third century CE various parts of South-east Asia witnessed a time of great prosper-ity, stimulated by increased sea trade between China and India, with trading ports established in Java (as well as other parts of the Indonesian archipelago, including coastal towns in Sumatra). The resultant accumulated wealth encouraged the development of native kingdoms in Java: the Sailendra and Sanjaya dynasties are two impor-tant examples. The Sailendra rulers were Buddhist and the Sanjaya rulers were Hindu. The former commissioned the building of Borobudur and the latter the building of the Prambanan temple complex. Borobudur is the largest ancient Bud-dhist monument in Southeast Asia. It is often described as a three-dimensional form of man-dala and thus a representation in miniature of the Buddhist cosmos. Borobudur was built between the last half of the eighth and the first half of the ninth centuries CE. The Prambanan Hindu temple complex, built in the early part of the ninth century by the Sanjaya dynasty rulers, initially held more than 200 temples. Over the centuries, many of these were destroyed, but by the early twenty-first century three large temples dedicated to the Hindu trinity of Brahma, Siva and Vishnu were in a reasonably good state of repair and dominated the site (together with several smaller construc-tions). Sculpted panels are a feature of the main buildings.

visual art forms and techniques

In historical and modern times the most important form of visual art associated with the archipelago has been textiles, although it is worth noting that relatively remote indigenous peoples (e.g. the Toraja from the highland interior of Sulawesi) have produced small quantities of elaborate wood carv-ing, as have peoples at several locations in Bali and Java. The most important textile types his-torically and in modern times are *batiks*, *ikats* and *songkets* for, in the context of the archipelago, these have acted as storehouses of evidence re-lating to cultural continuity, exchange and change.

Batiks form an important class of visual art in Java, and have a substantial catalogue of motifs, symbols and patterns, many of value when trac-ing cultural adherence, continuity and change as well as diffusion associated with Indonesia. Ikat is a woven textile in which threads have been dyed in predetermined areas prior to the weaving pro-cess. Songket is a brocaded textile, traditionally woven in silk or cotton, with gold, silver or other metallic thread used to assist with patterning. The most renowned locations of production of song-ket have been Sumatra, Kalimantan, Bali, Lom-bok, Sambawa and Sulawesi.

motifs, symbols and patterns

As noted previously, the forces of Buddhism, Hin-duism, Islam and, to a lesser extent, European co-lonialism had a dramatic impact on the culture and beliefs of the inhabitants of Java and other trading centres across the archipelago. There has been much debate about the origins of the designs which characterize the textiles of Indonesia. It is recognized generally that some of the designs and individual motifs have diffused from other parts of the world (particularly India and to some extent China and Europe), but there is no doubt that many of the features found in these cloths are in-digenous. In some cases, the weavers and users of these textiles may be well aware of the foreign origin of particular designs, whilst in others there may no longer be any consciousness that certain motifs or patterns have their origin elsewhere. The significance, symbolism or visual structure of borrowed elements once adopted sometimes shifts in subtle ways.

Probably the most important single source influencing the design of Indonesian textiles is the resist-dyed cloths of India. Most renowned of these resist-dyed cloths are the double-ikat silks from Gujarat and Orissa. As noted in Chapter 11, such cloths were known as *patola* and were featured as precious trade goods, traded extensively throughout much of South and Southeast Asia, initially through the activities of Indian, Arab and Chinese traders and, from the seventeenth century onwards, Portuguese, British and Dutch merchants. These textiles had a profound effect on the design of ikats in many parts of Indonesia. Known as *patola*, and produced in Orissa and Gujarat, they were used as temple hangings, bridal gifts and shrouds, and were worn at court appearances, classical dance events, weddings and funerals. The word *patola* (singular *patolu*) appeared in various forms as early as the fourteenth century CE in India and in accounts of early sixteenth-century European commentators. Guy reviewed the latter documents (1998: 26). Not surprisingly, in coastal Indian towns such as Orissa, ikat designs were inspired by the sea and included various sea animals and fish. Flowers and stripes were also common and arrowhead-type effects were in widespread use on the borders of saris (Weiner 1992). In South India, lotus blossoms, four-petalled flowers and swastika-type designs, as well as stylized peacocks, parrots, lions and elephants, were common (Weiner 1992). Checks and squares containing small motifs were also used. Ikats from Gujarat commonly depicted diamonds and rosettes. The vast bulk of patola cloths examined by the author exhibit either four-direction reflection symmetry or two-direction reflection symmetry. This shows a close similarity to the observations relating to Sindhi ajrak designs given in Chapter 11.

Borobudur (cs 30)

Borobudur is a Mahayana Buddhist temple located in Borobudur village in Magelang, central Java, Indonesia. Believed to have been constructed over a period of around seventy-five years and completed in the early ninth century, the monument consists of a series of five square platforms, each smaller than the previous, organized on top of a square base, in square pyramid fashion, and topped by three concentric (almost circular) platforms. A series of corridors (or galleries) sits between each successive square platform, and each of these four square-shaped corridor galleries is patterned profusely with narrative and other panels depicting contemporary courtly life, hermits, temples, flora and fauna, garlands, parasols, images of royalty, soldiers, servants and various mythical spiritual beings, as well as numerous scenes from the life of the Buddha and stories of his former lives, ending in the uppermost galleries with depictions associated with the Buddha's achievement of supreme knowledge (or nirvana). Stairways, with arched gateways, are located at the centre of each side of each square platform, and these give access to successive stages. The upper circular platforms feature a large central stupa which, at thirty-five metres above ground floor level, marks the highest point of the monument and is surrounded by seventy-two smaller stupas, arranged sixteen, twenty-four and thirty-two, in the three concentric different sized platforms. When constructed, each of these smaller stupas was formed from stone blocks, mainly cut X-shaped, thus creating a perforated effect to each of these smaller stupas. A statue of a seated Buddha, in lotus pose, was placed inside each. Viewed from above, Borobudur is similar visually to a Buddhist mandala. Pilgrims ascended the structure from the eastern entrance, walking clockwise around each square corridor gallery, using the staircase at each stage to move to the next level. Each successive level represents a further stage of enlightenment (Figures 12.1–12.15).

It seems that Borobudur was abandoned following a series of volcanic eruptions in the vicinity in the period between the early tenth and early eleventh centuries. By around the middle of the second millennium CE, Buddhism had declined in Java and

Figure 12.2 Borobudur Buddhist temple, Java, Indonesia

Figure 12.1 Borobudur Buddhist temple, Java, Indonesia

Figure 12.3 Borobudur Buddhist temple, Java, Indonesia

Figure 12.4 Borobudur Buddhist temple, Java, Indonesia

Figure 12.5 Borobudur Buddhist temple, Java, Indonesia

Figure 12.6 Borobudur Buddhist temple, Java, Indonesia

there had been widespread conversion to Islam. Meanwhile the monument lay hidden beneath volcanic ash and jungle growth, though it seems clear that local Javanese people were fully aware of its location. In the early nineteenth century, the location of the monument was communicated to various Europeans, including Thomas Stamford Raffles, the British lieutenant governor general. Subsequently a series of cleaning and restoration projects was undertaken, culminating in a major project in the last quarter of the twentieth century which ensured the monument's status as a UNESCO World Heritage site. In 2010, volcanic ash from Merapi fell on the monument, covering the reliefs and giving the monument a slate-grey colour. The present author's most recent visit to Borobudur was in late 2011, when parts of the monument were undergoing repair to the drainage system; these parts were cut off to all visitors. A public notice (put in place before the repair work mentioned above) located close to the monument instructed visitors to approach from the east entrance, going clockwise round the temple from east, to south, to west and north and, after each complete circuit, to ascend the east staircase to the next platform.

The structure features an estimated 2,672 individual reliefs; 1,460 of these can be classified as narrative and 1,212 as other forms of patterning.

Figure 12.7 Borobudur Buddhist temple, Java, Indonesia

Figure 12.8 Borobudur Buddhist temple, Java, Indonesia

Figure 12.9 Borobudur Buddhist temple, Java, Indonesia

Figure 12.10 Borobudur
Buddhist temple, Java,
Indonesia

Figure 12.11 Borobudur
Buddhist temple, Java,
Indonesia

Narrative panels on the walls read from right to left and on the balustrade read from left to right, as the pilgrim walks clockwise around each successive corridor gallery. In the late nineteenth century, a hidden series of panels was discovered under the base at the south-east corner of the monument. Known as the hidden footing, this was found to hold 160 narrative reliefs and various further panels with short inscriptions. Sculptural poses (with bent neck and one bent knee) appear to be strongly influenced by Indian Gupta style.

The structure is described invariably as a three-dimensional mandala (readily understandable when viewed from above) representing

Figure 12.12 Borobudur Buddhist temple, Java, Indonesia

kāmadhātu, *rupadhatu* and *arupadhatu* (or the world of desires, the world of forms and the formless world). So the pilgrim ascends the structure with each successive platform representing a further stage of enlightenment, from the base (with reliefs associated with *kāmadhātu*), via the next five platforms and its four galleries (associated with *rupadhatu*) to the three circular platforms surrounding the top central stupa (associated with *arupadhatu* and *nirvana*, the final stage of enlightenment). The three stages of enlightenment have a height ratio of 4:6:9 (base:body:head). The ratio 4:6:9 also features in Pawon and Mendut, two much smaller Buddhist monuments in the region (aligned in a straight line geographically with Borobudur).

Many Buddha statues were incorporated into the monument, each depicted in a seated, cross-legged or lotus position. A total of 432 statue niches can be seen in the first five balustrades (104,

Figure 12.13 Borobudur Buddhist temple, Java, Indonesia

Figure 12.14 Borobudur Buddhist temple, Java, Indonesia

Figure 12.15 Borobudur Museum courtyard, Java, Indonesia

104, 88, 72 and 64). At the circular levels there is a total of seventy-two (32, 24 and 16) perforated stupas with a space for a statue in each. Subtle differences can be detected between the groups of statues, particularly in the position of the hands (*mudras*) on each. The monument is oriented with sides facing north, south, east and west. In the Buddhist world, another direction, known as *zenith*, or centre, is added. Buddha statues facing each of the four standard compass directions and the central zenith direction have hand position (*mudras*) relating to their respective direction.

Figure 12.16 Plan of Borobudur Buddhist temple, Java, Indonesia. Believed to have been constructed as a three-dimensional mandala; the plan shows four-direction reflection symmetry. It fits neatly into a square template and all important features seem measured and planned with substantial attention to underlying geometric structure. Borobudur's geometry shows many parallels with other Buddhist temples in Asia.

Javanese batiks (cs 31)

The product

Batiks are a type of textile produced in many parts of the world though associated closely with Indonesia, particularly the island of Java. A peculiar veining effect is often associated with batik products. This occurs in cases where a brittle wax mixture has been used which, on cracking when immersed in the dye bath, allows the penetration of dye to the cloth's surface. Although this cracking effect is associated popularly with batik textiles the world over, and is often encouraged as a visual effect on screen-printed imitations, it has traditionally been discouraged on well-produced Javanese batiks (Figures 12.17–12.31).

For this reason, the present author believes that early Javanese batik textiles were probably in imitation of fine woven imported textiles (probably from India); these imported textiles, decorated through the use of various weaving techniques, would have shown clear demarcation of motifs against background and the predominance of veined effects in imitations would have been discouraged. In other parts of the world, where Javanese batik imitations were produced (e.g. Manchester in the United Kingdom) in the twentieth century, the veining effect was encouraged and led to the wide acceptance of such decorated textiles in markets such as West Africa. The traditional end use of batik in Java was as a garment for festive or ceremonial use, but in

Figure 12.17 Detail of Javanese batik (Coleman Collection, University of Leeds International Textiles Archive)

Figure 12.18 Detail of Javanese batik (Coleman Collection, University of Leeds International Textiles Archive)

recent times it has been made into Western-style apparel items, including men's shirts and women's dresses, blouses and skirts. Hann (1992a) previously reviewed the nature of the product, its decorative characteristics, including types of motifs and patterns used and various regional variations; these are summarized further in the next section.[1]

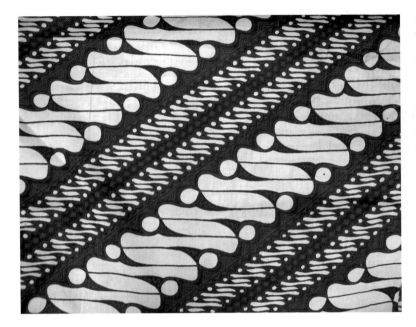

Figure 12.19 Detail of Javanese batik (Coleman Collection, University of Leeds International Textiles Archive)

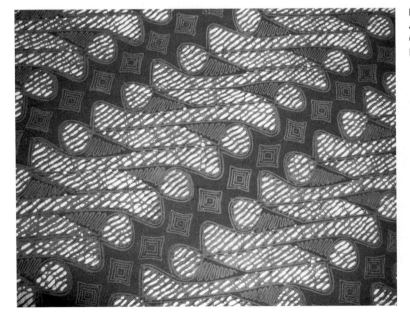

Figure 12.20 Detail of Javanese batik (Coleman Collection, University of Leeds International Textiles Archive)

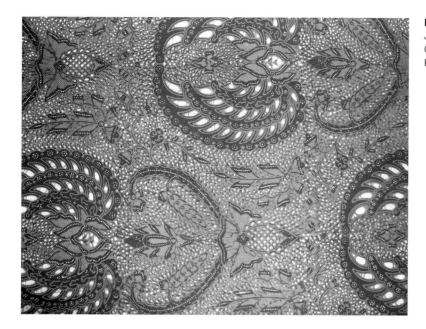

Figure 12.21 Detail of Javanese batik (Coleman Collection, University of Leeds International Textiles Archive)

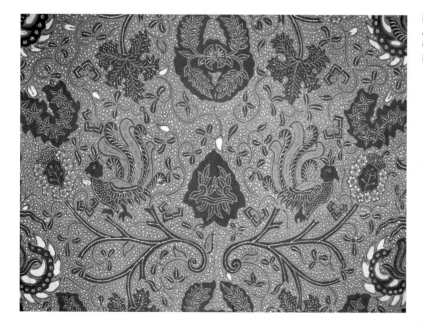

Figure 12.22 Detail of Javanese batik (Coleman Collection, University of Leeds International Textiles Archive)

Figure 12.23 Detail of Javanese batik (Coleman Collection, University of Leeds International Textiles Archive)

Figure 12.24 Detail of Javanese batik (Coleman Collection, University of Leeds International Textiles Archive)

Figure 12.25 Detail of Javanese batik (Coleman
Collection, University of Leeds International Textiles Archive)

Figure 12.26 Detail of
Javanese batik (Coleman
Collection, University of Leeds
International Textiles Archive)

Figure 12.27 Detail of Javanese batik (Coleman Collection, University of Leeds International Textiles Archive)

Figure 12.28 Detail of Javanese batik (Coleman Collection, University of Leeds International Textiles Archive)

Figure 12.29 Detail of Javanese batik (Coleman Collection, University of Leeds International Textiles Archive)

Figure 12.30 Detail of Javanese batik (Coleman Collection, University of Leeds International Textiles Archive)

Figure 12.31 Detail of Javanese batik (Coleman Collection, University of Leeds International Textiles Archive)

Regional variations

Historically, the most important batik-producing regions in Java have included the areas in and around the central Javanese sultanates or principalities of Surakarta (Solo) and Yogyakarta (Yogya), and the northern coastal areas or towns such as Cirebon. Batiks from the producers associated with the sultanates are known as *vorstenlanden batiks*, and depict motifs and patterns considered to reflect Hindu-Javanese culture; they also include a small number of forbidden or *larangan* designs, which were traditionally restricted in use to members of the principal sultanates of either Surakarta or Yogyakarta. Traditional coastal batiks, known as *pesisir batiks*, show naturalistic compositions and include animal, floral and maritime themes. Batiks from coastal regions of the north, on the other hand, show acceptance of Chinese and European motifs and compositions (Hann and Thomson 1993: 8).The iconography and structural characteristics of both categories

of Javanese batik retain much information relating to the ancient beliefs and religious philosophy of the Javanese people. Some of the more common motifs and patterns are identified later in this chapter.

The *tampal* (meaning *patch* or *plaster*) pattern consists of a design field divided by a network of regular (or sometimes irregular) shapes with each filled by either a repeating pattern or else by a symmetrical or asymmetrical motif. The tampal design is traditionally associated with Surakarta, Yogyakarta, Pekalongan and Cirebon, and may have origins in the patched clothing sometimes worn by Buddhist monks as an outward expression of poverty (Hann and Thomson 1993: 8).

A dominant pattern type, typical of Surakarta and Yogyakarta batiks, is the *parang* (meaning *dagger* or *chopper*) pattern. Varieties within this pattern class were *larangan* designs and were restricted in use to the high-ranking members of the sultanates. These patterns thus acted as insignias of social standing within Javanese society. A wing-shaped motif, known as *lar*, and a double-wing-shaped motif with a tail extending outwards, known as *sawat*, were depicted traditionally on *vorstenlanden* batiks and, by the late-twentieth century, on *pesisir* batiks as well. Both have been ascribed a Hindu origin and have been associated with the wings of Garuda (a winged character found in the Ramayana epic and, in decorative form, the emblem associated with Vishnu). By the late twentieth century, it had been adopted as the emblem of the Republic of Indonesia.

Motifs with Islamic associations include minaret and mihrab shapes, the 'Buraq' (the winged horse with a human head associated with the prophet Mohammad) and verses in Arabic from the Koran. Such motifs are most commonly found on traditional batiks produced on Java's northern coast, an early port of call for Arabic (as well as Indian) maritime merchants in the early years before widespread adoption of Islam as the dominant religion throughout Java. Arabesque-type shapes, although initially of Arabic origin, may have been adopted from European (Dutch or Portuguese) sources (Hann and Thomson 1993: 8). A class of designs known as *kawung* (meaning *fruit*) show intersecting circles (Warming and Gaworski 1981: 171), and may have originated in imitation of Arabic tiling designs.

Motifs of probable Chinese origin include the Chinese phoenix, which, in its Javanese form, seems to have fused with the Hindu 'Garuda' bird; the Chinese unicorn, associated historically with the birth of Confucius; pairs of fish, symbolic of marriage and unity; cloud motifs, which appear to have undergone further development in the region of Cirebon on Java's north coast, to produce the pattern known as *megamendung* (or threatening clouds); *banji* (a collective term for various forms of key patterns, often with swastika-type shapes); a wide range of floral decoration probably sourced from imported Chinese ceramics (Hann and Thomson 1993: 8).

Often the *tumpal* design, a selvedge-to-selvedge border pattern consisting of a series of elongated triangular shapes, is found on batiks produced as sarongs. This is often the case with batiks produced in workshops in and around Indramayu.

Patterns consisting of a type of repeating motif known as the *jelamprang* motif (an eight-rayed, star-like figure set in a circle, modified square or other regular polygon) have associations with the Pekalongan region (Djoemena 1986: 98). These patterns are probably Indian in origin and may have been copied from imported silk ikat cloths.

Not surprisingly, maritime themes and motifs associated with the sea dominate the patterning of batiks produced in workshops in and around towns on Java's north coast. Examples include: *ikan* (fish) of various kinds, *udang* (shrimp) and *ganggong* (algae) (Djoemena 1986: 35). The *grinsing* design, with its fish scale-like visual effect, is probably one of the oldest indigenous Indonesian designs (Warming and Gaworski 1981: 176). Semen (from *semi* meaning *sprout*) designs, found commonly on north coast batiks, consist of tightly packed compositions featuring stylized plans, mythological creatures and landscape-like motifs such as *meru* (a mountain shape, commonly interpreted as *the mountain of the gods*) (Gittinger 1985: 118). *Nikik* (from *tik* meaning *dot*) designs are typical of Surakarta and Yogyakarta and appear to be imitations of imported woven designs (probably from India) (Warming and Gaworski 1981: 171). A typical composition associated with batiks from Cirebon includes depictions of the creature known as the *singa barong*, a figure which is seemingly a fusion of Chinese, Islamic and Hindu symbolism (Djoemena 1986: 31). The body of the figure is taken from a horned dragon of Chinese origin; the wings of the creature are from Buraq, of Islamic origin; the elephant's trunk is taken from Ganesha (a Hindu deity). In the late twentieth century, the present author reported seeing a representation of the figure in three-dimensions, dominating the form of a chariot on display at Kesepukan Palace in Cirebon (Hann and Thomson 1993: 9).

As indicated earlier, it certainly appears to be the case that motif types, judged in terms of thematic and symbolic content, differ from region to region within Java, and the workshops in each particular location for production are noted for their own speciality batik types. During the late twentieth century, the present author conducted a survey of the symmetry characteristics of Javanese batiks from the island's principal batik-producing regions, including the areas in and around the central Javanese sultanates of Surakarta and Yogyakarta, the various coastal areas close to Cirebon, Indramayu, Pekalongan and Lasem and the area in and around Garut in east Java (Hann 1992b).

A symmetry analysis

A symmetry analysis was conducted on a representative sample of 110 repeating batik designs (fifty-six from coastal regions and fifty-four from Central Java), with each classed by reference to its symmetry characteristics. Data were taken from authoritative Indonesian and other published sources (Donahue 1981; Gittinger 1985; Djoemena 1986; Hamzuri 1989).[2] In total, 505 traditional designs were examined, and of these 110 exhibited regular all-over pattern characteristics, with all constituent elements repeating

clearly. The remaining 395 designs were nonrepeating varieties, but examination of the symmetry characteristics of constituent motifs indicated a predominance of figures with bilateral reflection symmetry.

Eleven of the seventeen all-over-pattern classes were represented to varying degrees. By far the dominant symmetry class was that with four-direction reflection symmetry (p4mm), evident in 54 (49 per cent) of the total of 110 designs. Interestingly a surprising 90 per cent of these fifty-four batiks were produced in coastal regions. On the assumption that the data are representative of traditional Javanese batik repeating patterns in general, the classification reported here confirms a consensus among traditional Javanese batik producers (as a whole) in the predominant use of a small number of symmetry classes, as well as an additional awareness of a wide range of symmetry possibilities. The most surprising result is that 90 per cent of the patterns showing four-direction reflection symmetry (p4mm) were produced in coastal workshops. Note that the same predominant preference (60 per cent from a total sample size of 71 items) for class p4mm was exhibited in the survey of a representative sample of Sindhi ajrak designs (Hann 1992b), also summarized in the present book (and presented in a case study in Chapter 11). The predominance of Islam among many of the coastal Javanese batik producers as well as among the Sindhi ajrak producers may well be a factor accounting for this result. It is not clear, however, why this particular class was predominant, though from other surveys the author detected that four-direction reflection symmetry (class p4mm) seems also to show a predominance among Islamic tiling designs. Clearly further examination and interregional comparisons of symmetry classes of design produced in Islamic regions is required.

Indonesian ikats (cs 32)

Ikats are a type of patterned textile, produced traditionally in numerous locations, including Central, South and Southeast Asia. Probably the widest variety of ikats is produced across the islands of the Indonesian archipelago, and this case study focuses on these textiles in particular (Figures 12.32–12.44).

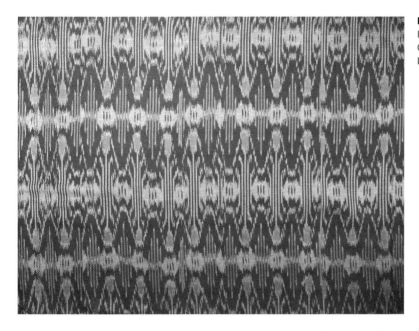

Figure 12.32 Detail of Indonesian ikat (Coleman Collection, University of Leeds International Textiles Archive)

Figure 12.33 Detail of Indonesian ikat (Coleman Collection, University of Leeds International Textiles Archive)

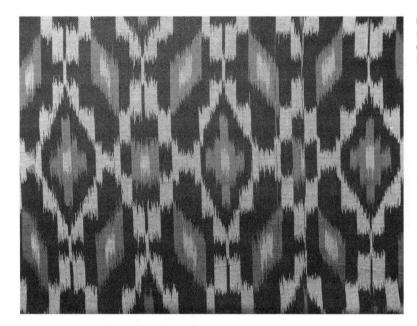

Figure 12.34 Detail of Indonesian ikat (Coleman Collection, University of Leeds International Textiles Archive)

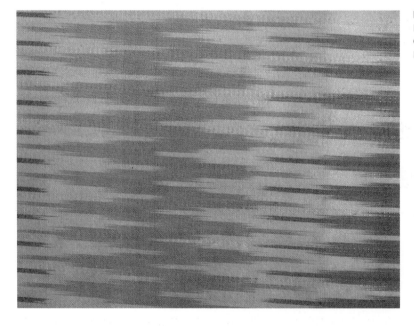

Figure 12.35 Detail of Indonesian ikat (Coleman Collection, University of Leeds International Textiles Archive)

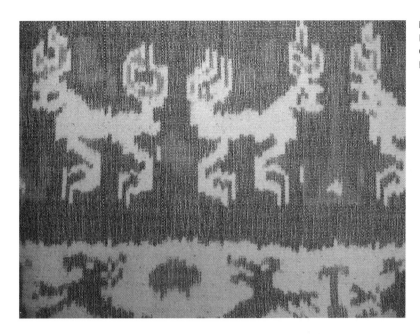

Figure 12.36 Detail of Indonesian ikat (Coleman Collection, University of Leeds International Textiles Archive)

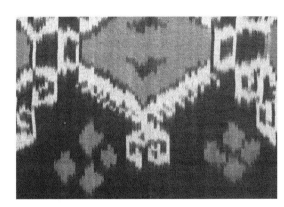

Figure 12.37 Detail of Indonesian ikat (Coleman Collection, University of Leeds International Textiles Archive)

Figure 12.38 Detail of Indonesian ikat (Coleman Collection, University of Leeds International Textiles Archive)

When considered regionally across the archipelago, certain compositional similarities can be detected, particularly with respect to layout of warp and weft threads. The majority of traditional ikats produced in the eastern part of the archipelago are composed of warp-ways stripes of various widths either in solid colour (blue/black or brown/red) or with ikat patterning ranging from small geometric figures a few centimetres in size to large figurative motifs drawn invariably from the

Figure 12.39 Detail of Indonesian ikat (Coleman Collection, University of Leeds International Textiles Archive)

Figure 12.40 Detail of Indonesian ikat (Coleman Collection, University of Leeds International Textiles Archive)

Figure 12.41 Detail of Indonesian ikat (Coleman Collection, University of Leeds International Textiles Archive)

various sources mentioned previously. The widths of stripes depend on the pattern produced. Typical compositions show one, two, three or more broad stripes (each of around 10 centimetres) with repeated ikat patterns in white against a dark blue or blue/black background. Where more than one ikat stripe is used, each stripe is located symmetrically and equidistant from the warp-ways centre and has accompanying narrower stripes at each side. The resultant visual effect is a warp-ways line of bilateral symmetry, with the right-hand side of the cloth a reflection of the left. Different areas within the region have different prescribed compositions which include rules governing the order of the stripes, their width, colour and motif content.

Traditionally it has been the case throughout much of Indonesia that certain textiles were used specifically for ritualistic, ceremonial and spiritual functions rather than for everyday wear. Referring specifically to warp ikats, Warming and Gaworski commented that they: 'have a ritual and spiritual value that extends beyond the mere physical object. Textiles are required for ceremonies, but not

Figure 12.42 Detail of Indonesian ikat (Coleman Collection, University of Leeds International Textiles Archive)

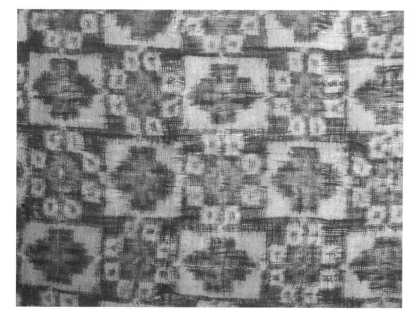

Figure 12.43 Detail of Indonesian double ikat from Bali (Coleman Collection, University of Leeds International Textiles Archive)

Figure 12.44 Detail of Indonesian double ikat from Bali (Coleman Collection, University of Leeds International Textiles Archive)

just as traditional dress for participants. The cloths themselves are a necessary part of the ritual. Warp-ikat cloths act as burial shrouds, as part of exchange of gifts before marriage, and as a way of preserving local history and legends' (1981: 79). Important island locations of traditional ikat production include East Sumba, Timor, Sulawesi, Flores, Sawu, Rote, Sumatra and Bali. The following sections summarize characteristics of each regional ikat type.

East Sumba

The best known of Indonesian ikats are the cotton warp-ikat cloths from East Sumba. Known as *hinggi*, they had multiple uses traditionally, from items of clothing (worn by men as waist and shoulder cloths), to status markers and to ritual and prestige objects. The principal compositional characteristic is a series of horizontal bands, three to eleven in number, containing a great variety of motifs derived from the realms of legend, sacred rite and such diverse foreign sources as Chinese porcelains or Dutch coins (Larsen 1976: 150). Traditionally, motifs included horses, deer, lions, monkeys, various varieties of birds, fish, lizards, crocodiles, snakes, six-pointed stars and diamond shapes and sea creatures such as sea horses, shrimps and lobsters. Certain designs were restricted to the aristocracy, and this was especially true of motifs taken from Indian *patola* cloths. Another prominent motif was the skull tree, probably a reminder of past ritualistic head hunting. The significance of the tree of skulls motif, according to Moss, is that it emphasizes the wearer's status in a strictly ordered society:

Performance of sacred rites was rigidly adhered to on Sumba in order to maintain order in the universe and among mortals on earth. Events from these rites were depicted in the cloths, and even though today much of this tradition is no longer honoured, the motifs are used commonly and their meanings usually understood. . . . The skull tree, upon which the heads of the vanquished enemy were hung and which appears in motifs on hinggi, refers to a sacred rite that insures a prosperous future'. (1979: 68)

Timor

During colonial times, Timor was divided into two distinct parts, with the Dutch-controlled territory in the west and the Portuguese-controlled territory in the east. Despite this historical division, by the early twenty-first century a common cultural identity had spread across the island and traditional textiles played an important role in ritual and ceremony. As Kartiwa pointed out, trade in Timor cloths outside the area was long-standing, especially to non-weaving areas such as Irian Jaya (1987: 80). It was common to combine warp ikat during the weaving process with other forms of decoration (such as supplementary weft). Brilliant red bands and stripes or large-scale blue ikat designs were typical. Motifs included various birds, horses, lizards and human figures. Writing in 1985, Gittinger observed that subtle differences in decoration and technique, including tonal qualities of colour and variation in band width, were apparent from area to area within Timor, but these variations were barely perceptible to the majority of outsiders (1985: 175).

Sulawesi

Cotton warp ikats were produced traditionally by the Toradja people of central Sulawesi. These depict large-scale geometric patterns in blue, white and black against a dominant red background. The geometry of motifs on Toradja ikats suggests human figures in schematic form (Larsen 1976: 149). Such textiles were used as death shrouds locally and were traded across the archipelago for use as hangings at funerals (Gittinger 1985: 207).

Flores

Traditionally, in many parts of Flores, warp-ikat patterned textiles were produced, and a wide range of sources of patterning can be identified. In the isolated central region, the ikats produced by the Ngada were generally blue-black in colouring and showed simple triangular, square and zigzag shapes, revealing very little influence from outside sources (Gittinger 1985: 168–9). Substantial foreign influence is evident elsewhere across the island. Occasionally European designs were adapted, or compositional arrangements typical of Sumba were imitated (Gittinger 1985: 169). The use of cloth as a means of expressing social status was an important feature of textiles in some parts of Flores. The design of Indian patola cloths also had a major impact here. The Lio people, who also produced ikat cloths depicting various snake forms, produced virtual imitations (Hann and Thomson 1993: 13). Other motifs depicted on ikats from Flores include lizards, insect-like forms, birds, dogs and human figures, all in highly stylized form (Gittinger 1985: 171).

Sawu (also spelled Savu, Sabu, Sawoe)

Sawu is located just south of the equator, west of Timor and between Sumba and Rote. The most important characteristic of traditional ikat textiles produced on Sawu is that their designs denoted membership in a female-aligned clan system that controlled life-crisis rituals (Hann and Thomson 1993: 12). Delicate white geometric and floral motifs against a dark blue or black background were the principal decorative feature (Warming and Gaworski 1981: 83), and motifs were taken from Portuguese, Dutch and other European sources (Hann and Thomson 1993: 12).

Rote

Inhabitants of Rote came into relatively early contact with Europeans during the seventeenth century
following the arrival of traders seeking to exchange
patola textiles from India for various spices. From
the eighteenth century, the people of Roti began
to replace the *patola* with cloths of their own making, some of them exact replicas, using various
octagon-shaped floral motifs known as *black motifs*
on Rote, and elsewhere in Indonesia as the *jelamprang motif*, though with a more limited dye range
than the Indian originals. The colours used were
red, white, black and blue-black. Typically floral
motifs were combined with small leaf shapes, inter-
twined with buds and branches and often placed in
longitudinal central bands (Kartiwa 1987: 84).

Sumatra

The Batak people of Sumatra traditionally produced cotton warp ikats with simple arrowhead
or diamond shapes in white against a monochromatic background colour. Warming and Gaworski observed that among the Batak people the
colours rather than the motifs used appeared to
be of greater symbolic significance, with white
symbolizing purity, red denoting bravery and black
associated with eternity, yellow with dignity and
green with prosperity (1981: 94).

Bali

The most renowned of Bali's traditional textiles is
a type of cloth known as *geringsing*, a double-
ikat cloth produced exclusively in Tenganan
Pegeringsingan, a single village located in the
south-east of the island. Double-ikat production
is immensely labourious and involves the pre-
dyeing of both the warp and the weft threads prior
to weaving. The *geringsing* cloths produced in
Tenganan have many functions within the village,

mainly associated with warding off evil. However,
the cloths are also highly prized throughout the
rest of Bali, although often for quite different ceremonial purposes.

A question often asked is whether the double-
ikat technique of Tenganan is indigenous or whether
it reached Bali from elsewhere (Coleman 1986:
37). Double ikat is extremely rare and, other than
its production in Bali, has traditionally been woven
in only a few parts of the world (including small
quantities in Gujarat and Japan). Gittinger hinted
at 'a possible historical relationship between the
processes of Bali and Gujarat', and stressed that
this 'has not been proven but is probable' (1982:
153). Holmgren and Spertus (1991: 59) came to
a similar conclusion, whilst Ramseyer (1991: 134)
reported that some villagers in Tenganan have in
their blood an enzyme frequently found in people
of the Indian subcontinent but only very rarely elsewhere, implying that the people and their weaving
technique originated in India. On the other hand,
Hitchcock (1991: 82) observed: 'the people of
Tenganan, who claim to be the descendants of the
pre-Hindu inhabitants of Bali, are more isolationist
than their fellow islanders, and it seems possible
that the [double-ikat] method was developed independently in Indonesia'.

Geringsing cloths show a range of stylized floral and geometric motifs as well as various human
figures. The style of the human figures has been
compared to thirteenth- and fourteenth-century
temple reliefs in central Java to the west of Bali,
thus alerting observers to the possibility that such
designs may have been woven previously in Java,
and migrated with Hindu populations from there
(Gittinger 1985: 103). A range of weft ikats is also
produced in Bali, depicting not only geometric
and floral forms but also various figural compositions drawn from Hindu mythology.

Prambanan temple complex (cs 33)

Figure 12.45 Prambanan temple complex, Java

Candi Prambanan is a ninth-century Hindu temple complex, dedicated to Brahma (the creator), Shiva (the destroyer) and Vishnu (the preserver). Located eighteen kilometres east of the central Javanese city of Yogyakarta, and characterized by high pointed architecture, the complex of temples was probably built at the stage in history which marked the change-over of power in the region from a Buddhist dynasty to an era of Hindu control (Figures 12.45–12.57).

Figure 12.46 Prambanan temple complex, Java

Figure 12.47 Prambanan
temple complex, Java

Figure 12.48 Prambanan
temple complex, Java

Figure 12.49 Prambanan
temple complex, Java

Figure 12.50 Prambanan
temple complex, Java

Figure 12.51 Prambanan temple complex, Java

Figure 12.52 Prambanan temple complex, Java

The complex was constructed following a square format, consisting originally of 240 temples laid out as follows: three *trimurti* temples dedicated to Brahma, Shiva and Vishnu. The term *trimurti* denotes triple form. Occasionally the three deities are sculpted with three heads with one body. Knappert commented: 'The trimurti is also called the parama . . . because the three gods merged into one being are supreme' (1995: 248).

Three *vahana* temples were placed in front of the *trimurti* temples. The term *vahana* is used to refer to a vehicle in the form of an animal, bird, fish, mythological creature of one kind or another or a chariot, functioning in the transportation of a deity (Knappert 1995: 255). The three *vahana* temples are dedicated to Hamsa (the sacred swan and vehicle of Brahma), Nandi (the bull and vehicle of Shiva) and Garuda (the eagle and vehicle of Vishnu). Two *apit* temples stand between the *trimurti* and *vahana* temples on the north and south sides.

Figure 12.53 Prambanan
temple complex, Java

Figure 12.54 Prambanan
temple complex, Java

Figure 12.55 Prambanan temple complex, Java

Figure 12.56 Prambanan temple complex, Java

The temple complex also includes four *kelir* temples (small shrines located on the four cardinal directional points), four *patok* temples (small shrines located on the four corners of the inner zone) a total of 224 *pervara* temples (arranged in four concentric squares of forty-four, fifty-two, sixty and sixty-eight small temple constructions).

By the first decade of the twenty-first century, eight main (central) temples and eight small shrines had been reconstructed, but only two of the original 224 *pervara* temples had been completed. What remained of the rest was in a ruinous state.

It is believed that the temple complex was planned to mimic Meru, the holy mountain abode of Hindu gods and the home of Shiva. There is a hierarchy of three temple zones (outer, middle and inner zones), best understood when the site is considered in bird's-eye view (i.e. plan view). A

similar hierarchy was explained in the case study of Borobudur (the Buddhist monument also located in central Java close to the city of Yogyakarta), where each zone represents a different stage or degree of spirituality or enlightenment.

The three zones at Prambanan are as follows: first bhurloka (in Buddhism *kāmadhātu*), located at the outer parts of the monument, is the lowest realm for common mortals, animals and demons, all considered by adherents to be consumed by lust, desire and unholy ways of life; second bhuvarloka (in Buddhism *rupadhatu*), is located at the outer part of the inner square or courtyard, close to the central temples, and is the

Figure 12.57 Prambanan temple complex, Java

Figure 12.58 Performance of Ramayana ballet, Trimurti open air theatre, Prambanan temple complex, 2011

middle realm occupied by holy people, ascetics and lesser deities; third svarloka (in Buddhism *arupadhatu*), is the innermost and holiest realm of gods, associated with each of the six central temples.

The temples are also adorned with narrative reliefs telling the story of the Hindu epic Rama-yana. This narrative starts in the Shiva temple and continues in the Brahma temple. The Ramayana dance performance (or the *Ramayana ballet* as it is referred to in the late twentieth and early twenty-first century) is the ancient dance of the Javanese courts or palaces. Since the 1960s, dancers have

performed this dance at every full moon at the Trimurti open air theatre in the west side of the Prambanan temple complex (Figure 12.58). The epic story (of definite Indian origin) involves Sita, wife of Rama, abducted by Ravanna. The monkey king Hanuman, in support of Rama, comes to the rescue with his army to save Sita.

On the outer walls of many of the structures, a series of niches is presented. Typically a lion is depicted in each niche flanked by two kalpataru trees and each of these is flanked by a pair of kin-naras (birds with human heads), or pairs of birds, deer, sheep, monkeys, horses or elephants.

DISCUSSION OR ASSIGNMENT TOPICS

Javanese Batiks

Identify the principal categories of Javanese batik. Using illustrative material of your choice, discuss the symmetry characteristics of Javanese batiks.

Borobudur

Where is the monument known as Borobudur? Explain why the monument has been compared to a mandala.

Ikats

Using illustrative material of your choice, discuss the geometrical characteristics of surface patterning on traditional Indonesian ikats.

Symmetries of Borobudur and Prambanan

Identify a range of dependable websites and other published sources which present plan drawings of Borobudur and the Prambanan Temple Complexes. Select two images for each site. Redraw each. Place each of your drawings within a square format (possibly denoted by a dotted line). Construct lines of reflection symmetry in each of the four drawings. Discuss your results.

The Diffusion of Motifs, Symbols and Patterns

Making reference to the diffusion of motifs, symbols and patterns, discuss the nature of the visual arts of Indonesia. Develop a discussion on diffusion and adaptation, and identify relevant types of decorative arts (e.g. batik, ikat, basketwork, architectural decoration, wood carving, etc.). Comment on techniques and processes used. Focus particular attention on motifs, patterns, symbols and colour palettes used. Identify those motifs and patterns which you believe are indigenous to Indonesia as well as those motifs that may have diffused from elsewhere.

further reading

Forshee, J. (2001). *Between the Folds: Stories of Cloth, Lives, and Travels from Sumba*, Honolulu: University of Hawai'i Press.

Gittinger, M. (1985). *Splendid Symbols: Textiles and Tradition in Indonesia*, Singapore: Oxford University Press.

Grabsky, P. (1999). *The Lost Temple of Java*, London: Orion Books.

Guy, J. (1998). *Woven Cargoes: Indian Textiles in the East*, London: Thames and Hudson.

Hitchcock, M. (1991). *Indonesian Textiles*, London: British Museum Press.

Larsen, J. L. (1976). *The Dyers Art: Ikat, Batik and Plangi*, New York: Van Nostrand Reinhold.

Lockard, C. (2009). *Southeast Asia in World History*, Oxford: Oxford University Press.

Miksic, J. (1990). *Borobudur: Golden Tales of the Buddhas*, Singapore: Periplus Editions.

Steinmann, A. (1947). 'Batiks', *CIBA Review*, 58 (July): 2090–123.

Tarling, N. (1992). *The Cambridge History of Southeast Asia*, vol. 1, Cambridge: Cambridge University Press.

notes

1. The word *batik* refers to a particular type of patterning technique and its resultant products. The derivation of the term is apparently from the Javanese *ambitik*, meaning to mark with small dots (Steinman 1947: 2091).The technique, as used in Java, involves the application of molten wax to the surface of a plain-woven cloth. On solidification of the wax, the cloth is immersed in a dye bath and the colour takes to those areas not covered with wax, while those areas covered with wax remain impervious to the dye. In Java distinction is made between two categories of batik products, each relying on a different wax-application technique: *tulis* batik and *cap* (pronounced tjap) batik. With *tulis* batik, the wax is applied using a drawing pen known as a *canting* (pronounced tjanting). This implement consists of a handle shaped from bamboo and a small vessel of thin copper with one or occasionally more capillary spouts, through which the melted wax flows onto the surface of the cloth. With *cap* batik, molten wax is applied to the cloth's surface using a hand-held copper printing block, thus allowing a speedier means of production than with application using a *canting*. In the production of monochromatic (i.e. with a single colour on a white background) batiks, the wax is applied once only and the cloth coloured using only one dye bath. With polychromatic (or multicoloured) batiks, more than one dyeing takes place together with an equivalent number of wax applications. After dyeing, as well as drying, the wax is removed from the cloth's surface either by scraping (especially where brittle waxes have been used) or by boiling in water.

2. In addition, several practitioners were consulted, and key items held in a small number of renowned local collections were examined.

13

the visual arts of dynastic China

As mentioned in the introduction to Chapter 4, China owes its origins to a civilization that developed in the Yellow River Valley around 2000 BCE, although numerous Neolithic cultures had dominated for extended periods during the four millennia previous to this (Rawson 1992: 293). Periods of internal conflict, development, expansion and stability followed, and China was ruled under a series of dynasties, with the Shang dynasty (mid-second millennium to late second millennium BCE) often listed as the first (Rawson 1992: 293). Chronologies, dates, geographic boundaries and borders are complex issues and are the subject of scholarly debate. It is not the intention in this book to contribute to this debate, but rather to identify a few developments or contributions to the visual arts during dynastic times, though the principal focus will be on the Qing dynasty, the final dynasty prior to the formation of the Republic of China in the early twentieth century. From very early dynasties to this final dynasty, a surprising consistency in the visual arts can be detected, with motifs and their inherent symbolism retained over the centuries. Rawson provided a detailed chronology (1992: 293–307). Rawson's 1992 book, *The British Museum Book of Chinese Art*, offers an ideal starting point for specialist project students dealing with any of the multifarious aspects of Chinese visual arts and culture.

The Manchus, a semi-nomadic people from the north, conquered the declining Ming state in the seventeenth century and established the last dynastic period, known as the Qing (pronounced Ch'ing) dynasty (mid-seventeenth to early twentieth century), a substantial empire which included territories in Central Asia, Siberia and Tibet, as well as much of present-day China. The Manchu rulers embraced traditional Chinese cultural norms and, in a climate of political stability, economic prosperity resulted during which the visual and other arts enjoyed a long period of patronage and achievement. Chinese visual arts have, over the centuries, exhibited impressive innovation in techniques as well as styles. Chinese craftspeople, probably more than any other cultural group, have excelled in an impressive range of artistic achievement which has included bronze and other metal casting, lacquer work, ceramics and textiles. Over the dynasties a rich catalogue of motifs, patterns and symbols has been retained and used across the visual arts. Motifs, symbols and compositional arrangements have rarely been specific to a particular visual art form. Often, compositional arrangements used in ceramics, for example, are readily detectable in various textile forms. Substantial collections of Chinese patterned objects, mainly from the Qing dynasty (though quantities are also at hand from the Ming and other previous dynasties), have accumulated in museums across the world, and these collections offer a rich platform from which to identify and discuss what could be termed *traditional Chinese visual art forms*.

Throughout much of the second millennium CE, a wide variety of raw materials was used in the production of functional and luxury objects. Techniques of manufacture, such as silk processing, jade working and metal casting, were refined, and technical innovations such as cloisonné and enamel painting were adopted with much apparent success. Lacquer, bamboo, bronze, ivory, jade, various woods, amber, mother of pearl, soapstone, lapis lazuli and porcelain continued to be produced, and silk continued to play a paramount role at least economically.

Inscriptions on bone and bronze provide evidence for silk manufacture and trade dating to very ancient times. Such evidence abounds from both the Shang and Western Zhou dynasties and provides a wide-ranging reference to numerous textile techniques and products. The excavation of a Western Zhou tomb in 1970 at Weiyingzi in Liaoning province yielded over twenty silk fragments, including a twill-woven brocade of fifty-two warp threads and fourteen weft threads per centimetre (Liaoning Provincial Museum 1979: 36). The principal textile-patterning techniques associated with China since ancient times are embroidery, silk tapestry (or *ke-si*) weaving, brocade weaving and velvet weaving. Various styles of embroidery developed in different regions. Hann (2004) previously gave details.

The styles and forms of bronze vessels for ritualistic purposes continued for many centuries to make reference to ancient dynasties (especially the Shang dynasty). These ancient traditional forms had been augmented in the mid-first

millennium CE by items (cups, bowls and other utensils) imported from Central Asia, Persia and the Eastern Mediterranean (Leidy, Siu and Watt 1997: 3). The casting of gold and silver was adopted at a relatively late stage, in the middle of the first millennium CE. The adoption and development of cloisonné and painted enamels in China can be traced to around the fifteenth and seventeenth centuries respectively.

In the field of ceramics, continuous development was shown from ancient times. Relatively crude forms of ancient pottery, made by coiling, date back to several millennia BCE. The term *porcelain* is a collective term applied to finer forms of ceramic products. These finer forms were produced in large quantities by the last few centuries BCE, though there is a debate on the precise date of first manufacture and use. Various technical developments can be traced down through the various dynasties of the Common Era. These developments included kiln construction, combinations of clays and other raw materials, types of glaze used and knowledge of optimum temperatures for successful firing, as well as innovations in colour and patterning applications. Product types included bowls, tea caddies, tea pots, jars, dishes, vases and ornaments with animal and human forms. A bewilderingly large number of different ceramic types can be identified, some particular to specific dynasties and some to particular regions. Examples include *sancai* wares, made during the Tang dynasty in green, amber colour and cream/off-white; *jian* tea wares, with their characteristic surface texture described as like a hare's fur, produced in Fujian province; *ding* ware, an exceedingly fine porcelain produced in northern China in the late centuries of the first millennium

CE, and elegantly shaped with understated patterning either incised or stamped into the clay prior to the application of the almost transparent glaze. Throughout much of the second millennium CE, particularly during the Ming and Qing dynasties, ceramics played a major role in trade between China and lands to the west as well as Japan and Korea to the east.

Nephrite (a form of jade), which occurs in shades of green, yellow and white, was imported from Khotan and Yarkand (both in Central Asia), though indigenous to parts of China in the Neolithic period. Another form of jade, known as *jadeite* and native to Myanmar (Burma), was used also, but to a lesser extent. The use of jade in China was of importance throughout much of the second millennium CE, and of particular importance during the late sixteenth and seventeenth centuries. Sculpted items depicting human and animal forms, real, imagined and mythical, as well as bowls, cups and dishes of various kinds, chimes, writing sets and books composed of jade tablets were common. Other raw materials, including agate, coral, lapis lazuli, turquoise and malachite, were also carved, probably by the artisans familiar with jade carving.

The use of ivory and bone, carved as handles or small vessels and ornaments, can be traced to the sixth millennium BCE. Elephants indigenous to China during the Neolithic period were the initial source for ivory in ancient times. Imported ivory from other parts of Asia as well as Africa was traded for Chinese goods throughout much of the second millennium CE. The use of ivory in the visual arts, in the form of carved figures or small containers, as well as its application as inlays to wood furniture, flourished particularly during the seventeenth and eighteenth centuries. Carved figures with religious themes (Christian, Buddhist and Taoist) were common for both export and home use. Items carved from bamboo, various woods (including tropical hard woods), amber and rhinoceros horn were common also during much of the second millennium CE.

Chinese lacquer, used as a protective and decorative coating on objects from various materials, originates from the lacquer tree (*Rhus verniciflua*), native to central and southern China. Lacquer was applied as a liquid in a series of thin coats, each allowed to set in warm temperatures and relatively high humidity. Once set, lacquer provided resistance to water and also to cooking temperatures. By the early centuries of the second millennium CE, lacquer was used not just as a coating but also as a raw material to be incised, carved and burnished. Narrative compositions in architectural and landscape settings, inlaid with mother of pearl and other materials, were common.

motifs and symbols (cs 34)

A vast range of motifs appears in traditional Chinese visual arts: humans, mythical animals, plants and fruits, man-made objects, abstract line drawings and various calligraphic signs. Three important sources for motifs and symbols were Buddhism, Taoism and Confucianism. Compositions were regulated frequently by the imperial court or simply restricted by tradition (a strong force throughout the Qing dynasty). In many cases, subtle meanings were conveyed by the use of combinations of auspicious motifs or compositions (Figures 13.1–13.13).

Figure 13.1 Detail of Qing dynasty textile (University of Leeds International Textiles Archive)

Figure 13.2 Detail of Qing dynasty textile (University of Leeds International Textiles Archive)

Figure 13.3 Detail of Qing dynasty textile (University of Leeds International Textiles Archive)

Figure 13.4 Detail of Qing dynasty textile (University of Leeds International Textiles Archive)

Figure 13.5 Detail of Qing dynasty textile (University of Leeds International Textiles Archive)

Figure 13.6 Detail of Qing dynasty textile (University of Leeds International Textiles Archive)

Figure 13.7 Detail of Qing dynasty textile (University of Leeds International Textiles Archive)

Figure 13.8 Detail of Qing dynasty textile (University of Leeds International Textiles Archive)

Figure 13.9 Detail of Qing dynasty textile (University of Leeds International Textiles Archive)

Figure 13.10 Detail of Qing dynasty textile (University of Leeds International Textiles Archive)

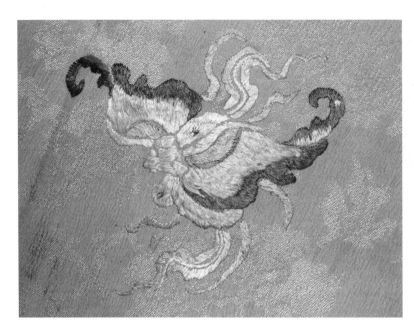

Figure 13.11 Detail of Qing dynasty textile (University of Leeds International Textiles Archive)

Figure 13.12 Detail of Qing dynasty textile (University of Leeds International Textiles Archive)

Figure 13.13 Detail of Qing dynasty textile (University of Leeds International Textiles Archive)

Buddhist, Taoist and Confucian symbols

Buddhist compositions included portraits of a Buddha figure. Often the Buddhist eight precious objects (*ba ji xiang*) would be depicted together or singly and in association with non-Buddhist motifs. The relevant eight Buddhist symbols are the wheel (or occasionally a bell), which symbolizes the law; the conch shell, which calls the faithful to prayer; the canopy, which represents protection and victory; the umbrella, which denotes nobility; the endless knot or knot of destiny, which symbolizes the path that leads to righteousness; the lotus, which stands for purity; the pair of fish, which means marriage and unity; the vase, which was reputed to contain the elixir of heaven and which symbolizes enduring peace (Zhong 1989: 38).

Taoist (also spelt Daoist) themes include the use of the so-called eight Taoist immortals or their associated emblems (*an ba xian*). These are as follows: Zhong Liquan, the patron of the military, with a fan or, occasionally, the peach of immortality; Zhang Guolao, a recluse and patron of artists and calligraphers, with a bamboo drum or tube and rods; Lu Dongbin, a scholar and patron of barbers, with sword; Chao Guejiou, the patron of actors and others associated with the theatre, with castanets; Li Tiaguai, the patron of the sick, with a gourd and staff; Hang Xiangzhi, the patron of musicians, with a flute; Lan Chaihe, the patron of florists and gardeners, with a flower basket; He Xiangu, the patron of housewives, with a lotus. (Zhong 1989: 38–9) (Figures 13.14a–h).

Motifs from Confucian or similar ethical origins included the five ethics (various pairs of birds, the father and son, the married couple, the brothers and friends). The eight secular, or precious, objects (*babao*), are generally listed as follows: the pearl, a symbol associated with the granting of wishes; the lozenge, a mark of victory; the *qing* or musical stone, indicating musical accomplishment; the coin, a sign of wealth; the rhinoceros horn, a

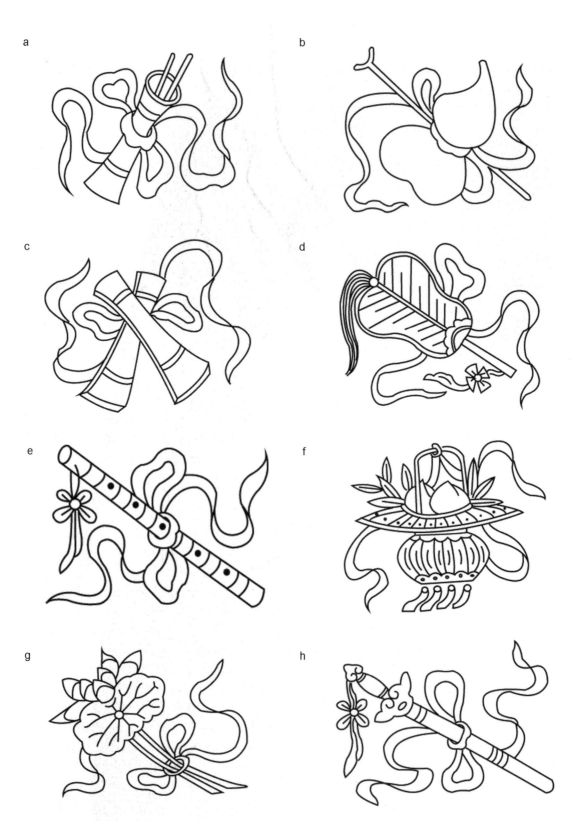

Figure 13.14a–h Each of the eight Taoist symbols is associated with an immortal spirit in human form. The symbols are tube and rods (a), gourd and staff (b), castanets (c), fan (d), flute (e), flower basket (f), lotus (g) and sword (h).

token of health; the mirror, which stands for un-broken conjugal happiness; the book, a token of scholarly learning; the artemisia leaf, representing good luck and the prevention of disease.

Calligraphic and homophonic motifs

Both written and spoken Chinese are sources of motifs and function as components of visual compositions. Many characters of Chinese script have a pictographic origin and, as a result, can be adapted readily in stylized form to the visual arts. Such motifs were used often during the Qing dynasty. A further important feature is the inclusion of numerous homophones in the language. As a result, auspicious phrases or ideas can be associated with correspondingly homophonic, but otherwise unrelated, objects. These proliferate in the Qing dynasty visual arts, often in the form of single objects and occasionally as a group of several objects. Examples of homophonic objects are: the *qing* or musical stone, for celebration (also a symbol of musical accomplishment); the magpie, for happiness; the vase, for peace; the lotus, for continuity; the osmanthus flower, for richness; the bat, for happiness (Zhong 1989: 40).

Examples of phrases which combine homophones are: *jin yu mang tang* (numerous offspring in the family), composed from a gold fish and crab-apple flowers; *ping shen san ji* (to be promoted by three ranks), composed of a vase containing three *ji* (halberds); *lian sheng guei zhi* (to have promising children), composed of a lotus, a boy holding a spray of osmanthus blossoms and occasionally another boy playing a *sheng* (a reed-like musical instrument) (Zhong 1989: 40). Note that occasionally the same motif (e.g. the vase), when combined with different groups of motifs, can symbolize something different.

Auspicious motifs and compositions

A wide range of geometric patterning is evident on Qing dynasty items. Key patterns were in widespread use on both woven and embroidered pieces. Botanical motifs were also used. Certain flowers were favoured, including the peony, the lotus, the chrysanthemum, the plum flower, and the crab-apple flower. Fruits included the *foshou* (or fingered citron), the pomegranate and the gourd. Pine or bamboo trees were also commonly depicted. The most frequently used mythological animal motifs were the dragon (*lung*), the unicorn (*qilin*) and the phoenix (or *feng huang*). All three are of ancient origin. As noted previously, the dragon (*lung*) is China's oldest mythological creature and featured on ancient bronzes long before the invention of writing (Walters 1995: 44). The dragon was deemed to be charged with *yang*, the positive principle of the cosmos, and was selected as a symbol of the emperor. Depending on the rank of the wearer, dragon motifs depicted on costumes would have five, four or three claws on each foot. Five-clawed motifs were reserved for the emperor and high-ranking officials. With the spread of Buddhism to China, symbolism associated with the motif was absorbed into the religion (Walters 1995: 45). The unicorn or *qilin* has been given various descriptions. The consensus appears to be: an animal with the body of a deer, the tail of an ox, the hooves of a horse, and with two horns (despite the associations with a unicorn). It is deemed the harbinger of great events and tradition claims its presence at the birth of Confucius. The Chinese phoenix, or *feng huang*, is the sacred bird of Chinese mythology and is generally depicted in a form similar to an ornamental pheasant. It was deemed to be charged with *yin*, the negative principle of the cosmos, and was adopted as the symbol for the empress. Other animal motifs include the lion, the deer, the bat, the crane, the *shoudai* bird (the paradise flycatcher), the pheasant, the wild goose, the mandarin duck, the kingfisher, the carp, the grasshopper, the mantis and the butterfly (Zhong 1989: 42).

For much of the Qing dynasty, civilian and military officials were required to wear cloth rank badges attached to the upper front and back of their garments. This practice had its origins in the Ming dynasty. Round badges, depicting dragon motifs, were the choice of imperial nobility. Meanwhile, civil officials were required to wear square badges, depicting various bird motifs, and military officials were required to wear badges with animal motifs. The ranking for each was as follows:

- First rank: white crane for civil officials and a unicorn for military officials.
- Second rank: golden pheasant for civil officials and lion for military officials.
- Third rank: peacock for civil officials and leopard for military officials.
- Fourth rank: wild goose for civil officials and tiger for military officials.
- Fifth rank: silver pheasant for civil officials and black bear for military officials.
- Sixth rank: egret for civil officials and panther for military officials.
- Seventh rank: mandarin duck for civil officials and rhinoceros for military officials.
- Eighth rank: quail for civil officials and rhinoceros (again) for military officials.
- Ninth rank: paradise flycatcher for civil officials and sea horse for military officials.

During the Qing dynasty, regulations for the use of certain motifs and symbols in costumes and other everyday objects were complex, and sets of bewildering rules indicate what was applicable for use by different social classes. Wilson's description of official court dress (principally during the Qing dynasty) is a useful starting point for students who wish to develop some knowledge of relevant regulations (V. Wilson 1986). For example, a bright yellow robe was reserved for use by the emperor, but occasionally a blue robe was used. The twelve symbols of authority, also known as the 'twelve imperial symbols', were depicted on the garment. These reputedly date back to the Western Zhou dynasty. They comprise the following symbols: the sun, the moon, a constellation of three stars, a mountain motif, a pair of dragons, a pheasant, a pair of bronze cups, water weed, grain (maybe millet), a flame, an axe and a symmetrical geometric symbol known as the *fu* symbol. Although all twelve, depicted together, were for the exclusive use of the emperor, lesser nobility were permitted designated selections from the twelve symbols.

ancient bronzes (cs 35)

China's Bronze Age began around 2000 BCE. According to Watt, Chinese Bronze Age culture and technology advanced at 'an astonishing speed' (1990: 13). Available evidence suggests that bronze casting in China was an independent discovery because of the dissimilarity of the technique when compared to techniques used elsewhere (Watt 1990: 13). In China, the casting of bronze was accomplished by a complex method known as the 'multiple piece-mould method' (Tregear 1995: 300–1), involving the production of several parts of a mould, which, when assembled, acted as the vessel for the molten bronze (approximately 76 per cent copper, 12 per cent tin and 12 per cent lead); when the bronze had solidified the moulds were removed. In ancient China, the designs on the bronze surface were achieved through the mould and were not applied later (as was the case elsewhere). The Hsia dynasty (regarded as a legendary dynasty, though named in traditional Chinese histories as the first dynasty) is occasionally associated with the earliest Bronze Age sites but, as Watt (1990: 14) pointed out, further archaeological evidence is required to confirm such a view. There is, however, ample archaeological evidence, including various forms of bronze artefact, associated with the Shang dynasty (fourteenth century to twelfth century BCE). Bronze was used extensively in decorated ritualistic objects. Although confined largely to Honan Province, the Shang state influenced developments in much of central and south-western China (Watt 1990: 15). The surface design on Shang dynasty bronzes is dominated by highly geometric, key-type designs, often with coiled terminals which appear animal-like (particularly dragon forms, but also deer, elephants, fish and felines of various kinds). Squared spirals (known as *lei wen*) were common. Tregear commented: 'The role of the bronze vessel changes gradually from ritual to status symbol and this is reflected in both motifs and shapes . . . Birds with curving plumes and crests were popular in east China and quadruped feline creatures or serpentine dragons make their appearance in the north and more metropolitan regions' (1995: 301).

Artefacts exhibiting Shang-type forms of patterning have been found in many areas in provinces adjacent to Honan. Such objects played a seemingly important role in ritual and ceremony and, according to Watt, bronze vessels 'with rich surface decoration held food and wine for sacrifices to the ancestor gods, and jade objects were used in ceremonies and offered as the most prestigious of gifts to gods and men' (Watt 1990: 15). Figures 13.15–13.24 illustrate examples of bronze objects from various periods.

Figure 13.15 Bronze ritual vessel, Shang dynasty, twelfth century BCE (British Museum)

Figure 13.16 Bronze ritual vessel, Shang dynasty, twelfth century BCE (British Museum)

Figure 13.17 Bronze ritual vessel, early to mid Western Zhou period, eleventh to tenth century BCE (British Museum)

Figure 13.19 Bronze bell, early Eastern Zhou period, seventh century BCE (British Museum)

Figure 13.18 Bronze ritual wine vessel, early Eastern Zhou period, eighth to seventh century BCE (British Museum)

Figure 13.20 Bronze bell, Eastern Zhou period, seventh century BCE (British Museum)

Figure 13.22 Bronze figure mounted on a mythical beast known as a chimera, Han dynasty, 206 BCE to 222 CE. May have acted as a base for a lamp (British Museum)

Figure 13.21 Bronze mirror, Han dynasty, 206 BCE to 222 CE (British Museum)

Figure 13.23 Bronze bell, Qing dynasty, 1644–1912
(British Museum)

Figure 13.24 Bronze bell, Qing dynasty, 1644–1912
(British Museum)

DISCUSSION OR ASSIGNMENT TOPICS

Ancient Bronzes

Discuss the production and use of bronze in ancient China (from around 500 BCE to around 500 CE). Making reference to illustrative material of your choice, discuss the geometric nature of patterns on bronze objects during the relevant period.

Dragon Robes

Assemble up to five images of so-called dragon robes. Identify the symbols on each and discuss the symmetry characteristics of the visual composition displayed on each of your selected items.

Qing Dynasty Visual Arts and Symbolism

With reference to the motifs used, discuss symbolism in the visual arts associated with Qing (1644–1912) China. Classify the wide range of motifs of relevance by origins (e.g. Buddhist, Taoist or Confucian etc.). Ensure that you do not simply provide a listing of motifs; full discussion is also required. Differentiate between calligraphic and homophonic motifs as well as the use of various forms of auspicious motifs and compositions. Where appropriate, support your answer by the addition of schematic or other drawn illustrations.

---

further reading

Allane, L. (1993). *Chinese Rugs. A Buyers Guide*, London: Thames and Hudson.

Bush, S. (1975). 'Thunder Monsters, Auspicious Animals, and Floral Ornament in Early Sixth-Century China', *Ars Orientalis*, 10: 19–33.

Jenyns, R.S. (1981). *Chinese Art*, Oxford: Phaidon.

Rawson, J. (ed.) (1992). *The British Museum Book of Chinese Art*, London: British Museum Press.

Tregear, M. (1995). 'Chinese Bronzes', in L. Gowing, ed., *A History of Art*, Rochester (Kent, UK): Grange Books, 300–1.

Walters, D. (1995). *Chinese Mythology. An Encyclopaedia of Myth and Legend*, London: Diamond Books.

Wilson, V. (1986). *Chinese Dress*, London: Bamboo Publishing and Victoria and Albert Museum.

14

east of east: Korea and Japan

Korea

Developments in the visual arts during the second millennium CE in Korea are generally considered under two specific dynasties: the Koryo (Goryeo) dynasty (early tenth to late fourteenth centuries) and the Chosun (Joseon) dynasty (late fourteenth to early twentieth centuries).

During much of the Koryo dynasty, a strong influence was exercised from China, and notable developments took place in the arts of painting and calligraphy and in the crafts of metalwork and wood carving. Probably most notable is the development of Korea's early form of green-glazed celadon wares, with associated techniques inherited from China. The production of celadon green-glazed ceramics during the Koryo dynasty was a move forward for Korean ceramic production as a whole. In particular, it represented a shift in how ceramics were perceived, moving from the belief that such objects were purely functional to one of believing that ceramics could exhibit refined aesthetic characteristics. A school of Buddhist stone carving developed, and numerous steles were erected in temples or open countryside, commemorating the memory of Zen masters. A dominant motif was a tortoise supporting a carved stone slab. Numerous Buddhist statues, often in the form of giant representations, were carved in groups of threes on rock faces or were sculpted from stone blocks.

During the Chosun dynasty, the administration of the country passed to the hands of a scholarly class who sat examinations based on those in China. During this dynasty, Confucianism gained a strong foothold, and a discipline and moderation were imposed which in turn led to a lack of innovation in the visual arts. On the other hand, as Auboyer and colleagues noted, 'the architecture of fortresses, monumental gateways, palaces, pavilions and Buddhist and Confucian temples (based at this point on the principles of astrology and geomancy) became simpler and more restrained. Sculpture became rather dull, and the wooden masks worn by shamanist dancers were lifeless compared with those made in previous centuries' (1994: 487). Developments in ceramic ware are notable. A particular type, known as *punch ong*, from a paste similar to that of celadon ware, was in everyday use. Commonly referred to by the Japanese name *mishima*, these wares were made in the south of the Korean peninsula from the fourteenth to the seventeenth centuries. A common end use was as tea bowls, prized by Japanese tea masters (Auboyer et al. 1994: 487). A Korean white porcelain type, decorated with cobalt (imported from China) and reserved largely for use by the aristocracy, was in demand by the Ming court (Auboyer et al. 1994: 487). Auboyer and colleagues noted a decline in the 'minor arts', but nonetheless acknowledged: 'Bronze bells, ritual objects, shaman masks, etc. continued to be produced, but in addition there appeared lacquered chests and caskets inlaid with mother-of-pearl, tortoise-shell and metal and a very special type of handicraft—the production of *hwagaks* or painted horn' (1994: 487).

Japan

When considering developments in the visual arts of Japan during the first and second millennium CE, five periods are worth identifying: the Heian period (late eighth century to late twelfth centuries); the Kamakura period (late twelfth century to second quarter of the fourteenth century); the Muromachi period (second quarter of the fourteenth century to third quarter of the sixteenth century); the Momoyama period (third quarter of the sixteenth century to first quarter of the seventeenth century); the Edo period (first quarter of the seventeenth century to third quarter of the nineteenth century).

The Heian period is characterized by refinement and elegance. A new capital known as Heian Kyo (site of present-day Kyoto) was established, with a layout modelled on the Chinese system of streets intersecting at right angles. Esoteric Buddhism exercised considerable influence on the nature of the arts generally. Influences from China gradually weakened and painting developed into two distinct styles: *kara-e* (painting in the Chinese manner) and *yamato-e* (painting in the Japanese manner) (Auboyer et al. 1994: 521). Pottery, known as *sue* pottery (fired at very high temperatures, and developed at least several hundred years previously), continued to be produced for use as urns, incense burners and other ceremonial items. The deities associated with Shinto beliefs began to be represented.

During the Kamakura period, Japanese Zen Buddhism exercised a strong influence on the nature of the visual arts. Realism was an important feature, and numerous sculptors and other artists were practising. Large numbers of palaces and monasteries were built, some influenced by Chinese or Indian styles (Auboyer et al., 1994: 522). A small amount of glazed pottery, influenced by Chinese styles, was produced for use by the aristocracy. Large domestic storage jars, portraits, religious scenes and illustrated scrolls were also produced.

In the Muromachi period, renewed contact was made with the Chinese Ming court, and Chinese influence in painting and calligraphy was evident. Zen Buddhist monks were actively involved in the production of illustrated scrolls with religious themes. The aristocracy commissioned groups of painters. Towards the middle of the sixteenth century, a Portuguese ship was wrecked off the southern part of the Japanese archipelago. Its crew was apparently the first large group of Europeans to have arrived in that part of Japan. In the centuries to follow, others would come, focussed on religious conversion or trade.

During the Momoyama period, tens of thousands of Japanese aristocracy, merchants and peasants converted to Christianity. The contact with Europeans gave rise to new art styles. This period was particularly noted for the large amounts of pottery produced. The aesthetics of the tea ceremony (and its architectural setting) were a major focus for development.

An important aspect of the Edo period was the tendency towards isolationism. Only a small number of authorized ships and individuals were allowed to enter or to leave Japan. This remained the case until the mid-nineteenth century. There appears to have been little significant development in the visual arts with the exception of ceramic manufacture and, towards the final decades of the period, resist-dyeing techniques of various kinds, all focussed on the surface patterns of textiles, particularly kimono fabrics

Korean roof tiles, stone lanterns and pagodas (cs 36)

Roof tiles were an important development as they were relatively cheap to produce and, in terms of fire safety, were superior to previous forms of roof covering. Often tiles would include impressions of mythological creatures of one kind or another, in the belief that these would ward off evil spirits and keep the occupants of the house protected (Figures 14.1–14.6).

Figure 14.2 Korean roof tile (National Museum, Seoul)

Figure 14.1 Korean roof tile (National Museum, Seoul)

Figure 14.3 Korean roof tile (National Museum, Seoul)

Figure 14.6 Korean roof tile in use (outskirts of Seoul)

Figure 14.4 Korean roof tile (National Museum, Seoul)

Stone lanterns are associated particularly with eastern Asia. In historical times they were found commonly in Korea (Figures 14.7–14.10). Traditional components may include the onion-shaped component at the very top of the object; the lotus-shaped support; a conical or pyramidal umbrella (occasionally with corners appearing to curl upwards) covering the fire box; the fire box; the part on which the fire box rests; a single post, often replaced by three legs. Occasionally further elements were added to the base. There are many subtypes. Occasionally carvings of deer or peonies decorated the fire box.

Figure 14.5 Korean roof tile (National Museum, Seoul)

Figure 14.7 Korean stone lantern, Seoul

Figure 14.8 Korean stone lantern, Seoul

Figure 14.10 Korean stone lantern, Seoul

Figure 14.9 Korean stone lantern, Seoul

The stupa evolved into a pagoda as Buddhism spread to the eastern part of Asia (Figures 14.11–14.13). In Korea, probably the most famous pagoda is the Gyeongcheonsa pagoda, which is thirteen metres high and with ten storeys (Figure 14.14). An inscription on the first storey states that the pagoda was built/created in the mid-fourteenth century, at the now lost Gyeongcheonsa temple. Made from marble rather than granite (the latter being more usual), panels on its tiered construction are carved with Buddhas, bodhisattavas, flowers and arabesque designs. In 1962, this ten-storey monument was designated a national treasure by the South Korean government.

Figure 14.11 Korean stone stupa, Seoul

Figure 14.12 Korean stone pagoda, Seoul

After the pagoda's return from Japan (where it had been taken during the most recent Japanese occupation of Korea), the monument was placed in the grounds of Gyongbokgung Palace, but because of the detrimental air pollution of the time the monument was moved and erected on the ground floor in the National Museum of Korea in Seoul, where it stood in the early twenty-first century.

Figure 14.13 Korean stone pagoda, Seoul

Figure 14.14 Ten-story pagoda, Goryo period, fourteenth century (National Museum, Seoul)

katagami stencils (cs 37)

The processes associated with the dyeing of textiles in Japan are highly sophisticated and developed over many centuries. *Katazome* is a general term that includes several Japanese dyeing techniques that use stencils, often to create repeating patterns for use on kimonos. *Katagami* stencils are hand-cut from hand-made paper stiffened with *shibugaki* (persimmon juice). Free-standing motifs are held together with fine silk (Figures 14.15–14.30).[1]

Figure 14.15 Japanese *katagami* (stencil) used for resist printing on textiles, late nineteenth to early twentieth century (University of Leeds International Textiles Archive)

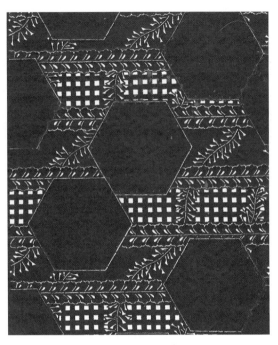

Figure 14.17 Japanese *katagami* (stencil) used for resist printing on textiles, late nineteenth to early twentieth century (University of Leeds International Textiles Archive)

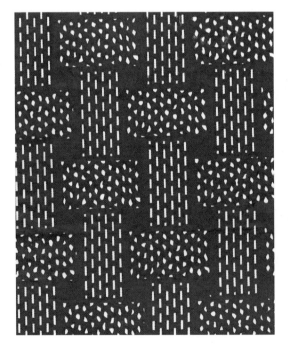

Figure 14.16 Japanese *katagami* (stencil) used for resist printing on textiles, late nineteenth to early twentieth century (University of Leeds International Textiles Archive)

Figure 14.18 Japanese *katagami* (stencil) used for resist printing on textiles, late nineteenth to early twentieth century (University of Leeds International Textiles Archive)

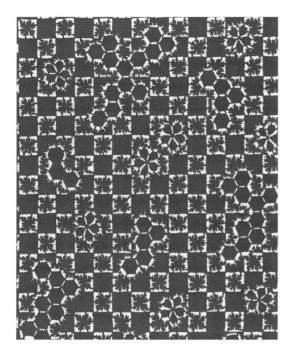

Figure 14.19 Japanese *katagami* (stencil) used for resist printing on textiles, late nineteenth to early twentieth century (University of Leeds International Textiles Archive)

Figure 14.21 Japanese *katagami* (stencil) used for resist printing on textiles, late nineteenth to early twentieth century (University of Leeds International Textiles Archive)

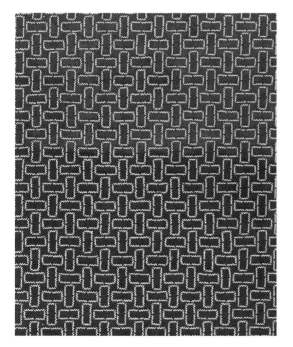

Figure 14.20 Japanese *katagami* (stencil) used for resist printing on textiles, late nineteenth to early twentieth century (University of Leeds International Textiles Archive)

Figure 14.22 Japanese *katagami* (stencil) used for resist printing on textiles, late nineteenth to early twentieth century (University of Leeds International Textiles Archive)

Figure 14.23 Japanese *katagami* (stencil) used for resist printing on textiles, late nineteenth to early twentieth century (University of Leeds International Textiles Archive)

Figure 14.25 Japanese *katagami* (stencil) used for resist printing on textiles, late nineteenth to early twentieth century (University of Leeds International Tevxtiles Archive)

Figure 14.24 Japanese *katagami* (stencil) used for resist printing on textiles, late nineteenth to early twentieth century (University of Leeds International Textiles Archive)

Figure 14.26 Japanese *katagami* (stencil) used for resist printing on textiles, late nineteenth to early twentieth century (University of Leeds International Textiles Archive)

Figure 14.27 Japanese *katagami* (stencil) used for resist printing on textiles, late nineteenth to early twentieth century (University of Leeds International Textiles Archive)

Figure 14.29 Japanese *katagami* (stencil) used for resist printing on textiles, late nineteenth to early twentieth century (University of Leeds International Textiles Archive)

Figure 14.28 Japanese *katagami* (stencil) used for resist printing on textiles, late nineteenth to early twentieth century (University of Leeds International Textiles Archive)

Figure 14.30 Japanese *katagami* (stencil) used for resist printing on textiles, late nineteenth to early twentieth century (University of Leeds International Textiles Archive)

The word *katagami* refers to the method of making paper stencils, as well as the stencils themselves. Traditionally, the production of the stencils was centred on the city of Ise in Mie Prefecture. Multiple sheets of thin paper were laminated together and waterproofed with persimmon tannin. Often a fine net of hairs was laid between two of the layers; this net acted as a support for the stencil. The final rectangular sheet typically measured around 70 centimetres by around 40 centimetres. A predetermined composition (memorized, reproduced from a sketch or carefully measured if of a repeating nature) was then cut or punched from this sheet, leaving paper where a background (or ground colour) was intended in the final piece.

In the nineteenth and twentieth centuries, collectors and museums in Europe and North America amassed large collections of *katagami*. Meanwhile in Japan, where at the time they were not considered as an art form, quantities of *katagami* were simply destroyed. Japanese stencil and woodblock printing influenced many Western artists and designers, including Vincent van Gogh, James McNeill Whistler, Louis Tiffany and Frank Lloyd Wright.

Various compositions exist, some with a free-standing element and others involving repetition of motifs which may be geometric shapes, animals, flowers, landscapes or everyday objects.

DISCUSSION OR ASSIGNMENT TOPICS

Korean Roof Tiles

Using illustrative material of your choice, discuss the symbolism and the symmetry of traditional Korean roof tiles.

Katagami Symmetry

Discuss the symmetry characteristics of the designs depicted on the *katagami* stencil images included in this chapter.

---

further reading

Anon (1967). 'Japanese Resist-dyeing Techniques', *CIBA Review*, 4.

Auboyer, J., Beurdeley, M., Boisselier, J. Massonaud, C. and Rousset, H. (1994). *Forms and Styles: Asia*, Koln: Evergreen (Benedikt Taschen Verlag GmbH).

Hornung, C. (1985). *Traditional Japanese Stencil Designs*, New York: Dover, 1985.

McBride, R. D. (2008). *Domesticating the Dharma: Buddhist Cults and the Hwaom Synthesis in Silla Korea*, Honolulu: University of Hawai'i Press.

Nelson, S. M. (1993). *The Archaeology of Korea*, Cambridge: Cambridge University Press.

Portal, J. (2000). *Korea—Art and Archaeology*, London: British Museum Press, 2000.

Tuer, A. W. (1967). *Traditional Japanese Patterns*, New York: Dover, 1967.

note

1. The term *resist dyeing* refers to a range of techniques used in the patterning of textiles by dyeing preselected areas on a fabric's (or a yarn's) surface. This selective dyeing, which involves preventing the dye from reaching parts of the textile surface, is permitted by knotting, folding, tying, stitching thread into the fabric and pulling it tight or applying resist materials such as wax, mud, starch or various pastes, occasionally using stencils or shields. Variants of resist dyeing are found worldwide and have been used to decorate textiles throughout much of recorded textile history.

Stencils can be used for direct application of dye paste to a textile surface, but it was more usual to use a resist-dyeing technique, which involved the application (by spatula) of a resist paste (made from rice) to the textile through the openings in the stencil. When the resist paste was dry, the textile was immersed in a dye bath, and the colour took only to those areas of the textile not covered with the resist paste.

To ensure precise repetition and registration, each laminated and cut sheet had two small pinholes that served as registration marks. At each stage of printing a fine point was passed through each of the two holes and aligned with the corresponding marks left by the previous impression. In this way, precise design registration was ensured. Stencils could be used either vertically or horizontally.

Stencils were used occasionally in association with other techniques, including direct printing, or free-hand drawing techniques. *Bingata* prints were renowned for their bright colours and well-defined lines as well as their depiction of numerous animal, plant and landscape motifs (Anon 1967: 27). The term *yuzen* refers to a complex combination of printing and dyeing operations, often combined with free-hand application of details. With *yuzen*, stencils were used first to print motifs in one or more colours. Additional colours were painted by hand. Each motif was then covered with resist paste and the ground (or background) colour was then applied by squeegee. It has been observed that 'stencils produce full, sharply defined, bold and beautiful figures superior to the somewhat hazy-edged effects obtained' using other resist-dyeing methods (Anon 1967: 29).

Stencils were used also with a dye-pouring technique known as *chosen*. With this method, resist paste was applied through the stencil several times across a white, un-dyed textile which subsequently was folded the equivalent number of times to the number of applications, with each fold corresponding to the length and breadth of the stencilled area. Dye liquor was then poured on to the folded textile package and allowed to penetrate down through the textile, dyeing only those areas not covered by resist paste (Anon 1967: 29). The result was a single-colour image on a white background.

15

conclusion

Since the publication of *The Grammar of Ornament* in 1856, scholars interested in motifs and patterns have had a tendency to produce a Linnaean-type classification system. It is the contention here that this is indeed a useful first step, and that an accurate taxonomic ordering and classification, based, for example, on whether or not a motif or pattern is floral, animal, abstract or geometric and so forth can contribute to our understanding of the visual arts. Such classifications and descriptions, however, fail to account for the possibility that the visual arts (including motifs and patterns) may have a further dimension of meaning not readily obvious to cultural outsiders. It has been the intention in this present book to explore to a small degree how this encoded meaning may be accessed by considering the underlying geometry of the object or group of objects under examination.

It is well established that symmetry is a culturally sensitive parameter and that different cultures and societies have their own unique symmetry preferences. This relationship unfolds when representative selections of patterns from different cultural settings are classified with respect to their symmetry characteristics. Further to this, various eminent scholars accept that underlying symmetry characteristics in the visual arts aid the communication of something beyond surface appearance, an encoded message to be read by adherents of the source culture or society (Washburn

2004). This communication may be subliminal or obvious immediately to those holding membership; otherwise the uninitiated viewer may simply see ornamentation or decoration consisting of a group of motifs or patterns, which are classed as floral, animal, abstract or geometric and so forth.

Underlying geometric symmetry of repeating patterns can be assessed and classified by reference to standard pattern-symmetry classification (and its simplifications) or, with nonrepeating compositions, aided by reference to the degree of reflection symmetry, for example. An important goal is to understand further how the structural geometry underpinning various visual art forms communicate certain deeply held cultural rules.

Most observers readily accept that visual symbols also incorporate meaning, which may be obvious to some but not to others, and that many symbols are peculiar to different cultures and societies. There appears therefore to be no significant antagonism, at least in the mind of this author, between the role of symbols and the role of other statements in the visual arts (motifs, regular patterns or nonrepeating compositions). The understanding of each is a matter of being able to decode the intended meaning, which is easier for those with knowledge of the culture or society in which the symbol or other visual statement has been created. Both symbols and other visual statements can act as intermediaries and may encode or encapsulate meaning beyond what is obvious to cultural outsiders; those with knowledge of the relevant source culture, however, have the ability to pick up these meanings or cultural messages. It is the contention here, therefore, that most visual arts incorporate a symbolism, or underlying meaning, in a similar way to common visual symbols generated historically, for example, in most European cultures.

It is well established that different cultures express different underlying geometric preferences in their visual art forms. It seems also that a certain geometric adherence or continued selection of these preferences is evident historically, and that this has affected all cultures and societies involved to a greater or lesser extent in the visual arts. The reasons for continued selection of underlying geometric structures in the visual arts are probably similar to those identified by Purves when considering persistence of varieties of architectural spaces, as due to 'an elusive web of conscious and unconscious needs, desires and associations' (1982). Geometric adherence or persistence is thus when visual forms resonate with such strength that they are retained again and again. They encapsulate what may be considered as 'traditional'. Seen in symmetry terms they are the symmetry preferences of the given culture or society. Occasionally however, some significant form of cultural change in the society may occur, possibly through the diffusion and adoption of new religious beliefs; as a result the dominant persistent forms, and associated symmetry preferences, develop or change as a result. The identification of underlying symmetry characteristics can thus be used as an indicator of cultural adherence, continuity and change and, possibly also, as a measure of diffusion in the visual arts and architecture from culture to culture or society to society, all subject of course to the availability of representative sources of data.

DISCUSSION TOPIC

Catalogue Entries

Select ten object illustrations from at least three chapters of this book. Using the nine-point framework presented in Chapter 1, produce a series of catalogue entries for your selected objects. These entries should be understandable to a general public audience.

references

Abas, S. J. and Salman, A. S. (1995). *Symmetries of Islamic Geometrical Patterns*, London: World Scientific.

Ackerman, P. (1955). 'Persian Textiles', *CIBA Review*, 9: 3507–35.

Adamson, G., Riello, G. and Teasley, S. (2011). *Global Design History*, London: Routledge.

Albenda, P. (1978). 'Assyrian Carpets in Stone', *The Journal of the Ancient Near East Society*, 10: 1–34.

Allane, L. (1993). *Chinese Rugs: A Buyers Guide*, London: Thames and Hudson.

Ames, F. (1986). *The Kashmir Shawl*, Woodbridge, Suffolk, (UK): Antique Collectors' Club.

Anon (1874). 'The Alhambra, at Granada, Spain', *The Aldine*, 7 (11): 214–15.

Anon (1967). 'Japanese Resist-dyeing Techniques', *CIBA Review*, 4: 24.

Ariswara, A. (1993). *Prambanan*, 3rd ed., translated by Lenah Matius. Jakarta: P. T. Intermasa.

Arnheim, R. (1988). 'Symmetry and the Organisation of Form: A Review Article', *Leonardo*, 21 (3): 173–276.

Aruz, J., Farkas, A., Alekseev, A. and Korolkova, E., (2001). *The Golden Deer of Eurasia: Scythian and Sarmatian Treasures from the Russian Steppes*, The State Hermitage, Saint Petersburg, and the Archaeological Museum, Ufa. New York: Metropolitan Museum of Art.

Aruz, J. with Wallenfels, R. (eds.) (2003). *Art of the First Cities: The Third Millennium* B.C. *from the Mediterranean to the Indus*, New Haven, CT: Yale University Press.

Ascher, M. (2000). 'Ethnomathematics for the Geometry Curriculum', in C. A. Gorini, ed., *Geometry at Work: Papers in Applied Geometry,* MMA Notes no. 53: 59–63.

Askari, N. and Crill, R. (1997). *Colours of the Indus: Costume and Textiles of Pakistan*, London: Merrel Holberton and Victoria and Albert Museum.

Atmadi, P. (1988). *Some Architectural Design Principles of Temples in Java: A Study through the Buildings Projection on the Reliefs of Borobudur Temple*, Yogyakarta (Java, Indonesia): Gajah Mada University Press.

Auboyer, J., Beurdeley, M., Boisselier, J., Massonaud, C. and Rousset, H. (1994). *Forms and Styles: Asia*, Köln: Evergreen (Benedikt Taschen Verlag GmbH).

Azarpay, G., Lambert, W. G., Heimpel, W. and Kilmer, A. D. (1987). 'Proportional Guidelines in Ancient Near Eastern Art', *Journal of Near Eastern Studies*, 46 (3): 183–213.

Baer, E. (1985). 'The Mihrab in the Cave of the Dome of the Rock', *Muqarnas*, 3: 8–19.

Bafna, S. (2000). 'On the Idea of the Mandala as a Governing Device in Indian Architectural Tradition', *Journal of the Society of Architectural Historians*, 59 (1): 26–49.

Balbás, L. T. (1951). 'Bibliography of Spanish Muslim Art 1939–1946', *Ars Islamica*, 15/16: 165–85.

Ballard, C. (1988). 'Dudumahan: A Rock Art Site on Kai Kecil, Southeast Moluccas', *Bulletin of the Indo-Pacific Prehistory Association*, 8: 139–61.

Ballard, C., Bradley, R., Nordenborg, M., Myhre, A. and Wilson, M. (2003). 'The Ship as Symbol in the

Prehistory of Scandinavia and Southeast Asia',
World Archaeology, 35 (3): 385–403.

Bargebuhr, F. P. (1956). 'The Alhambra Palace of the
Eleventh Century', *Journal of the Warburg and
Courtauld Institutes*, 19 (3/4): 192–258.

Barista, H. O. (1978). *Techniques in Turkish Embroideries*, Ankara: Technical Teacher Training College.

Barista, H. O. (1984). *Turk Isleme Sanati Tarihi (The History of Turkish Embroidery)*, Ankara: Gazi Universi-
tesi Basin.

Barnes, G. L. (1995). 'An Introduction to Buddhist Archaeology', *World Archaeology*, 27 (2):165–82.

Barraud, C. (1985). 'The Sailing-boat: Circulation and
Values in the Kei Islands, Indonesia', in R. H.
Barnes, D. de Coppet and R. J. Parkin (eds.),
*Contexts and Levels: Anthropological Essays on
Hierarchy*, JASO Occasional Papers No. 4. Oxford:
Anthropological Society of Oxford, 117–30.

Bataille, G. (2005). *The Cradle of Humanity: Prehistoric
Art and Culture*, New York: Zone Books.

Bauman, J. (1987). *Central Asian Carpets: Study Guide*,
Islamabad: Asian Study Group.

Baumer, C. (2000). *Southern Silk Road: In the Footsteps
of Sir Aurel Stein and Sven Hedin*, Bangkok: Orchid
Press.

Beach, M. C. (2007). 'The Ear Commands the Story:
Exploration and Imagination on the Silk Road', *Art
Institute of Chicago Museum Studies*, 33 (1): 8–19,
90.

Bellingham, D., Whittaker, D. and Grant, J. (1992). *Myths
and Legends*, London: New Burlington Books.

Bennett, I. (1972). *Book of Oriental Carpets and Rugs*,
London: Hamlyn.

Bennett, I. (1978). *Rugs and Carpets of the World*, London: Quarto Publishing.

Bentley, J. H. (1993). *Old World Encounters: Cross-
Cultural Contacts and Exchange in Pre-Modern
Times*, New York: Oxford University Press.

Bentley, J. H. (1996). 'Cross-Cultural Interaction and
Periodization in World History', *The American Historical Review*, 101 (3): 749–70.

Benzel, K. Graff, S. B., Rakic, Y. and Watts, E. W.
(2010). *Art of the Ancient Near East: A Resource
for Educators*, New York: The Metropolitan Museum of Art.

Berendt, K. A. (2007). *The Art of Gandhara in the Metropolitan Museum of Art*, New York: Metropolitan
Museum of Art.

Berker, N. (1979). 'Turk El Islemelerinde Semboller'
('Symbolism in Turkish Embroidery'), *Sanat Dunyamiz*, cilt. (vol.) 3, sayi. (no.) 15: 32–4, 47.

Berker, N. (1981). *Islemeler (Embroideries)*, Istanbul: Yapi
Kredi Bankasi Kultur ve Sanat Yayinlari, Tifdruk.

Berker, N. (1991). *The Turkish Embroidery*, Istanbul:
Yapi Kredi Bank Press.

Bernet Kempers, A. J. (1959). *Ancient Indonesian Art*,
Cambridge, MA: Harvard University Press.

Berry, B. Y. (1932). 'Old Turkish Towels', *Art Bulletin,
College Art Association of America*, 14: 344–58.

Bilgrami, N. (1990). *Sindh Jo Ajrak*, Karachi: Department
of Culture and Tourism, Government of Sindh.

Blaut, J. M. (1987). 'Diffusionism: Uniformitarian Critique', *Annals of the Association of American Ge-
ographers*, 77 (1): 30–47.

Boas, F. (1924). 'Evolution or Diffusion', *American Anthropologist*, 26 (3): 340–4.

Bochert, H. and Gombrich, R. (1984). *The World of
Buddhism*, London: Thames and Hudson.

Böhmer, H. and Thompson, J. (1991). 'The Pazyryk
Carpet: A Technical Discussion', *Notes in the History of Art*, 10 (4): 30–6.

Bonani, G., Hajdas, I., Rouff, U., Seifert, M., Molodin,
V. and Sljusarenko, I., (2001). 'Dendrochronologi-
cal and Radiocarbon Dating of the Scythian Burial
Place in the Pazyryk Valley in the Altai Mountains,
South Siberia', *Radiocarbon*, 43 (2B): 1.

Boone, J. L. and Benco, N. L. (1999). 'Islamic Settlement in North Africa and the Iberian Peninsula', *Annual Review of Anthropology*, 28: 51–71.

Boulnois, L. (1966). *The Silk Road*, translated by D. Chamberlain, New York: E. P. Dutton.

Bowie, T. (2006). *The Medieval Sketchbook of Villard de Honnecourt*, New York: Dover.

Brotton, J. (2012). *A History of the World in Twelve Maps*, London: Allen Lane.

Broug, E. (2008). *Islamic Geometric Patterns*, London: Thames and Hudson.

Brunes, T. (1967). *The Secret of Ancient Geometry and Its Uses*, 2 vols., Copenhagen: Rhodos.

Bucher, F. (1968). 'Design in Gothic Architecture: A Preliminary Assessment', *Journal of the Society of Architectural Historians*, 27 (1): 49–71.

Bühler, A. (1942). 'Ikats', *CIBA Review*, 44: 1586–611.

Bush, S. (1975). 'Thunder Monsters, Auspicious Animals, and Floral Ornament in Early Sixth-Century China', *Ars Orientalis*, 10: 19–33.

Butler, A. (1983). *Encyclopedia of Embroidery Techniques*, London: Batsford.

Calter, P. (2000). 'Sun Disk, Moon Disk', in C. A. Gorini (ed.), *Geometry at Work, MAA Notes* no. 53: 12–19.

Campana, M. (1969). *Oriental Carpets*, London: Hamlyn.

Carr, M. (1990). 'Chinese Dragon Names', *Linguistics of the Tibeto-Burman Area*, 13 (2): 87–189.

Cecil-Edwards, A. (1983). *The Persian Carpet*, London: Duckworth.

Celal, M. (1939). *Turk Islemeleri* (*Turkish Embroideries*), Istanbul: Kenan Masimevi ve Klise Fabrikasi.

Chang, K. (1973). *Inscribed Bronzes of the Shang and Chou: A Comprehensive Study*, Taipei: Nankang, 168–88.

Chen, Y. and Liu, S. (1980). 'The Excavation Bulletin of Gureixi Cave Burials in Jianxi Province', *Wenwu (Cultural Relics)*, 11: 15.

Chen, Y. and Zhang, S. (1982). 'The Warring States Silks Excavated from Suanwackan Tomb No 1, Masan, Jianling', *Wenwu (Cultural Relics)*, 10: 10.

Chen, Z. (1961). *References to the History of Recent Industrialisation in China*, vol. 4, Peking: Sanlian Press, 130–2.

Ch'en, K.K.S. (1968). *Buddhism: The Light of Asia*, Woodbury, NY: Barron's Educational Series.

Chitham, R. (2005). *The Classical Orders of Architecture*, 2nd ed., Amsterdam: Elsevier.

Chmelnizkij, S. (1989). 'Methods of Constructing Geometric Ornamental Systems in the Cupola of the Alhambra', *Muqarnas*, 6: 43–9.

Christian, D. (2000). 'Silk Roads or Steppe Roads? The Silk Roads in World History', *Journal of World History*, 11 (1):1–26.

Clabburn, P. (1981). *Shawls in Imitation of the Indian*, Shire Album Series, no. 77, Risborough (Buckinghamshire, UK): Shire Publications.

Coleman, H. (2008). *The Textiles of Bali and Nusa Tenggara*, Leeds: University of Leeds International Textiles Archive.

Collins, P. (2008). *Assyrian Palace Sculptures*, London: British Museum Press.

Cook, T. A. ([1914] 1979). *The Curves of Life*, London: Constable and Co. Reprint, New York: Dover.

Cooper, J. C. (1978). *An Illustrated Encyclopaedia of Traditional Symbols*, London: Thames and Hudson.

Crystal, E. (1985). 'The soul that is seen: The Tau Tau as shadow of death, reflection of life in Toraja tradition', in J. Feldman (ed.), *The Eloquent Dead: Ancestral Sculpture of Indonesia and Southeast Asia*, Los Angeles: UCLA Museum of Cultural History, 129–46.

Cummings, J. and Wassman, B. (2001). *Buddhist Stupas in Asia: The Shape of Perfection*, with foreword by A. F. Thurman, London: Lonely Planet Publications.

Curtin, P. D. (1985). *Cross-Cultural Trade in World History*, Cambridge: Cambridge University Press.

Curtis, J. (2000). *Ancient Persia*, London: British Museum Press.

Curtis, J. and Tallis, N. (2005). *Forgotten Empire: The World of Ancient Persia*, London: British Museum Press.

Davies, P. (1989). *The Penguin Guide to the Monuments of India*, vol. II. London: Viking.

Davis, D. D. (1983). 'Investigating the Diffusion of Stylistic Innovations', *Advances in Archaeological Method and Theory*, 6: 53–89.

Davis-Kimball, J., Murphy, E. M., Koryakova, L. and Yablonsky, L. T. (eds.) (2000). *Kurgans, Ritual Sites and Settlements: Eurasian Bronze and Iron Age*, New York: BAR Series.

D'Azevedo, W. L. (1958). 'A Structural Approach to Esthetics: Towards a Definition of Art in Anthropology', *American Anthropologist*, 60 (4): 702–14.

Deetz, J. (1965). *The Dynamics of Stylistic Change in Arikara Ceramics*, Illinois Studies in Anthropology, no. 4, Urbana: University of Illinois Press.

De Montequin, F.-A. (1987). 'Muslim Spain and the Maghrib: The Artistic Relationship in the Amoravid and Almohad Periods', *Bulletin (British Society for Middle Eastern Studies)*, 14 (2): 162–71.

Diyarbekirli, N. (1972). *Hun's Sanati (Hun's Art)*, Istanbul: Milli Egitim Basimevi (National Education Press).

Djoemena, N. S. (1986). *Batik: Its Mystery and Meaning*, Jakarta: Penerbit Djambatan.

Donahue, L. O. (1981). *Encyclopedia of Batik Designs*, London: Cornwall Books.

Dudley, C. J. (2010). *Canterbury Cathedral, Aspects of its Sacramental Geometry*, London: Xlibris.

Dumarcay, J. (1989). *The Temples of Java*, edited and translated by Michael Smithies, Singapore: Oxford University Press.

Durul, Y. (1979). 'Isleme Sanatinda Uckur ve Makramalar' ('Embroidered Napkins and Waistbands'), *Sanat Dunyamiz*, cilt. (vol.) 3, sayi. (no.) 15: 12–21.

Ecker, H. (2004). *Caliphs and Kings: The Art and Influence of Islamic Spain*, Washington, DC: Arthur M. Sackler Gallery and the Smithsonian Institute.

Edmonson, M. S. (1961). 'Neolithic Diffusion Rates', *Current Anthropology*, 2 (2): 71–102.

Eiland, M., Jr, and Eiland M. (1998). *Oriental Rugs: A Complete Guide*, London: Lawrence King.

Elam, K. (2001). *Geometry of Design: Studies in Proportion and Composition*, New York: Princeton Architectural Press.

Else, J. (1988). 'A Composite of Indian Textiles: Tradition and Technology', *Ars Textrina*, 10: 71–84.

Erickson, B. (1986). 'Art and Geometry: Proportioning Devices in Pictorial Composition', *Leonardo*, 19 (3): 211–15.

Erikson, J. (1968). *Mātā ni Pachedi (Temple Cloth of the Mother Goddess)*, Ahmedabad: National Institute of Design and New Order Book Company.

Ettinghausen, R. (1954). 'Notes on the Lusterware of Spain', *Ars Orientalis*, 1: 133–56.

Fage, J. S. (2001). *A History of Africa*, 4th ed., London: Routledge.

Feltham, H. (2010). *Lions, Silks and Silver: The Influence of Sasanian Persia*, Sino-Platonic Papers, number 206, Philadelphia: University of Pennsylvania, Department of East Asian Languages and Civilizations.

Field, R. (2004). *Geometric Patterns from Islamic Art and Architecture*, Norfolk (UK): Tarquin Publications.

Finkel, I. L. and Seymour, M. J. (eds.) (2008). *Babylon: Myth and Reality*, London: British Museum Press.

Finkel, I. L. and Seymour, M. J. (2009). *Babylon: City of Wonders*, London: British Museum Press.

Fischer, J. L. (1961). 'Art Styles as Cultural Cognitive Maps', *American Anthropologist* (New Series) 63 (1): 79–93.

Fletcher, R. (2004). 'Musings on the Vesica Piscis', *Nexus Network Journal*, 6 (2): 95–110.

Fletcher, R. (2005). 'Six +One', *Nexus Network Journal*, 7 (1): 141–60.

Fletcher, R. (2006). 'The Golden Section', *Nexus Network Journal*, 8 (1): 67–89.

Foltz, R. C. (2010). *Religions of the Silk Road: Premodern Patterns of Globalization*, New York: Macmillan.

Fontana, D. (1993). *The Secret Language of Symbols*, San Francisco: Chronicle Books.

Fontana, D. (2005). *Meditation with Mandalas*, London: Duncan Baird Publishers.

Forshee, J. (2001). *Between the Folds: Stories of Cloth, Lives, and Travels from Sumba*, Honolulu: University of Hawai'i Press,

Franck, I. M. and Brownstone, D. M. (1986). *The Silk Road: A History*, New York: Facts on File.

Freeman-Grenville, G.S.P. and Munro-Hay, S. C. (2006). *Islam: An Illustrated History*, New York and London: Continuum.

Friedrich, M. H. (1970). 'Design Structure and Social Interaction: Archaeological Implications of an Ethnographic Analysis', *American Antiquity*, 35 (3): 332–43.

Gans-Ruedin, E. (1971). *Modern Oriental Carpets*, London: Thames and Hudson.

Gantzhorn, V. (1998). *Oriental Carpets*, Cologne: Taschen.

Garfield, S. (2012). *On the Map: Why the World Looks Like It Does*, London: Profile Books.

Gervis, P. (1954). *This is Kashmir*, London: Cassell and Co. Ltd.

Ghyka, M. ([1946] 1977). *The Geometry of Art and Life*, New York: Sheed and Ward. Reprint, New York: Dover.

Gittinger, M. S. (1972). *A Study of the Ship Cloths of South Sumatra: Their Design and Usage*, PhD thesis, Columbia University, New York.

Gittinger, M. S. (1982). *Master Dyers to the World: Technique and Trade in Early Indian Dyed Cotton Textiles*, Washington, DC: The Textile Museum.

Gittinger, M. S. (1985). *Splendid Symbols: Textiles and Tradition in Indonesia*, Singapore: Oxford University Press.

Gombrich, E. H. (1979). *The Sense of Order*, London: Phaidon, 1979.

Gonul, M. (n.d.). *Turk Eliseri Sanati XVI–XIX Yuzyil (Turkish Handicrafts 16–19th Centuries)*, Ankara: Is Bankasi Kultur Yayinlari (Is Bank Cultural Press).

Gostelow, M. (1975). *A World of Embroidery*, London: Mills and Boon.

Grabar, O. (1973). *The Formation of Islamic Art*, New Haven, CT and London: Yale University Press.

Grabar, O. (1992). *The Mediation of Ornament*, Princeton, NJ: Princeton University Press.

Grabsky, P. (1999). *The Lost Temple of Java*, London: Orion Books.

Gray, B. (ed.) (1981). *The Arts of India*, Oxford: Phaidon Press.

Grosier, J. B. (1989). *The World of the Ancient Chinese*, Paris: Minerva.

Guy, J. (1998). *Woven Cargoe: Indian Textiles in the East*, London: Thames and Hudson.

Hambidge, J. ([1926], [1928], 1967). *The Elements of Dynamic Symmetry*, New York: Dover.

Hamzuri, D. (1989). *Batik Klasik*, Jakarta: Penerbit Djambatan.

Hann, M. A. (1982). *The Economics of Technological Change*, Textile Progress Series, vol. 11, no. 3, Manchester: The Textile Institute.

Hann, M. A. (1987). *Fashion: An Interdisciplinary Review*, Textile Progress Series, vol. 16, no. 4, Manchester: The Textile Institute.

Hann, M. A. (1992a). 'Unity in Diversity: The Batiks of Java', *Ars Textrina*, 18: 157–70.

Hann, M. A. (1992b). 'Symmetry in Regular Repeating Patterns: Case Studies from Various Cultural Settings', *Journal of the Textile Institute*, 83 (4): 579–90.

Hann, M. A. (2003a). 'The Fundamentals of Pattern Structure. Part I: Woods Revisited', *Journal of the Textile Institute*, 94 (part 2, nos 1 and 2): 53–65.

Hann, M. A. (2003b). 'The Fundamentals of Pattern Structure. Part II: The Counter-change Challenge', *Journal of the Textile Institute*, 94 (part 2, nos 1 and 2): 66–80.

Hann, M. A. (2003c). 'The Fundamentals of Pattern Structure. Part III: The Use of Symmetry Classification as an Analytical Tool', *Journal of the Textile Institute*, 94 (part 2, nos 1 and 2): 81–8.

Hann, M. A. (2004). *Dragons, Unicorns and Phoenixes*, Leeds: The University Gallery.

Hann, M. A. (2011). 'The Pazyryk Carpet. A Stylistic Appraisal of the Deep-frozen Treasure from Kurgan Number Five in the High Altai', in T. J. Farnham and D. Shaffer (eds.), *Oriental Carpet and Textile Studies VII*, International Conference on Oriental Carpets (ICOC), London, 85–94.

Hann, M. A. (2012). *Structure and Form in Design: Critical Ideas for Creative Practice*, London and New York: Berg.

Hann, M. A., Senturk, C. A. and Thomson, G. M. (1995). *The Pesel Embroideries*, Leeds: The University Gallery.

Hann, M. A. and Thomas, B. G. (2005). *Patterns of Culture—Decorative Weaving Techniques*, Ars Textrina series, Leeds: ULITA and the Leeds Philosophical and Literary Society.

Hann, M. A. and Thomson, G. M. (1992). *The Geometry of Regular Repeating Patterns*, Textile Progress Series, vol. 22, no. 1, Manchester: The Textile Institute.

Hann, M. A. and Thomson, G. M. (1993). *Unity in Diversity: The Textiles of Indonesia*, Leeds: The University Gallery.

Hann, M. A., Thomson, G. M. and Zhong, H. (1990). *Qing Dynasty Embroideries. Selections from the Clothworkers' Collection*, Leeds: The University Gallery.

Hargittai, I. (ed.) (1986). *Symmetry: Unifying Human Understanding*, New York: Pergamon.

Hargittai, I. (ed.) (1989). *Symmetry 2: Unifying Human Understanding*, New York: Pergamon.

Harris, N.(1977). *Rugs and Carpets of the Orient*, London: Hamlyn.

Harrison, T. (1958). 'The Caves of Niah: A History of Prehistory', *Sarawak Museum Journal*, 8: 549–95.

Haselberger, H. (1957). 'Method of Studying Ethnological Art', *Current Anthropology*, 2 (4): 341–84.

Hatt, R. (1980). 'A Thirteenth Century Tibetan Reliquary. An Icographic and Physical Analysis', *Artibus Asiae*, 42 (2/3): 175–220.

Hegmon, M. (1992). 'Archaeological Research on Style', *Annual Review of Anthropology*, 21: 517–36.

Hill, J. N. (1966). 'A Prehistoric Community in Eastern Arizona', *South-western Journal of Anthropology*, 22: 9–30.

Hillenbrand, R. (1999). *Islamic Art and Architecture*, London: Thames and Hudson.

Hillgarth, J. N. (1961–3). 'Visigothic Spain and Early Christian Ireland', *Proceedings of the Royal Irish Academy. Section C: Archaeology, Celtic Studies, History, Linguistics, Literature*, vol. 62, 167–94.

Hitchcock, M. (1991). *Indonesian Textiles*, London: British Museum Press.

Hodgkin, T. (1887). 'Visigothic Spain', *The English Historical Review*, 2 (6): 209–34.

Hodgson, B. H. (1861). 'Notice on Buddhist Symbols', *Journal of the Royal Asiatic Society of Great Britain and Ireland*, 1 (8): 393–9.

Hodgson, M.G.S. (1974). *The Venture of Islam: Conscience and History in a World Civilization*, 3 vols., Chicago: University of Chicago Press.

Hollenback, G. M. (2005). 'Grids on Drawing Boards', *The Journal of Egyptian Archaeology*, 91: 189–90.

Holmgren, R. J. and Spertus, A. E. (1991). 'Is Geringsing really Balinese?' in G. Völger and K. V. Welck (eds.), *Indonesian Textiles*, Cologne: Gesellschaft für Völkerkunde, 59–80.

Holt, C. (1967). *Art in Indonesia: Continuities and Change*, Ithaca, NY: Cornell University Press.

Hornung, C. (1985). *Traditional Japanese Stencil Designs*, New York: Dover.

Horowitz, W. (1988). 'The Babylonian Map of the World', *Iraq*, 50: 147–65.

Hubel, R. G. (1970). *The Book of Carpets*, New York: Praeger Publishers.

Huntley, H. E. (1970). *The Divine Proportion: A Study in Mathematical Beauty*, New York: Dover.

Huylebrouck, D. (2007). 'Curve Fitting in Architecture', *Nexus Network Journal*, 9 (1): 59–65.

Irwin, J. (1955). *Shawls: A Study of Indo European Influence*, London: HMSO.

Irwin, J. (1973). *The Kashmir Shawl*, London: HMSO.

Iversen, E. (1960). 'A Canonical Master-Drawing in the British Museum', *The Journal of Egyptian Archaeology*, 46: 71–9.

Iversen, E. (1968). 'Diodorus' Account of the Egyptian Canon', *The Journal of Egyptian Archaeology*, 54: 215–18.

Iversen, E. (1976). 'The Proportions of the Face in Egyptian Art', *Studien zur Altägyptischen Kultur*, 4: 135–48.

Jaffé, A. (1968). 'Symbolism in the Visual Arts', in C. G. Jung (ed.), *Man and His Symbols*, New York: Dell, 255–322.

Jarnow, J., Judelle, B. and Guerreiro, M. (1981). *Inside the Fashion Business*, 3rd ed., New York: Wiley.

Jenyns, R. S. (1981). *Chinese Art*, Oxford: Phaidon.

Jones, O. ([1856] 1986). *The Grammar of Ornament*, London: Day and Son. Reprint, London: Omega.

Johnstone, P. (1961). *Greek Island Embroidery*, London: Alec Tiranti Ltd.

Jung, C. G. (ed.) (1968). *Man and His Symbols*, New York: Dell.

Kappraff, J. (1991). *Connections: The Geometric Bridge between Art and Science*, New York: McGraw-Hill.

Kappraff, J. (2000). 'A Secret of Ancient Geometry', in C. A. Gorini (ed.) *Geometry at Work*, *MAA Notes* no. 53: 26–36.

Kappraff, J. ([2002] 2003). *Beyond Measure. A Guided Tour through Nature*, *Myth and Number*, River Edge, NJ and London: World Scientific.

Kartiwa, S. (1987). *Indonesian Ikats*, Jakarta: Penerbit Djambatan.

Kazanov, A. M. (1994). *Nomads and the Outside World*, 2nd ed., Madison: University of Wisconsin Press.

Kendrick, A. F. and Tattersall, C.E.C. (1922). *Handwoven Carpets. Oriental and European*, vol. 2: *Plates*, London: Benn Brothers Ltd.

Kenesson, S. S. (1992). 'Nasrid Luster Pottery: The Alhambra Vases', *Muqarnas*, 9: 93–115.

Khoury, N.N.N. (1996). 'The Meaning of the Great Mosque of Cordoba in the Tenth Century', *Muqarnas*, 13: 80–98.

Kirby, N. (1992). *Persian Carpets*, unpublished BA dissertation, Department of Textile Industries, University of Leeds.

Kirk, W. (1975). 'The Role of India in the Diffusion of Early Cultures', *The Geographical Journal*, 141 (1): 19–34.

Knappert, J. (1995). *Indian Mythology*, London: Diamond Books.

Konig, R. (1973). *A la Mode: On the Social Psychology of Fashion*, New York: Seabury Press.

Kosasih, E. A. (1991). 'Rock Art in Indonesia', in P. Bahn and A. Rosenfeld (eds.) *Rock Art and Prehistory*, Oxbow Monograph 10, Oxford: Oxbow.

Koyluoglu, N. (1974). 'Edirne Muzesindeki Hayvan Motifli Islemeler' ('Embroidered Textiles with Animal Motifs Held in Edirne Museum'), *Turk Etnografya Dergisi*, sayi. (no.) 14: 129–38.

Kramer, A.L.N. and Koen, W. (1987). *Tuttle's Concise Indonesian Dictionary*, Rutland, VT: Charles Tuttle Company.

Kroeber, A. L. (1940). 'Stimulus Diffusion', *American Anthropologist*, 42 (1): 1–20.

Kroeber, A. L. ([1948] 1963). *Anthropology: Culture Patterns and Processes*, New York: Harcourt, Brace and World.

Labib, S. (1979). 'The Era of Suleyman the Magnificent: Crisis of Orientation', *International Journal of Middle East Studies*, 10: 435–51.

Larsen, J. L. (1976). *The Dyers Art: Ikat, Batik and Plangi*, New York: Van Nostrand Reinhold.

Lavio, M. (2002). *The Golden Ratio: The Story of Phi, The World's Most Astounding Number*, New York: Broadway Books.

Lawlor, R. (1982). *Sacred Geometry: Philosophy and Practice*, London: Thames and Hudson.

Lee, S. (2003). *A History of Far Eastern Art*, 5th ed., New York: Prentice Hall.

Leidy, D. P., Siu, W. A. and Watt, J. C. Y. (1997). *Chinese Decorative Arts,* New York: Metropolitan Museum of Art.

Leix, A. (1944). 'Embroidery in Turkestan', *CIBA Review*, 4: 1464–5.

Lévi-Strauss, C. (1962). *The Savage Mind*, Chicago: University of Chicago Press.

Lévi-Strauss, C. (1967). *Structural Anthropology*, Garden City, NJ: Doubleday/Anchor.

Lewcock, R. and Brans, G. (1976). 'The Boat as an Architectural Symbol', in P. Oliver (ed.), *Shelter, Sign and Symbol*, London: Barrie & Jenkins, 107–16.

Liaoning Provincial Museum (1979). 'The Western Zhou Tomb and the Ancient Ruins at Weiyingzi, Chaoyang, Liaoning Province', *Kaogu*, 5: 36.

Liu, B. and Luo, R. (1986). *The History of Chinese Silk*, Beijing: The Press of the Textile Industries.

Liungman, C. G. (1991). *Dictionary of Symbols*, New York and London: Norton.

Lockard, C. (2009). *Southeast Asia in World History*, Oxford: Oxford University Press.

Longacre, W. A. (1968). 'Some Aspects of Prehistoric Society in East-central Arizona', in S. R. Binford and L. R. Binford (eds.), *New Perspectives in Archaeology*, Chicago: Aldine Press, 89–102.

Lorenzen, E. (1977). 'Canon and "Thumbs" in Egyptian Art', *Journal of the American Oriental Society*, 97 (4): 531–9.

Lorenzen, E. (1980). 'The Canonical Figure 19 and an Egyptian Drawing Board in the British Museum', *Studien zur Altägyptischen Kultur*, 8: 181–99.

MacGregor, N. (2012). *A History of the World in 100 Objects*, London: Penguin and the British Museum.

Mackey, E. (1989). *Early Indus Civilization*, New Delhi: Eastern Book House.

Manguin, P. Y. (1986). 'Shipshape Societies: Boat Symbolism and Political Systems in Insular Southeast Asia', in D. G. Marr and A. C. Milner (eds.), *Southeast Asia in the 9th to 14th Centuries*, Singapore and Canberra: Institute of Southeast Asian Studies and Research School of Pacific Studies, Australian National University, 187–213.

Marshall, D.J.P. (2006). 'Origins of an Obsession', *Nexus Network Journal*, 8 (1): 53–64.

Marshall, J. (1960). *A Guide to Taxila*, Karachi: Sani Communications in association with the Department of Archaeology of Pakistan.

Marzuki, Y. and Heraty, T. (1993). *Borobudur*, 6th ed., Jakarta: Penerbit Djambatan.

Mason, C. (2002). *The Geometrical Characteristics of Oriental Carpets: An Examination of Cultural Diffusion*, PhD thesis, University of Leeds.

McBride, R. D. (2008). *Domesticating the Dharma: Buddhist Cults and the Hwaom Synthesis in Silla Korea*, Honolulu: University of Hawai'i Press.

McNeill, W. H. (1977). *Plagues and Peoples*, Oxford: Blackwell.

Melchizedek, D. (2000). *The Ancient Secret of the Flower of Life*, vol. 2, Flagstaff, AZ: Light Technology Publishing.

Meyer, F. S. ([1894] 1987). *Handbook of Ornament: A Grammar of Art, Industrial and Architectural*, 4th ed., Hessling and Spielmayer, New York. Reprint, *Meyer's Handbook of Ornament*, London: Omega.

Miksic, J. (1990). *Borobudur. Golden Tales of Buddhas*, Singapore: Periplis Editions (HK) Ltd.

Milhofer, S. A. (1976). *The Colour Treasury of Oriental Rugs*, Oxford: Elsevier-Phaidon.

Moss, L.A.G. (1979). 'Cloths in the Cultures of the Lesser Sunda Islands', in J. Fischer (ed.), *Threads of Tradition: Textiles of Indonesia and Sarawak*, Berkeley: University of California Press, 63–72.

Mundkur, B. (1978). 'The Alleged Diffusion of Hindu Divine Symbols into Pre-Columbian Mesoamerica: A Critique'. *Current Anthropology*, 19 (3): 541–83.

Munro, T. (1963). *Evolution in the Arts*, Cleveland, OH: Cleveland Museum.

Munro, T. (1970). *Form and Style in the Arts: An Introduction to Aesthetic Morphology*, Cleveland, OH and London: Case Western Reserve University Press with Cleveland Museum.

Nelson, S. M. (1993). *The Archaeology of Korea*, Cambridge: Cambridge University Press.

Newberry, E. W. (1936). 'Turkish Towels and their Designs', *Embroidery Journal* 4 (3): 51–62.

Newberry, E. W. (1939). 'The Embroideries of Morocco', *Embroidery Journal*, (1938–9): 29–35.

O'Connor, S. (2003). 'Nine New Painted Rock Art Sites from East Timor in the Context of the Western Pacific Region'. *Asian Perspectives*, 42 (1): 96–128.

Padovan, R. (1999). *Proportion, Science, Philosophy, Architecture*, London and New York: Routledge.

Padwick, R. and Walker, T (1977). *Pattern: Its Structure and Geometry*, Sunderland (UK): Ceolfrith Press, Sunderland Arts Centre.

Paine, S. (1990). *Embroidered Textiles*, London: Thames and Hudson.

Palotay, G. V. (1955). 'Turkish Linen Embroidery', *CIBA Review*, 9: 3662–86.

Pearson, P. (2003). *The Indian Ocean*, London: Routledge.

Peltenburg, E. J. (1995). 'The Royal Standard of Ur', in L. Gowing (ed.), *A History of Art*, Rochester (Kent, UK): Grange Books, 60–1.

Petrie, F. ([1930] 1974). *Decorative Patterns of the Ancient World*, London: Studio Editions. Reprint, London and New York: Dover.

Pinder-Wilson, R. (1960). 'Tugras of Suleyman the Magnificent', *British Museum Quarterly*, 23: 23–5.

Portal, J. (2000). *Korea—Art and Archaeology*, London: British Museum Press.

Purves, A. (1982). 'The Persistence of Formal Patterns', *Perspecta*, 19: 138–63.

Racinet, A. ([1873] 1988). *Polychromic Ornament*, London: Henry Sotheran. Reprint, *The Encyclopedia of Ornament*, London: Studio Editions.

Ramseyer, U. (1991). 'Geringsing: Magical protection and communal identity', in B. Hauser-Schäublin, M. Nabholz-Kartaschoff and U. Ramseyer (eds.), *Balinese Textiles*, London: British Museum Press, 116–35.

Rands, R. L. and Riley, C. L. (1958). 'Diffusion and Discontinuous Distribution', *American Anthropologist*, 60 (2): 274–97.

Raizman, D. (1999). 'The Church of Santa Cruz and the Beginnings of Mudejar Architecture in Toledo', *Gesta*, 38 (2): 128–41.

Rawson, J. (ed.) (1992). *The British Museum Book of Chinese Art*, London: British Museum Press.

Reade, J. E. (1986). 'Rassam's Excavations at Borsippa and Kutha, 1879–82', *Iraq*, 48: 105–16.

Reade, J. (1983, 1998). *Assyrian Sculpture*, London: British Museum Press.

Reed, S. (1972). *Oriental Rugs and Carpets*, London: Octopus Books.

Reynolds, M. A. (2000). 'The Geometer's Angle. Marriage of Incommensurables', *Nexus Network Journal*, 2: 133–44.

Reynolds, M. A. (2001). 'The Geometer's Angle: An Introduction to the Art and Science of Geometric Analysis', *Nexus Network Journal*, 3 (1): 113–21.

Reynolds, M. A. (2002). 'On the Triple Square and the Diagonal of the Golden Section', *Nexus Network Journal*, 4 (1): 119–24.

Reynolds, M. A. (2003). 'The Unknown Modular: the "2.058" Rectangle', *Nexus Network Journal*, 5 (2): 119–30.

Rhi, J. H. (1994). 'From Bodhisattva to Buddha: the Beginning of Iconic Representation in Buddhist Art', *Artibus Asiae*, 54: 207–25.

Rice, D. T. (1975). *Islamic Art*, London: Book Club Associates and Thames and Hudson.

Robins, G. (1985). 'Standing Figures in the Late Grid System of the 26th Dynasty', *Studien zur Altägyptischen Kultur*, 12: 101–16.

Robins, G. (1991). 'Composition and the Artist's Squared Grid', *Journal of the American Research Center in Egypt*, 28: 41–54.

Robins, G. (1994). 'On Supposed Connections between the "Canon of Proportion" and Metrology', *The Journal of Egyptian Archaeology*, 80: 191–4.

Rogers, E. M. and Shoemaker, F. F. (1971). *Communication of Innovations*, New York: The Free Press.

Rogers, J. M. (1988). *The Topkapi Saray Museum*, London: Thames and Hudson.

Rogers, J. M. (1992). 'The Art of Islamic Spain. Granada and New York', *The Burlington Magazine*, 134 (1073): 549–52.

Rosser-Owen, M. (1999). 'A Córdoban Ivory Pyxis Lid in the Ashmolean Museum', *Muqarnas*, 16: 16–31.

Rubenson, K. S. (1990). 'The Textiles from Pazyryk: A Study in the Transfer and Transformation of Artistic Motifs', *Expedition*, 32 (1): 49–61.

Rudenko, S. I. (1953). *Kul'tura naseleniia Gornogo Altaia v Skifskoe vremia*, Moscow-Leningrad: Izd-vo Akademii nauk SSSR.

Rudenko, S. I. (1970). *Frozen Tombs of Siberia: The Pazyryk Burials of Iron Age Horsemen*, translated by M. W. Thompson. Berkeley and Los Angeles: University of California Press.

Ruggles, D. F. (1999). 'The Alcazar of Seville and Mudejar Architecture', *Gesta*, 43 (2): 87–98.

Rui, J. (2008). 'Identifying Several Visual Types in Gandhāran Buddha Images', *Archives of Asian Art*, 58: 43–85.

Sackett (1977). The Meaning of Style in Archaeology: A General Model', *American Antiquity*, 42 (3): 369–80.

Scarre, C. (ed.) (1991). *Past Worlds: The Times Atlas of Archeology*, London: Times Books Limited.

Schapiro, M. (1953). 'Style', in A. L. Kroeber (ed.) *Anthropology Today*, Chicago: University of Chicago Press, 287–312.

Schattschneider, D. (1978). 'The Plane Symmetry Groups. Their Recognition and Notation', *American Mathematical Monthly*, 85 (6): 439–50.

Schattschneider, D. (2004). *M. C. Escher: Visions of Symmetry*, London: Thames and Hudson.

Schurmann, U. (1982). *The Pazyryk: Its Uses and Origin*, New York: Armenian Rugs Society.

Sehrai, F. (1991). *The Buddha Story in the Peshawar Museum*, Peshawar: F. Sehrai and University of Peshawar.

Senturk, C. A. (1993). *A Case Study of the Pesel Collection of Near Eastern Textiles*, M. Phil. thesis, The University of Leeds.

Shepherd, D. G. (1957). 'A Dated Hispano-Islamic Silk', *Ars Orientalis*, 2: 373–82.

Shepherd, D. G. (1978). 'A Treasure from a Thirteenth-Century Spanish Tomb', *The Bulletin of the Cleveland Museum of Art*, 65 (4): 111–34.

Shin-Tsu-Tai, S. (ed.) (1998). *Carved Paper: The Art of the Japanese Stencil*, New York and Tokyo: Santa Barbara Museum of Art.

Shubnikov, A. V. and Koptsik, V. A. (1974). *Symmetry in Science and Art*, New York: Plenum Press.

Silver, H. R. (1979). 'Ethnoart', *Annual Review of Anthropology*, 8: 267–307.

Speltz, A. ([1915] 1988). *Das Farbige Ornament aller Historischen Stile*, Leipzig: A. Schumann's Verlag. Reprint, *The History of Ornament*, New York: Portland House.

Sproles, G. B. (1979). *Fashion: Consumer Behaviour Towards Dress*, Minneapolis, MN: Burgess.

Steinmann, A. (1947). 'Batiks', *CIBA Review*, 58: 2090–123.

Stephenson, C. and Suddards, F. (1897). *A Textbook Dealing with Ornamental Design for Woven Fabrics*, London: Methuen.

Stevens P. S. (1984). *Handbook of Regular Patterns: An Introduction to Symmetry in Two Dimensions*, Cambridge, MA: MIT Press.

Stewart, M. (2009). *Patterns of Eternity: Sacred Geometry and the Starcut Diagram*, Edinburgh: Floris Books.

Stoddard, H. (1999). 'Dynamic Structures in Buddhist Mandalas: Apradakşina and Mystic Hear in the Mopther Tantra Section of the Anuttarayoga Tantras', *Artibus Asiae*, 58, (3 to 4): 169–213.

Stone, P. F. (1997). *The Oriental Rug Lexicon*, London: Thames and Hudson.

Sutton, D. (2007). *Islamic Design*, Glastonbury, Somerset (UK): Wooden Books.

Tabbaa, Y. (1985). 'The Muqarnas Dome: Its Origin and Meaning', *Muqarnas*, 3: 61–74.

Tadgell, C. (1990). *The History of Architecture in India*, London: Phaidon Press.

Tarling, N. (1992). *The Cambridge History of Southeast Asia*, vol. 1, Cambridge: Cambridge University Press.

Thompson, D. W. (1917 and 1961). *On Growth and Form*, Cambridge: Cambridge University Press.

Tregear, M. (1995). 'Chinese Bronzes', in L. Gowing (ed.), *A History of Art*, Rochester (Kent, UK): Grange Books, 300–1.

Tuer, A. W. (1967). *Traditional Japanese Patterns*, New York: Dover.

Wace, A.J.B. (1935). *Mediterranean and Near Eastern Embroideries*, London: Halton and Company.

Walters, D. (1995). *Chinese Mythology: An Encyclopaedia of Myth and Legend*, London: Diamond Books.

Wang, J. and Mou, Y. (1980). 'On the Excavation at Qianshangyang Site in Wuxing', *Kaogu*, 4: 353–5.

Wardwell, A. E. (1983). 'A Fifteenth-Century Silk Curtain from Muslim Spain', *The Bulletin of the Cleveland Museum of Art*, 70 (2): 58–72.

Warming, W. and Gaworski, M. (1981). *The World of Indonesian Textiles*, London: Serindia Publications.

Washburn, D. K. (ed.) (1983). *Structure and Cognition in Art*, Cambridge: Cambridge University Press.

Washburn, D. K. (ed.) (2004). *Embedded Symmetries, Natural and Cultural*, Albuquerque: University of New Mexico Press.

Washburn D. K. and Crowe D. W. (1988). *Symmetries of Culture: Theory and Practice of Plane Pattern Analysis*, Seattle and London: University of Washington Press.

Washburn D. K. and Crowe D. W. (2004) (eds.). *Symmetry Comes of Age: The Role of Pattern in Culture*, Seattle and London: University of Washington Press.

Watson, P. J. (1977). 'Design Analysis of Painted Pottery', *American Antiquity*, 42 (3): 381–93.

Watt, C. M. and Watt, D. J. (1987). 'Geometrical Ordering of the Garden Houses at Ostia', *Journal of the Society of Architectural Historians*, 46 (3): 265–76.

Watt, J. C. (1990). The Arts of Ancient China, *The Metropolitan Museum of Art Bulletin*, New Series, 48 (1): 1, 2, 4–72.

Wearden, J. (1995). 'The Surprising Geometry of the Ardabil Carpet', *Ars Textrina*, 24: 61–6.

Weiner, Y. (1992). 'The Indian Origin of Ikat', *Ars Textrina*, 17: 57–85.

Whallon, R. (Jr.) (1968). 'Investigation of Late Prehistoric Social Organisation in New York State', in S. R. Binford and L. R. Binford (eds.), *New Perspectives in Archaeology*, Chicago: Aldine Press, 223–44.

Whishaw, E. M. (1921). 'Mozarabic Art in Andalucia', *American Journal of Archaeology*, 25 (4): 364–75.

Wickert, J. D. (1990). *Borobudur*, Jakarta: P. T. Intermasa.

Wilson, J. K. (1990). 'Powerful Form and Potent Symbol: The Dragon in Asia', *The Bulletin of the Cleveland Museum of Art*, 77 (8): 286–323.

Wilson, V. (1986). *Chinese Dress*, London: Bamboo Publishing and Victoria and Albert Museum.

Wittkower, R. (1962). *Architectural Principles in the Age of Humanism*, 3rd ed., London: Tiranti.

Wittkower, R. (1977). *Allegory and the Migration of Symbols*, London: Thames and Hudson.

Yacopino, F. (1987). *Threadlines Gallery*, Karachi: Ministry of Industry and Elite Publications.

Zebrowski, M. (1981). 'Decorative Arts of the Mughal Period', in B. Gray (ed.), *The Arts of India*, Oxford: Phaidon, 177–89.

Zeitlin, R. (1994). 'Accounting for the Prehistoric Long-Distance Movement of Goods with a Measure of Style', *World Archaeology*, 26 (2): 208–34.

Zhong, H. (1989). *The Patterning of Qing Dynasty Textiles—A Case Study of the Clothworkers' Library Special Collection*, M.Phil. thesis, Department of Textile Industries, University of Leeds.

Zhu, X. (1985). *The History of Zhejiang Silks*, Hangzhou: Zhejiang Peoples Publishing House.

Zipper, K. and Fritzsche, C. (1989). *Oriental Rugs. Vol. 4, Turkish*, Munich: Battenburg Verlag.

Zwalf, V. (1985). *Buddhism: Art and Faith*, London: British Museum Press.

Zwalf, V. (1996). *A Catalogue of the Gandhara Sculpture in the British Museum*, vols. I and II, London: British Museum Press.

index